INTERCULTURAL MEDIATION IN EUROPE: NARRATIVES OF PROFESSIONAL TRANSFORMATION

EDITED BY

EUGENIA ARVANITIS AND ACHILLES KAMEAS

INTERCULTURAL MEDIATION IN EUROPE: NARRATIVES OF PROFESSIONAL TRANSFORMATION

EDITED BY
EUGENIA ARVANITIS AND ACHILLES KAMEAS

First published in 2014 in Champaign, Illinois, USA
by Common Ground Publishing LLC
as part of the Diversity in Organizations, Communities, and Nations book series

Library of Congress Cataloging-in-Publication Data

Intercultural mediation in Europe : narratives of professional transformation / edited by Eugenia Arvanitis and Achilles Kameas.
pages cm
Includes bibliographical references and index.
ISBN 978-1-61229-475-9 (pbk : alk. paper) -- ISBN 978-1-61229-476-6 (pdf : alk. paper)
1. Multiculturalism--Europe. 2. Mediation--Europe. 3. Immigrants--Services for--Europe. 4. Human services--Europe. I. Arvanitis, Eugenia. II. Kameas, Achilles.

HN380.Z9M8444 2014
306.44'6094--dc23

2014026172

Cover image photo credit: Chrissianna Karameri

Table of Contents

Acknowledgements

This book is a collective effort of many professionals around Europe who work in diverse disciplines such as intercultural mediation, new technologies, social work, anthropology and education. They also come from a wide range of institutions such as schools, universities, local authorities and NGOs. Their scope is to reflect on issues pertaining to intercultural mediation and to take effective action suggesting an agenda of transformation and social inclusion.

Book authors came together thanks to the SONETOR project (518736-LLP-1-2011-1-GR-LEONARDO-LMP) and its concluding conference in January 2014. This publication echoes the discussions and reflections made in the conference. Special thanks go to SONETOR partners: the Hellenic Open University, the coordinator of the project (Greece), the University of Limerick (Ireland), the Pontifical University of John Paul II (Poland), the Computer Technology Institute and Press "Diophantos" (Greece), the MARQUE 21 SL (Spain) and the BEST Institut für berufsbezogene Weiterbildung und Personaltra (Austria).

Many thanks go to the SONETOR Final Conference participants and the members of the SONETOR community of Cultural Mediators.

The editors and authors would like to express their gratitude to Konstantina Polymeropoulou for providing assistance in the compilation and formatting of the individual chapters and proof checking the final version of the document.

Finally, special thanks go to the European Commission, which funded this publication.

Introduction

Eugenia Arvanitis and Achilles Kameas

Introduction

In modern pluralistic societies intercultural or cultural mediation is closely associated with aspects of democracy, solidarity and social inclusion as it values and harnesses diversity. For the past four decades intercultural mediation was perceived as an act of conflict resolution or a positive discrimination act towards migrants who arrive in Europe "for a better life". Its scope has been associated with migrant assimilation or at the very best with their integration. Recent European policies (the Europe 2020 strategy and the European agenda for the integration of non-EU migrants) frame a new integration agenda that highlights considerable challenges such as the recognition of diversity, the contribution of migration to a competitive and sustainable economy and the importance to secure social cohesion and respect of human rights.

Eurocentric views about the *other* have prevailed the course of integration, even though it has been recently perceived by European policy frameworks as a dynamic, two-way process of mutual accommodation by both migrants and receiving societies.

In this context, intercultural mediation emerges as an important factor of social integration in the areas such as the judicial system, the health and welfare service provision or in education. However, when addressing mediation it is important to depart from monological assumptions of assimilation and its marginal status as an act of social activism. Instead intercultural mediation should become a systemic response to accommodate migrant participation and inclusion in a new social space of reciprocity and shared responsibility. It is also important for states to develop a framework for financing, monitoring and benchmarking mediation process in securing its effectiveness and reflexive posture. Mediating between parties of different cultural backgrounds and communities as well as systemic service providers require highly skilled intercultural professionals with new competences. It is only through professionalism that intercultural mediators will be valued and respected as (cultural or social) *agents of change* able to transform ethno specific views that hinder reciprocal communication and understanding. The SONETOR project (funded in the context of EU Lifelong Learning program) created a new social space of interpersonal and intercultural communication and professional practice through the innovative use of social media. It raised the issue of mediators' professionalism and their validation in our collective mind. Through its actions SONETOR unfolded multiple narratives of mediation in a reflective account. SONETOR became the vehicle for improving the quality of services through up-skilling and re-skilling of cultural mediators. It also provided a third space for learning through the use of social media networking. Peer learning activities grounded on real-life experiences, best practices from the field and collaborative reflection transformed the paradigm of knowing and acting, which lies in the heart of mediation. The project also became a tool to establish and sustain a European community of cultural mediators through its multi-lingual social networking platform, which provides a universal focal point for the exchange of working experiences between community members and other stakeholders in all Europe.

This book is a collection of narratives regarding intercultural mediation as it was perceived by academics and professionals across Europe. It captures reflexive accounts and voices of experts and non-experts heard at the International Conference on «*Enhancing the Skills and Identity of Cultural Mediators in a multicultural Europe*» (ESI-CM 2014), 8-9 January 2014 in Patras, Greece. It presents the diversity of policies, providers and services attached to mediation in the context of pluralistic and cohesive societies. Finally, it raises the importance of professionalizing and training intercultural mediators to secure effectiveness and validation. The intellectual trajectory of this book is grounded on the notion that social transformation can be best served through a bottom up approach, namely by enhancing people's interactivity, reciprocal learning and reflective practice on socially grounded issues.

This book is divided in four parts as described below:

Reframing Intercultural Mediation

The initial chapters of this book reframe intercultural mediation, the role of mediators and migrancy. **Eugenia Arvanitis** argues that mediation creates a highly interconnected social space or a contact zone where reciprocal communication takes place. Mediation disrupts ethnocentric narratives of cultural homogeneity and conformity negotiating all kind of differences. It also creates dynamic spaces of critical engagement by individuals (being either exotic *others* or familiar *others*) and social actors broadening the scope of democratic pluralism. Mediation tests the notion of the *third space* confronting issues of equitable civic participation, accessibility of resources and social justice. *This chapter focuses on the mediation process as an act of social transformation* highlighting its multidimensional nature and reflexive posture to diversity. It, finally, discusses the role and competences of intercultural mediators.

The following chapter by **Morteza Rezaei-Zadeh** and **Dermot Coughlan** goes deeper to explore (inter)cultural mediators per se. Cultural mediators here are defined from two perspectives including their roles and their competences. Consistent with the latter one, this chapter presents the results of two Interactive Management sessions, which were conducted to identify and rank the most important competences of cultural mediators. Further to generating two sets of those competences, their interrelationships are also examined and displayed in the schematic diagrams known as Enhancement Structures. The participants in these two Interactive Management sessions were the immigrants from an international community in Ireland as well as individuals whose work can be defined as that of cultural mediation. Further conclusions are made at the end of the chapter and the applications of these findings are also discussed. From methodological perspective, the current study is the first one which uses and explores the value of Interactive Management as a qualitative concept-mapping method in the area of cultural mediation studies.

Moreover, **Vasiliki Papageorgiou** reflects on the role of intercultural mediator form an anthropological point of view offering her fieldwork experience working with Albanian migrants in Greece. She explores the intercultural relations in the context of cultural contact, namely interactions and cultural processes. She goes further to draw an analogy between cultural mediation and ethnographic work.

In concluding this section three more chapters offer a background in understanding migration movements and policies at regional level.

Zambeta Papadodima analyses the most representative policies on migration during the last decade, in order to identify the recent regional transition in the migration politics along the European South. By exploring these last restructures in spaces, discourses and practices on migration, she proposes a prominent field for reflection about research challenges, policies and services in the multicultural metropolis nowadays.

Charikleia Manavi elaborates on migration and return migration policies that enable migrants and return migrants to reach their highest potential. She first summarizes the contributions made by migrants to their host societies, the changes in global migration and the migration background in Europe today. Secondly, she points out the process of transition analyzing the concept of return migration. Particular emphasis is given on procedures, which harness human and embodied (inter)cultural capital as a key concept for social change and national prosperity for both host and home countries. Subsequently, she stresses the role of social workers, vocational counselors and cultural mediators in the above task. This chapter presents a Leonardo daVinci transfer of innovation project, as a good practice. The so called "Back to Work"; a training and validation tool that supports (social) counselors in working with unemployed migrants and returning migrants including those that have skills in various areas, which have been acquired in a non-formal setting.

The following chapter by **Akrivi-Irene Panagiotopoulou** and **Andrica Rozi** elaborates on the European Union interventions, which actively promote the social inclusion of migrants by engaging stakeholders in well-designed programs characterized by a high viability and transferability potential. This chapter describes two of such programs and their outcomes. The first project, *Learning Community – Migrants as Educational Multipliers Pave the Way for Migrants to Access Lifelong Learning*, was a Grundtvig Multilateral Project implemented by a partnership of organizations from five EU countries. The employability, the empowerment and the social integration of the participants were strengthened through an innovative methodological consulting approach. The second project,

Creating a Register of Trained Intercultural Mediators and Networking Intercultural Mediators through an Electronic Platform, was financed by the Greek Ministry of Interior and the European Fund for the Integration of Third Country Nationals in Greece. The creation of the first registry of trained intercultural mediators in Greece is hereby presented, pointing out the necessity and importance of a well-structured intercultural mediation activity in the country.

The SONETOR Project: Forging Peer Learning Synergies through Social Networking

The following six chapters are captioned "The SONETOR project: Forging peer learning Synergies through social networking" and describe an innovative peer learning and training framework for intercultural mediators.

Achilles Kameas and **Konstantina Polymeropoulou** present the baseline of the SONETOR project (www.sonetor-project.eu) and the integration of social computing tools to enhance the peer learning of cultural mediators. The SONETOR was funded by EU in the context of the Leonardo da Vinci strand of the Life Long Learning program (518736-LLP-1-2011-1-GR-LEONARDO-LMP). The project developed a training platform that integrates social networking applications with specially produced content and services. This new approach to training enables cultural mediators to develop formal and non-formal skills and competences and apply them during their work with immigrants. This chapter presents the project actions undertaken to organize the learning engagement of the user community, a draft profile of cultural mediators, the SONETOR platform and its services and the peer learning scenarios.

The next chapter by **Krzysztof Gurba** raises the need of developing peerlearning training programs for cultural mediators (such as SONETOR) utilizing new network social software and elaborated educational scenarios. A participative methodology was adopted allowing users to engage in learning content production and bring interesting personal experiences. The users created unguided learning scenarios around a simple story based on real mediation cases. This stance of the user as the producer of learning content is supported by a far-reaching interactivity (collective updating of the content through reflection and dialogue) and mutual co-stimulation using social media tools.

Furthermore, **Mara Aspioti** and **Achilles Kameas** present the experience of the Greek National Moderator and the SONETOR Project coordinator. During the SONETOR project, an (inter)cultural mediators' community was established in each of the partner countries consisting of trained professionals who used the platform and its services in order to upload and exchange content. In each country, one of the community members has been appointed as a National Moderator (NM) with the mission to manage and facilitate the operation of the community. This chapter is a reflective account of the Greek NM experience during the lifetime of the project and afterwards. It focuses on issues related to the National Moderator's profile, necessary knowledge, skills and competences he/she shall possesses as well as challenges he/she has to cope with, in order to carry out the educational process and the management of the human resources in the project.

The chapter by **Jeries Besarat, Catherine Christodoulopoulou, Andreas Koskeris** and **John Garofalakis** elaborates on the technicalities of the SONETOR platform, its functionalities, specifications and services. Under SONETOR project, a training platform that integrates existing social networking applications with modern adult education methodologies was developed and content and services were specially produced. The SONETOR platform allows users to register to a learning community and interact in a reciprocal ad reflective way (e.g. users are able to develop relationships, sending friendship requests and exchange messages). The platform allows registered users to create their own material, articles and share it to the others authenticated users. Also, users have the ability to connect with other social networks like Facebook and Twitter without leaving the platform and share their material in these social networks too. Users can create and moderate their own group. Groups can be small communities as only accepted members of the group have access to it. Finally, the platform is connected with Moodle LMS, thus, enabling users to login automatically with the same username and password and attend classes.

The contribution by **Achilles Kameas, Mara Aspioti and Georgia Antonelou** discuss the ways in which new computing technologies support cultural mediation. The authors suggest that ICT can facilitate not only delivery of instruction, but also the learning process itself independent of any institutional level. In fact, ICT can promote international collaboration and intercultural social networking and also provide a flexible and effective life-long professional development for learners who participate in any educational structure. ICT competences comprise a subset of digital literacy and skills necessary for real-life functioning in all kinds of professional activities and levels of education form; that is why, ICT educational applications should be based on appropriate pedagogical frameworks and models that promote the effective and efficient use of those applications.

Cultural mediation is a reaction-dependent process, thus conditions and situations may affect the strategies adopted during cultural mediating. Cultural mediation is also a process of interaction. Consequently, the parts involved and in particular the part in-between playing the bridging role (i.e. the Cultural mediator) have to possess specific skills and competences such as negotiation skills, crisis management skills, empathy and more. These skills must be taught and well-exercised beforehand in order to become a cultural-mediator's asset. All the above can be developed and managed with the aid of certain environments and educational methodologies. In other words, cultural mediation can be taught and, cultural mediators can and should have their knowledge, skills and competences constantly informed and upgraded. In the context of Information Society, the easiest, most affordable and fastest way to do this is by utilizing the facilities offered by ICT technologies. Internet and social media could be considered as two of the most popular ICT technologies followed by applications used by modern digital devices such as mobile phones, tablets, etc. Online social networks (OSNs) are defined as online platforms that (a) provide services for a user to build a public profile and to explicitly declare the connection between his or her profile with those of the other users, (b) enable a user to share information and content with the public or selected users and, (c) support the development and usage of social applications with which the user can interact and collaborate with either friends or strangers.

The authors argue that SONETOR platform provides users from all countries who want to be educated and trained as Cultural Mediators with specific ICT applications (tools and other services) that enhance communication, collaboration, focus group creation, teleconferences and social networking. The platform has been developed to support peer learning, learning through collaboration, social constructivism and crowd learning. Apart from the SONETOR platform, a number of free applications, simulations or games on mediation in general and on Cultural Mediation in particular can be found on the Internet and can be accessed through mobile devices or PCs. Finally, an increasing interest in the development of market oriented mediation and/or cultural mediation applications are noted lately.

The final chapter of this part of the book is written by **Dermot Coughlan and Morteza Rezaei-Zadeh**. It examines the relevance and impact of the SONETOR Project in Cultural Mediation by reviewing the current position of migration in Ireland. The authors offer a reflective account of the issues arise pertaining to migrants and their integration into Irish society. They also attempt to predict and assess the mediation services, which might support greater social inclusion and the training required by those professionals working with migrants.

Systemic Responses to Mediation: Narratives of Recognition and Validation

The following chapters are captioned "Systemic responses to mediation: Narratives of recognition and validation". They discuss mediation interventions in Ireland, Portugal and Greece.

The contribution by **Mayte Martin** focuses on cultural mediation process in Ireland, which has been implemented since 2002. It was originally developed by projects co-funded by the EU with the first training program offered to all minority ethnic groups residing in Ireland. A second training program was tailored specifically for the Roma population. Roma people have started arriving in Ireland since the end of the 90s and had experienced many obstacles accessing Irish services. Cultural mediation in Ireland was designed for the health services, but it was used in other areas such in schools, probation, and police. These projects were instrumental in creating a cultural mediation model that included training program, code of practice, profile of cultural mediators and guidelines to assist service providers to work with cultural mediators. The development of all these procedures is necessary to achieve the recognition of cultural mediation as a profession.

On a similar note **Mónica Diniz and Cláudia Santa Cruz** reflect on the challenge of intercultural mediation in the Lisbon Community Policing. The authors discuss the new challenges on urban security faced by the Lisbon Municipal Police (LMP). The implementation of a community policing model is a new way of intervention to improve security responses in the city. It emphasizes the adoption of an insider's look by the organization to address its human capital and the need to develop a responsive training strategy, philosophy and practice of mediation. In the context of a community policing, where the police officers are more integrated in the social tissue, and therefore acting as social cohesion agents, there is an increasing need of the police to use a preventive approach. The implementation of the community policing pilot-experience in *Alta de Lisboa*, helped guiding the LMP training strategy for the near future, namely how to develop in police officers the skills to sustain and enhance the police-citizen articulation, involving all social groups, especially in cultural diverse communities.

The findings of this model of policing recommends that, for the police to be able to articulate with the citizens and to establish a trusting relationship in diverse cultural contexts, it's important that the LMP training strategy focus on intercultural learning skills of the police officers, as well as the development of mediation skills. This training approach assumes that the police officers will be more apt and able to manage conflict and mediate knowing that mediators' competences are not limited only to the promotion of their professional skills, but also include empowerment and personal growth. These competences enable police officers to bring change to the citizens and the city and deal with the unexpected and the uncertain.

Two more contributors elaborate on the systemic response of the Municipality of Patras in fabricating a holistic planning to deal with a city's intercultural responsibility.

Maria Andrikopoulou - Rouvali, a serving Vice-Mayor articulates the importance of taking into count diversity in cities such as Patras (inhabited by various types of population with different origins, languages, religions and cultures). The author notes that detailed knowledge of all these groups is of vital importance to enhance active citizenship and cohesion in an intercultural city. She reflects on her role and responsibilities of being the Vice-Mayor of Patras on "Support to citizen, Volunteerism, Gender Equality & Integration of Migrants". She reflects on local initiatives, which encourage common intercultural activities and networking. Namely: a) The Council for the Inclusion of Migrants; a valuable tool for participation, representation and promotion of the views of migrants at local level; b) The establishment of the Department of "Volunteerism & Equality Policy", which oversees more than 600 volunteers in various areas, putting emphasis on sports, social solidarity and culture. This Department initiates actions that embrace all vulnerable groups of population (so, migrants are included its target-groups). And c) Structures for solidarity & inclusion for the benefit of vulnerable groups of population regardless religion and nationality, such as long-term unemployed, elderly, young people, women, all facing poverty. Namely: Social General Clinic, Pharmacy, Pediatric Clinic, Social Grocery, Bank of Food, Social Wardrobe and Bank of Time.

Chrissa Geraga elaborates on the Intercultural strategy of the City of Patras, its objectives and actions. By the turn of the 20th century Patras had become an important port for the western Peloponnese, regarded as a Mediterranean gateway of Greece to the west, particularly to Italy. The Municipality of Patras recognizes that all the residents of the city are culturally enriched by its contemporary diversity and need a living environment friendly for all. Since 2008, Patras is an active member of the "Intercultural Cities-ICC" network coordinated by the Council of Europe aiming at managing the diversity advantage. The municipality has developed strong relationships with all key civil-society actors in the city, so that intercultural strategic operation comes to life. Patras is perceived as an intercultural meeting point, imbued with a spirit of openness, as a co-creation of the municipality, civil society and the residents of the city.

The final chapter of this part by **Konstantina Kyriakopoulou** reflects on social exclusion and the need of Doctors of the World to act as intercultural mediators in order to enhance the social integration of refugees and asylum seekers. The author states that social exclusion could bring severe disruption of cohesion. The author presents everyday practices that Doctor of the World use when they work with to people who lack access to the National Health Care System. The users of these services can be immigrants, refugees without legal license of their stay in the country, poor people or these without insurance, homeless people and Roma populations.

School Mediation

Three final chapters of this book focus on school mediation and the critical responsibility of teachers in undertaking mediation roles.

Eleni Skourtou present a mediation project with university students trained at the Education Department of the Aegean University in Rhodes, Greece. She provides a reflective account on the transformative effect of mediation on future teachers through the development of literacy supporting activities for Roma children. These future teachers tested their personal assumptions in their efforts to bridge school culture and official literacy forms with home knowledge and learning practices. They acted as bridges of identities in linguistically and culturally diverse school classes where diversity is interwoven with extreme poverty and social exclusion. This chapter elaborates on the gradual shift of university students' social attitudes towards Roma and the fact that it was easier to challenge social stereotypes than literacy ones. Through their work as mediators future teachers come to the conclusion that is difficult for them to become aware and effectively harness the literacy skills and prior knowledge that Roma children's brought to school. The preliminary findings of this project alarmed project participants by indicating a *deficit* approach, namely future teachers were able to ascertain what children were lacking compared to official knowledge. Ascertaining and valuing what Roma children knew when they started schooling had proven to be outside students' monocultural mindset. The author came to the conclusion that future teachers have to be trained in cultural mediation and that part of this training should be their involvement in literacy activities with Roma students both in the school and in the community context.

Then the contribution by **Georgios Nikolaou, Theodoros Thanos and Eleni Samsari** focuses more precisely on school mediation as an important processes to counteract violence and bullying. This chapter investigates how the process of school mediation could be applied as an alternative and effective means to confront incidents of school violence and school bullying where students from different cultural background are involved. School bullying is a complex social problem which attracts considerable interest over the years. The problem becomes more intense and difficult, when native and non-native students are involved either as bullies or as victims. The authors raise the fact and the application of general anti-bullying practices and policies in schools usually have disappointing results. They suggest that school mediation could be an alternative solution, which could be applied within the school environment, focusing on the uniqueness of each problem. The contribution of mediators is very important, so that both sides would decide to participate and discuss about the nature of the problem and its possible solutions. In schools, where mediation was used in order to solve some disputes, the participants were completely satisfied and they improved their relationships with each other. Taking into account some basic principles of school mediation (e.g., empathy, volunteerism, equity etc.), it is clear that native and non-native students who are involved in an incident of school bullying, accept rules and become familiar with a process, which serves the purpose of intercultural education.

This book concludes with a final chapter by **Theodoros Thanos** and **Charalampos Dalakas** who further elaborate on the school violence and its prevention as it emerges in Europe during the last 15 years and after the European Conference in Utrecht (1997). The authors focus on an inclusive and a restorative justice paradigm to offer an alternative management approach to conflict between pupils at a Primary school in Epirus, Greece. They reflect on emerging relationships among offenders and victims as well the school community based on research data. The performative nature of mediation builds on the concept of school security, democracy and solidarity and proves its value in a pluralistic society.

Part I: Reframing Intercultural Mediation

Chapter 1: The Intercultural Mediation: A Transformative Journey of Learning and Reflexivity

Eugenia Arvantis

Introduction

Cultural homogeneity and conformity no longer count as productive dimensions of our modern societies. Global and radical socio-economic and political changes brought by globalization create dynamic spaces of interconnectedness. In these spaces individuals develop diverse kinds of knowledge, competences and sensibilities as well as new forms of civility, work and personal fulfillment. It seems that critical engagement and the ability to participate in multiple and overlapping domains of social activity is an important factor of socio-economic mobility and cohesiveness broadening the scope of democratic (civic) pluralism (Kalantzis & Cope, 2012). Both migrants (the distinguishable or exotic *others*) and locals (the familiar *others*) confront issues of equitable participation as well as disparities in accessing work opportunities and social services.

Diversity[1], new knowledge and relationships explain a multifaceted *social capital*, which our learning societies seek to fabricate to sustain economic growth and social cohesion. Differences create spaces of a dynamic 'divergence' where people reflect on and (re)invent themselves and their worlds. In this context, acts of negotiation of differences occur to enhance mutual understanding, reflexivity and effective communication patterns. Mediation, for example, is a process where a third party brings unequal and diverse others together with their free consent and modulates their negotiations to achieve reciprocal engagement. This process implies trust and dialogue and establishes bridges of mutual understanding. Globalized and multicultural societies experience a wide range of mediations (in

[1] Diversity (based on gender, ethnicity, cultural aspirations, ways of working and life experiences, interests, styles of communication, different points of view, specialist knowledge or any other differences) is understood as a new kind of non-fixed capital that can be harnessed as an asset for the society as a whole (Kalantzis & Cope, 2012).

business, in the political, social or diplomatic arena) including *intercultural* mediation.

Intercultural mediation brings into the fore a wide spectrum of issues faced by modern societies in a multifaceted, inclusive and engaging way. In the European context (inter)cultural mediation is associated to migrant influx and the difficulties faced by social institutions and professionals to adapt their interventions to specific integration or settlement needs. It is also associated with the exclusion and marginalization that affect socially excluded groups (especially migrants) and the urgency to alleviate social fragmentation that ends up in conflict and violence (domestic, ethnic, etc.). Intercultural mediation is considered as a systemic response to secure access to public services. It assists both migrants to find their way in the new country and social actors and institutions to better understand migrant settlement needs and communicate in a respectful manner with them (Cohen-Emerique, 2007, p. 8). However, intercultural mediation is not merely a form of conflict resolution or merely an interpersonal act. It has a multidimensional nature, which develops a reflexive posture to diversity taking into account the sociopolitical context and the power relations in place. This reflexive and transformative nature of mediation requires a critical engagement by all participants based on their human and social capital and it assumes that multiple narratives and perspectives need to be heard.

In addition, intercultural mediation can take several forms. Cohen-Emerique, has identified four types of mediation (Cohen-Emerique, 2007, p. 11-14): The first type (the *liaison* type) facilitates communication between parties (through giving information, interpreting or translating). This type of mediation facilitates the accessibility of migrant groups to various public services and it also ensures that social actors decode the needs of those groups and respond to them. A second type of mediation aims to dissolve cultural misunderstandings due to ignorance, prejudice, discrimination or stereotyping. Here intercultural mediation assists both parties to break free from their ignorance by providing culturally appropriate information. It also enables parties to reflect on the dynamics of their interpersonal identities, which imply all sort of dualisms and power relations such as *us* versus *others*, *superiors* versus *inferiors* and *majority* versus *minority*. A third type of mediation is that of conflict management and resolution in all sort of domains such as family, justice, education, healthcare and welfare. Here intercultural mediation builds bridges and creates new spaces of compromise and consensus. The final type refers to a process of transformation of institutional approaches, norms, structures and regulations as well as personal beliefs in the context of mutual understanding, collaboration and trust. Here intercultural mediators act as *agents of change* and their expertise and competency is being recognized and valued by both parties. The most frequently used type of mediation is the first one, according to research evidence (Cohen-Emerique, 2007, p. 14). The other forms and especially the transformative mediation (which requires critical and reflective participation) is difficult to emerge as a common practice because institutions and professions are resistant to change.

In this context, intercultural mediators can act as translators/interpreters, cultural informants, conflict mediators, advocates and/or bilingual workers (Jabert, 1998 cited in Cohen-Emerique, 2007, p. 15-16). The main attitudes guiding these roles refer to the mediators' *status quo* and *negotiation* possibilities.

For example, linguistic (translators/interpreters) and systemic agents (bilingual workers) are subject to certain professional guidelines and codes of practice and in that sense they confirm mainstream discourses. On the other hand cultural informants, advocates, integrating agents or mediators have the capacity to explain, negotiate, and defend cultural differences and, thus, legitimize them. By doing so, they position themselves closer to the user operating as cultural agents. This operational framework points out the ambiguity of this profession and also further implications for intercultural mediators as they have to constantly maintain a balance between proximity and distance against mediation parties. Intercultural mediators are both *insiders* and *outsiders* during the mediation process. They can be closer to users and migrants (especially if they have similar cultural background) attracting criticism by social actors for being biased and lacking professionalism. At the same time they can function as *outsiders* maintaining their objective and neutral status deriving from their professional standards. This is why training and certified qualifications together with a professional code of practice are important steps in securing professional integrity and impartiality.

This chapter will discuss three main threads that place intercultural mediation at the heart of an inclusive and pluralistic society.

Firstly, it will discuss the pivotal role of intercultural mediation to effectively negotiate differences in a cohesive society. We adopt here a more inclusive approach to understand differences and the social dynamics of diversity. Differences are not static and they are grounded on group dynamics, which "are constituted through relationships in which one group is defined in relation to another". In other words, groups are "invariably relational" (Kalantzis & Cope, 2012, p. 167) as much they are "internally differentiated". A modern nation-state committed to pluralism is infused with diverse narratives of belonging, inclusion, collaboration and cosmopolitanism.

Secondly, intercultural mediation will be analyzed as a reflexive and dialogical process, which creates intercultural spaces, where individuals and groups acquire more agency. The latter depends on individual and group ability to be reflexive and develop a culture of reciprocity and mutual learning in harnessing diversity (either personal, cultural or institutional). Reflexivity, collaboration and dialogue in globalized societies can reconfigure relations between group *insiders* and *outsiders*. Our modern societies are relationship-focused and require people who can work flexibly and effectively across diverse cultural, social and work settings.

Finally, intercultural mediation will be discussed as a process where the devolution of social, personal and cultural responsibility takes place in the context of civic pluralism (Kalantzis & Cope, 2012). The top down bureaucratic relationship of the state to citizens is been replaced in many cases by pluralistic structures of self-governance (local or transnational) and forms of social participation. This in fact showcases the decline of the centralizing and homogenizing nation-state and it poses new challenges for social participation and inclusion. Intercultural mediation is closely associated to the commitment of modern states to redistributive justice (comparable outcomes and accessibility to resources and social services) without prejudice to the differences between the life experiences of citizens and non-citizens.

The following sections will analyze intercultural mediation as a process of intercultural transformation for all parties involved and also as a learning resource in newly constructed spaces of social interactions.

Mediating Diversity: An Inclusive Approach to Space, Reflexivity and Dialogue

Cosmopolitanization (cosmopolitan realism) has become a reality bringing new challenges, inequalities and positive /negative side effects. Beck (2009, p. 12) adopts this concept instead of globalization to describe the way the excluded-*others* have been included in our highly interconnected world. Cosmopolitanization is an unintended result not restricted to the developed countries or to cosmopolitan individuals who follow sophisticated lifestyles (idealistic or elitist interpretation). This is due to the continuous mixing and interfering with and against others. The *other*, the *foreigner*, is present in our everyday lives to such a degree that the group inside-outside distinctions no longer can be sustained. As Beck points out "you can be an alien, a non-citizen living elsewhere and at the same time be a neighbor, a competitor" (Beck, 2009, p. 13). Everyone belongs to the cosmos and also to certain polities (states, sovereignties). At the same time individuals can connect *here* and *there*, whereas many people become foreigners not by free choice, but as a result of hardship. Cosmopolitanization offers "a logical also/and model" (Beck, 2009, p. 22) to understand, discuss and reflect on cultural diversity and at the same time to affirm the presence of the *other* as different but equal. This context transforms our relations and the ways we communicate and act by building on our collective intelligibility.

The learning and transformational dimensions of the mediation process are accentuated in newly developed cosmopolitan spaces of reflection where diversity is a valuable resource. However, intercultural mediation has been mostly explained by intercultural discourse as an act of interpersonal communication. This focus and its micro phenomena were based on the belief that cultural differences and the lack of a common set of cultural reference hinder communication. Intercultural mediation acted as a problem solver in cross-cultural situations, which were affected by cultural differences. Indeed cultural differences may hinder effective communication (verbal and non-verbal communication values) as people tend to consider their own cultural beliefs and systems as universal ones. Cultural blindness obscures the richness of the *other* culture creating barriers and misbeliefs.

Important universal cultural differences (*etic*) according to Hall (1989a, 1989b) can be *space*, *time* and *context*. For example, his *proxemic* view (Hall, 1968) on cultural differences provides an approach to understand how perceptions on nearness affect behavior. Also different cultural perceptions on time[2] (which is

---

[2] Hall (1989b) has made the distinction between monochronic and polychronic cultures. The first understand time as "a classification system that orders life" (Kalscheuer, 2009, p. 31) and a tangible metaphor. The second refer to a less rigid order where time is more spontaneous.

a primary organizer of life activities) affect the degree of successful function in intercultural situations.

Finally, the cultural contextualization[3], namely the degree of information given by the context, whether it is being verbalized or not (*high* vs *low* context cultures) and also the inner logic of a culture (*emic* perspective) should be taken into account (Hall, 1989a, in Kalscheuer, 2009, p. 31). However, this view gives the impression that cultural differences are static and unbridgeable as well as universal to the cultures and all people they are referring to. This universalistic approach however, is based on a 'hegemonic eurocentrism' (Miike, 2003), which promotes western cultural discourses as valid to all other cultures. (Kalscheuer, 2009, p. 32). Also this view understands culture in a more static and homogeneous form based on binary representation of cultural differences. These prevailing connotations amongst interculturalists in fact reduce cultural uniqueness and they obscure the fluidity, changeability and multiplicity of cultures and personal identities and the importance of hybridity, reciprocity (reciprocal influence and exchange) and reflexivity in (trans)forming them.

In addition, the use of multiple classifications of difference, which are dictated by western developed concepts[4], do not take into account the fact that intersections of these classifications (such as class and gender or gender and race) create even more variation. In conditions of increasing global interconnectedness, differences are subtle and complex and shape people's personalities and life histories in unique ways. Kalantzis & Cope (2012) have suggested a more *inclusive* approach to diversity in order to illustrate the complexity of differences. They define diversity including dimensions of differences such as *material* (differences of social class, geographical locale and family), *corporeal* (differences of age, race, sex and sexuality, and physical and mental capacities) and *symbolic* (socially constructed realities of culture or ethnicity, language, gender, affinity and persona). Both academics note that everyday life experiences, which they called *lifeworld* (namely, individual set of habits, behaviors, values and interests), are implicitly present because they "seem so obvious to insiders that they don't need saying" (Kalantzis & Cope, 2012, p. 138).

Lifeworlds have an enormous impact on individuals' engagement in any communication circumstance. Thus, people with diverse *lifeworlds* engage in perpetual intercultural communicative actions in every aspect of their

---

[3] The mediation process may involve conflicting cultural attributes such as individualism vs collectivism; femininity vs masculinity; different sense of security (need for more or less rules), hierarchy or power, multi-tasking approach vs mono-tasking approach, orientation and understanding of time and space, non-verbal vs verbal communication in response to a particular situation (WikiMediation, n.d.). Gestures may also lead to confusion in cross-cultural settings. For example, in India a nod from right to left means an affirmation, while a movement of head from up to down means a refusal; A thumb up could be an impolite gesture in Iran; In Japan, the smile / laugh can be a sign of embarrassment and confusion
(See http://en.wikimediation.org/index.php?title=Intercultural_mediation).

[4] For example, Hofstede (1980) has nominated four dimensions such as power distance, collectivism versus individualism, masculinity versus feminity, uncertainty avoidance, which seem to be universal and unbridgeable. Later on he added another two dimensions (long-term versus short-term orientation and indulgence versus self-restraint) (Hofstede, Hofstede, & Minkov, 2010)

interpersonal communication. They are doing so by using negotiation and sensitivity on (cultural) differences in such aspects as: cultural styles, orientation to space and time, gender differentiation or power distances. The basis for a successful intercultural communication, thus, lies on intercultural sensibilities and competences.

In this context, mediation process can be perceived as a unique *convergence* where participants' *lifeworld* constructs of values, beliefs and principles come together in newly formed spatialities. In these *social* or *lived spaces*[5] of engagement that is highly (re)shaped by the participants' *lifeworlds,* mediators assist parties to understand one another and to be aware of bias towards process, persons, behaviors and outcomes. The way by which mediators shape this new *intercultural space* to create "*a larger third culture* context" (Townsend, 2002, para. 3) determines their success and professional status.

Furthermore, the reality of cosmopolitanization exceeds traditional dualisms and static approaches to differences. New concepts and insights are required to better understand intercultural communication. Kalscheuer (2009) notes that the post-colonial notion of *self-reflexivity* could, for instance, enrich intercultural communication and make it more intercultural in nature, because it clarifies the participant's role to the prevalence of hegemony and it enhances its critical consciousness. In addition, cultural divergence generates new contact zones where cultural patterns intersect and become transformed. Intercultural mediation reinterprets *spatiality* as it is associated to a 'third culture', namely an enriched ('in between' and 'also/and') place where cultural boundedness is loosened. Here in this non-fixed space culturally diverse people could meet in a temporary and provisional mode and exchange cultural encounters. Thomas (1996) described this contact zone between spaces, which is being characterized by flexibility and tolerance, as 'transcultural space'.

An interesting angle is how power relations affect the representation of the *other/foreigner* and what can be the role of intercultural mediation. Especially postcolonial theorists (Bhabha, 1994 and Spivak, 1990) were interested on the *oppressed marginals* and their role in acquiring critical consciousness of their position to resist and be heard. Thus, attention was drawn in the concept of *in-between* spaces where permanent movement and ongoing cultural shift occurred. For example, Lefebvre (1991) has spoken about *third space* to overcome traditional dualism in describing space. Soja (1996) also elaborated on this notion by suggesting the term "critical thirding as othering" (in Kalscheuer, 2009, p. 37) to imply that *oppressed marginals* can disorder the dominant discourses of belonging by forming communities of resistance in order to be heard by majority representatives. Finally, *hybridity* (Bhabha, 1994) is perceived as a recombination of different cultural elements in the third space (the 'interstitial' space between cultures), which question and disrupt dominant discourses. It is a dynamic condition enabling people to modify existing relationships and alter identity and power relations acquiring more agency. However in most cases *marginals* have

---

[5] Here it is useful to note Lefebvre's unitary theory of space (1991), which brings together all its elements, namely i) the physical (real/material) or perceived space, ii) the mental (imagined/conceptual) or conceived space and iii) the social or lived space (Rick, 1997, p. 10-12). The social or lived space is a new "site where our perceived and conceived notions of space meet, are contested, combined and altered" (Skordoulis & Arvanitis, 2008, p. 108)

not equal chances to articulate their positions not even to be heard or set up new structures of authority.

Moreover, even these new conceptions fail to take into account the evolving nature of contact zones. The "third culture seems to be temporarily restricted to the moment of cultural encounter" (Kalscheuer, 2009, p. 34) as it accepts the individual change (by the confrontation of people from divergent cultures), but not the constant transformation of cultures themselves. Instead the notion of 'trans-difference' may enrich intercultural approach in terms of power. (Breinig, and Lösch, 2002, p. 23) explain that the term means "whatever runs 'through' the line of demarcation drawn by binary difference" (in Kalscheuer, 2009, p. 40). It is a notion that interrogates the validity of binary differences without dismissing them as a point of reference. It offers a complementary context of analyzing differences where people's ascribed identities and differences can be negotiated, modified and transformed.

Breinig, and Lösch (2002) nominate three levels where trans-difference can be explained. a) The *intra-systemic* level where trans-difference or alternate constructions of meaning and voices of resistance are oppressed to maintain the existing order. b) The *inter-systemic* level where negotiation of identities in diverse cultural contexts takes place. Here people with conflicting ideas and values start to communicate and by doing this they question the universal validity of their cultural traits. They also reflect on their own identities in this *third* space being open to personal transformation through negotiation and contradiction of their own cultural beliefs, boundaries and values. In this context, people renegotiate mechanisms of inclusion and exclusion going beyond this binary. The notion of trans-difference is based on Clifford's (1988) definition of culture, which is more open and accepts cultural modification and flexibility. Trans-difference is not a *third* space of emancipatory rhetoric where binarisms are deconstructed in a colonial setting (as Bhabha, 1994). It goes beyond these dualisms to offer *agency* to the different actors and the power to alter their cultural understanding and behaviors. Finally, c) the third level is the *individual* one, which denotes the multilayers of identity, the multiple participation (in different social, ethnic and professional groups) the overlapping of contradictory aspects of belonging and the need for people to constantly (re)position themselves. In pluralistic societies individuals have multiple affiliations and affinities which can be mutually exclusive or incompatible (Kalantzis & Cope, 2012). Individual participation in these diverse domains of social interactivity demand different registers of cultural contact and, thus, produce trans-difference. In this context, people have to reflect, take position and transform their action in order to emancipate themselves from the strict boundaries of dual cultural system beliefs. This can be a difficult process because people face social constraints as third spaces are not power-free zones.

The Devolution of Responsibility and the Narratives of Civic Pluralism

Intercultural mediation has become a postmodern apparatus of public policy and service delivery to counteract inequalities and exclusion. It has been used as an extension of the state's power concerning conflict resolution in an ethnocentric context, especially when addressing the social integration of migrants. For example, many (trans)national organizations (e.g. European Community) deploy mediation practices and policies in promoting social cohesion. These organizations, however, maintain a powerful agency to construct and impose the rules and the course of mediation in a singular way. This is mostly evident in the so-called *institutionalized mediations*[6] (Six, 1999 in Cohen-Emerique, 2007, p. 10), which are closely linked to bureaucratic power. In other words, mediation is often legitimated by the governing bodies as a form to manage diversity and/or marginality. Thus, state authorities often determine the nature of mediation processes and the way that professionals or community volunteers could intervene.

More specifically, systemic responses to training mediators and the accreditation of mediation services differ from country to country in Europe, even though there are generic frameworks of professional conduct especially in the area of justice (http://www.diamesolavisi.net/mediation_gr.html). Some national systems legitimized intercultural mediation as an act of access and equity employing qualified professionals and others leave it on the peripheral sphere of humanitarian/ (semi)voluntary aid. In France, for instance, socio-cultural mediation started in the mid-1970s by migrant volunteers (especially women) who assisted other migrants to overcome socio-cultural barriers in their integration. This migrant grass roots activism brought the establishment of mediation associations demanding equality of civil rights and access to public services and resources. In the early 2000's migrant mediators gained gradual recognition by state authorities through funding, some official training and the ratification of their professional charter of ethics and practice in 2006 (http://fr.wikimediation.org/index.php?title=Code_of_Ethics_and_Deontology_of_Mediation). Mediation in France is a more institutionalized process (mostly carried out by migrant associations and less by various other institutions), although progress has been slow with little adaptation to specific needs. Mediators' training is been introduced but left on the free will of educational providers. In Spain and Italy intercultural mediation is closely linked to the arrival of migrants. In both countries mediation has a precarious status because of the insufficient provision of training and funding (Cohen-Emerique, 2007).

However, the so-called *civic pluralism* transforms the scope of intercultural mediation. It implies a new kind of civility and a new relationship between the state and its civil society pointing into a new culture of negotiating diversity. Nationalistic hierarchies, which imposed themselves on all social spheres through command and compliance have given way to a culture of multiple participation and a new citizenry. *Civic pluralism* brings the devolution of social relations and individual responsibility and accepts that cohesion can be sustained only through diversity even though new disparities and resource competitions are in place. In *civic pluralism* individuals are to "be constantly prepared for the unpredictability of engagement with others whose lifeworld experiences are varied" (Kalantzis & Cope, 2012, p. 100). Also new ways of "belonging" emerge "among people who live in close local and global proximity but not necessarily of the same kin group,

---

[6] The other type of mediation, according to Six (1999, in Cohen-Emerique, 2007, p. 10), is the garden/true mediation, where bonds and bridges between the parties involved as well as common understanding around conflicting issues is constructed.

whose values are varied and whose life choices at times may seem at odds with each other" (Kalantzis & Cope, 2012, p. 128).

Furthermore, nationalist centralized bureaucratic control and delegation gives way to *federalism* (multiple and overlapping sites of self-government) and *subsidiarity* (delegation of certain coordinating, negotiating and mediating roles from local sites to general). In the context of civic pluralism government institutions need "to become a more and more neutral arbiter of differences rather than an advocate of a single cultural vision, as was the case in the era of nationalism" (Kalantzis & Cope, 2012, p. 129). The underlying principles are *equivalence*, *devolution* and *diversity* of service provision in the view of securing equity through comparable social outcomes and diverse services provided by various community support groups and NGOs. These organizations enjoy a considerable degree of autonomy in developing customized services for their clients based on government funding and auditing. This devolution generates more diversity (of approaches, services, institutions, cultures and communities). This means, as far as intercultural mediation is concerned, that there is a need for a more participative, *democratic and pluralistic* form of governance. This form can be grounded on a reflexive (Sampson, 2008), practice of dialogue, (instead of being limited to activism) and an ethical code of collaborative practice between all mediation actors (organizations, professionals, groups and individuals).

The scope of intercultural mediation is to encourage individuals and systems to be transformed through reflexive action and collaborative practices so that all parties become more conscious of dominant discourses that often oppress minority groups. Diverse mediation providers (e.g. social organizations, political institutions and education, judicial, health and welfare systems) contribute to civic pluralism through a *narrative* model (dialogical and relational) where different narratives can be heard in new and meaningful ways (Riva-Mossman, 2009). This model can better address intercultural mediation as it recognizes the importance of power relations in conflict resolution and it assumes that mediation is a process of mutual adventure and discovery, which actively engages all parties in a reciprocal and mutual act of understanding. The narrative approach supports diversity by challenging the expert posture of the mediator/provider or ethnocentric narratives allowing different intercultural voices to be heard. This is why intercultural mediation can be seen as a threat to dominant discourses. However the liberation of both expert and non-expert voices in a participative frame is a crucial point to social inclusiveness because people who are denied to voice their needs may be mobilized against the dominant discourse creating more conflict. Overall, narrative mediation can be seen as "being in between" (Buber, 1970) process. It focuses on this relational space, which guarantees a dialogical and reciprocal professional practice as well as more participation for citizens and non-citizens.

In this context, intercultural mediation is closely intertwined with the concept of *interculturality* and embraces a culture of reciprocity and responsiveness to the specificities of diverse migrant groups based on interdependence and cooperation between cultural groups, individuals and institutions. Interculturality understands cultural diversity in the context of reciprocity, dialogue and mutual understanding and enrichment rejecting the superiority and the unquestioned validity of one culture. At the same time it acknowledges that cultural systems may be incompatible and contradictory resulting in conflict (Panikkar, 1995). Interculturality is not "a disconnected plurality" and moves away from the absolute judgments to a space of mutual learning and exchange. The most important element in this new space is the openness to the *other* and to the self and the ability to engage in reflective dialogue. This means that parties embrace a new ground of understanding and intelligibility. On the other hand all parties maintain a critical approach to judgments and value systems arising from single superior viewpoints, prejudice or ignorance. This reflective dialogical praxis ("dialogical dialogue" as per Panikkar, 1979) involves interpersonal dialogue[7] even though ideas, values and opinions may be incompatible (Agusti-Panareda (2007, p. 42). In other words, parties that engage in a reflexive dialogue in fact experience and integrate elements of the symbolic world of the *other*. Thus, mediators are *change agents* acting as *bridges* of reciprocal adaptation and they are not instruments of transmitting fixed sets of norms and regulations. They are *insiders* to both the system and the community (Agusti-Panareda, 2007, p. 45).

However, intercultural mediation is frequently perceived by state institutions and even mediators themselves as a one-way process implying the conformity of migrants (i.e. assimilation or integration) into a new fixed and unquestionable socio-cultural system. Agusti-Panareda (2007) based on his extended field work on intercultural mediation in Catalonia, Spain, suggests that mediation practice as performed today falls closer to assimilation rather than interculturality, even though there are instances of mediators who act as *change agents*. He asserts that there is considerable ground to be covered towards sustaining an intercultural mindset in mediation services because of a variety of limitations and barriers in the intercultural discourse. Thus, both *normative or ideological* and *factual* or *contextual* limitations occur, which hinder reflexive dialogue. The first refers to strong preconceptions of cultural superiority and migrant obligation to assimilate. The latter refers to the precarious status of migrants (e.g. being foreigners, in need or simply a problem). Mediation process is, conveniently, a pre-set context of state rules and regulations and it may involve either a weak or a strong sense of interculturality. Thus, mediation can foster simple cultural interaction and interchange based on mutual respect and enrichment or it can move furthermore to entail "equal participation, autonomy and consensus" (Agusti-Panareda, 2007, p. 44) in non-fixed new spaces that can be reshaped by all parties.

Intercultural Mediators and their Competences

Intercultural mediator can be any person who works/communicates with people who are different from each other by way of social status, ethnicity, religion, nationality, gender, age or sexual orientation. In addition is someone who is able

[7] Namely, an act of mutual exchange of cultural experiences and "mutual uncovering of the underlying cultural presuppositions and frameworks of intelligibility" (Agusti-Panareda (2007, p. 42). This engagement also involves a) a critical understanding on behalf of the parties of dialoguing traditions of the interlocutors, b) an internal intra-cultural dialogue, which seeks to express common values of both cultures and c) an external intercultural dialogue where participants mutually cross over to the other tradition integrating their testimonies within a new space of common understanding (Agusti-Panareda, 2007).

to facilitate relations between migrants and the specific social context and service providers removing linguistic and cultural barriers and securing accessibility to culturally appropriate services (Verrept, 2012, p. 8)[8]. In other words intercultural mediators act as 'active transformers of narratives' or 'bridges of identities' (Cohen-Emerique, 2007) enabling parties to avoid cultural relativism [9] and enhance better cultural understanding and acceptance. Especially in conflict situations, the so-called "sociocultural dramas" (Turner, 1957 in Riva-Mossman 2009, p. 146) mediators create a 'liminal space' [10] where the ritual of mediation can be performed bringing conflict resolution and transformation.

Overall the intercultural mediator is both a *reflective practitioner* who provides services along a broad spectrum of diversity including cultural differences and an *intercultural learner* who communicates and liaises for cross-purposes.

More specifically, a mediator acts as an intercultural learner who, according to Townsend, (2002, para.2), enters "*a contested space* amid a complex setting of interests, values, beliefs and behaviors". Here, the intercultural "mediator's skills, sensitivity, awareness (of self and others) and patience will be summoned to the forefront of this *whirling space* of conflicting behaviors, substantive jousting, contesting statements and adversarial accusations" (Townsend, 2002, para.2). In this intercultural space new traits of sociability (new relations and communication patterns) are developed. Mediators are transformative learners who in fact maintain multiple foci of both their skills and status and the mediation process itself. They engage in a journey of personal and cultural transformation in which they feel they belong while maintaining at the same time their professional impartiality.

Jon Townsend (2002, para.4) described the following five intercultural principles and mediation practices, which create an operational intercultural space of mutual understanding, empathy and collaborative ethos using culturally appropriate behaviors. These principles are:

---

[8] Some research evidence from health professionals and ethnic minority patients show that intercultural mediators have a positive effect in resolving linguistic and cultural barriers by facilitating the exchange of correct and detailed information. They also ensure the quality of a culturally sensitive and responsive care by identifying patients' needs and respecting their rights (Verrept, 2012, p. 8)

[9] See more on parochial and anti-intellectual character of cultural relativism in Kalantzis and Cope (2012, p. 234-235).

[10] The concept of 'liminality' and of 'liminal' space derives from Arnold van Gennep's theory (1960) of 'rites of passage' (initially published in French in 1909). According to this theory all cultures mark important transitions in the annual cycle and in the life cycle of individuals through rituals which have a tripartite structure. They are distinguished into rites of separation (from the previous stage), rites of transition or liminal rites (when a person is in-between, neither in the previous stage nor completely incorporated in the new stage), and rites of incorporation (into the new status of one's life). Van Gennep pointed out the ritual 'danger' of the liminal stage. People who find themselves in a state of transition, in a 'liminal' state, are polluted and polluting. They are in a state of 'ambiguity', by virtue of being endangering and endangered at the same time. According to American anthropologist Victor Turner, liminal people attract the attention and sympathy of the community and express its solidarity. On the positive and negative dimensions of 'liminality', see Chryssanthopoulou (1984, p. 5-11).

- ***Flexibility***, namely the "mental elasticity" that allows mediators "to be a part of and yet apart from the cultural milieu into which they have entered". Attributes associated with this principle are wonder, awe or creativity.
- ***Tolerance***, namely the ability to resist the effects of prejudice in regard to the views, beliefs and practices of others. "Transparency, empathetic understanding and ethnorelative valuing" are some of the attributes associated with this principle.
- ***Hope***, namely the ability to act as a positive role-model_providing pathways for the participants to enter in a transformative journey of exploration of the unknown and the unfamiliar.
- ***Respect and reciprocity***, which "allows the mediator to realize that process is negotiable" based on a reciprocal and reflective dialogue. In order to acknowledge and understand the participants' cultural beliefs and values, the cultural/communicative protocols of engagement must be made explicit and discussed by all parties involved in an inclusive context, which values and reflects the cultural needs and values of the parties.
- ***Inquisitiveness to learning***, namely the ability and willingness to learning "about one's self, about others, about how others see themselves". Mediators serve as a bridge between their own *lifeworld* and the life histories and cultures of others. They are also keen to know "why" and "how".

At this point it is important to note that intercultural mediators tackle *personal ethnocentrism* (the sense that one's own ethnic culture is superior to all others) and ensure that the other parties of mediation do so. They also seek to move towards a more *ethnorelative and inclusive* understanding and practice (the premise "that cultures cannot be judged or evaluated from a single or absolute ethical or moral perspective") (Townsend, 2002, para.6). Clearly their role in mediation reflects a long, dynamic and evolving process of transformation and learning where reciprocity, negotiation, critical reflection and retrospective take place. On the other hand, intercultural mediators are *reflective practitioners* who develop culturally sensitive skills and apply a methodology and a code of practice. In other words, mediators are trained to engage in intercultural learning and action and secure the quality and the effectiveness of mediation acting as *action-research professionals*. They also act as *social scientists* able to analyze their cases and the mediation process itself and reflect on the social context (e.g. power relations, social justice issues).

Moreover, mediators possess a multifaceted *intercultural competence* (knowledge, skills and attitudes) enriched by personal experiences and reflection. Intercultural competence (Europe, 2011 and Stier, 2006) is defined by the ability not only to successfully communicate with people from other cultures, namely an ability for cultural exchange, interaction and symbolism, but to negotiate with the whole spectrum of diversity (one's *lifeworld*) and otherness (collective ethnic groups' identity). Thus, intercultural competence is a social skill of establishing and maintaining relationships, effective communication and collaborative outcomes, and must be approached in an interdisciplinary way. It also encompasses analytical skills of the global society, a reflexive posture to ambiguity, risk taking, empathy, intercultural awareness, and capacity to transform (Αρβανίτη, 2011). These abilities mean that a person is able to perceive and understand the cultural differences that affect thoughts, feelings and actions.

More specifically, *intercultural knowledge* in the mediation process refers to: i) *awareness/knowledge of different cultural framework(s),* culturally shaped norms and cultural circumstances (facts of history, behavioral patterns, values, principles, symbols, traditions, roles, etc.) and expectations, which explain participants' different perspectives. ii) *self-awareness*, namely the ability to recognize one's own cultural influences and their possible effects on mediation and iii) *multi-cultural perspectives* such as the ability to recognize, understand and appreciate culturally-shaped perspectives, behaviors and events as well as the ability to manage ambiguities in multi-cultural situations in order to facilitate communication and reciprocity (Institute of International Mediation, 2010 and Αρβανίτη, 2011).

On the other hand, *intercultural skills* refer to i) the ability to *manage and apply intercultural knowledge* through the use of interdisciplinary working methods. ii) *The ability to use information and multimodal expressions* and communication styles. Here it is important for mediators to be able to adjust their own communication style to participants' respective cultural styles, and to help participants to communicate optimally with each other. And iii) *Demonstration of creative and critical skills* in the mediation process such as intrapersonal (perspective alternation, problem solving, self-reflection, etc.) and interpersonal skills (use of body language, non - verbal patterns, symbols, etc.), as well as ability to identify possible cultural patterns, which may hinder mediation and design potentially appropriate interventions.

Overall successful mediators have the ability to manage the mediation process and adapt it accordingly to ensure reciprocal settlement and compliance. A skillful mediator needs, for example, to confront differences as they emerge in mediation (see http://imimediation.org/intercultural-certification-criteria). These can be different communication styles (e.g. emotional expressiveness or otherwise), mindset toward conflict (how participants may prefer to negotiate), orientation toward exchanging information (transparent – non-transparent and fact related – non-fact related), time orientation & perspective (deadlines, deliverables, punctuality time pressure- no time pressure), decision-making approaches (norms based – subjective, interests-based, individualist or collectivist).

Finally, *intercultural attitudes* refer to the intercultural awareness and commitment to universal human values and rights as well as the adoption of a positive, sensitive and inclusive attitude for effective communication, active participation, collaboration, compromise and adaptation (Αρβανίτη, 2011).

Conclusion

Global interconnection leads to cultural interaction in new and diversified situations outside traditional social settings. Intercultural mediation is not a power-free zone of contact, but a socially constructed one and it often has to facilitate asymmetrical communication frameworks. The core concepts intertwined with intercultural mediation include flexibility, adaptation and transferability, reflective dialogue, interconnectness and belongingness. In its transformative type mediation enables the reconstruction of *spatiality* as it creates hybrid spaces for new meanings and reflective dialogue allowing the transformation of cultural attitudes and representations. Different voices can be heard and more agency can be given to all parties involved. Mediators, on the other hand, are 'inhabitants of social spaces' (Cohen-Emerique, 2007), 'bridges of identities' and *reflective practitioners* who distribute equal opportunities of participation among the parties thus enhancing mutual understanding.

This chapter discussed the necessity for mediation and mediators to sustain an intercultural potential. Intercultural mediators are catalysts in cre*ating a social space of mutual interaction and community dialogue* where intercultural learning and living can take prominence. Even though mediators do not possess institutional power to affect change, they can intervene as brokers to create spaces of cultural interactivity and mutual trust between all parties involved. Mutual adjustment and recognition are important premises to an intercultural understanding and dialogue.

In addition, mediators may *bring a systemic and administrative change* facilitating the adaptation of the social actors and systems themselves to match emerging needs when dealing with diversity and the challenges of migration. This can happen by initiating the transformation of existing administrative protocols and services to more cultural sensitive and inclusive ones, and also by bringing an interdepartmental and holistic response to managing diverse needs. They can facilitate professionals and institutional bureaucracy to become aware of the fact that integration is a mutual process and not only migrants' obligation and that rigid and ethnocentric regulations might have severe social consequences. Finally, the very work of mediators itself could bring more *agency* to migrants and their integration process (Agusti-Panareda, 2007), whereas systemic transformation may serve to benefit both migrants and the community at large.

Successful mediators possess multiple and certified qualifications and follow an official code of practice. Official recognition, funding, the adoption of professional standards and basic and lifelong training of mediators emerge as important systemic change to ensure quality provision. Mediation can no longer remain on the margins of society.

References

Agusti-Panareda, J. (2007). The Intercultural Promise of Mediation. *InterCulture, 153*, 39-55.

Αρβανίτη, Ε. (2011). Αναλυτικά προγράμματα και αναστοχαστική νεωτερικότητα: Μια διαπολιτισμική προσέγγιση. Στο Κ. Μαλαφάντης, Μ. Σακελλαρίου και Θ. Μπάκας (Eds.), *Πρακτικά ΙΓ' Διεθνούς Συνεδρίου της Παιδαγωγικής Εταιρείας. Αναλυτικά Προγράμματα και Σχολικά Εγχειρίδια: Ελληνική Πραγματικότητα και Διεθνής Εμπειρία. (Τόμος Β')* (σελ. 539-551). Αθήνα: Διάδραση.

Beck, U. (2009). Cosmopolitanization Without Cosmopolitans: On the Discussion Between Normative and Empirical-Analytical

Cosmopolitanism in Philosophy and the Social Sciences. In K. Ikas and G. Wagner (Eds.), *Communicating in the Third Space* (pp. 11-25). New York: Routledge.

Bhabha, H. (1994). *The Location of Culture.* New York: Routledge.

Breinig, H. and Lösch, K. (2002). Introduction: Difference and Transdifference. In J. G. H. Breinig (Ed.), *Multiculturalism in contemporary societies: perspectives on difference and transdifference* (pp. 11-36). Erlangen: Universitätsbund Erlangen.

Chryssanthopoulou, V. (1984). An Analysis of Rituals surrounding Birth in Modern Greece. Master's Thesis, Department of Social Anthropology, University of Oxford.

Clifford, J. (1988). T*he Predicament of Culture.* Cambridge, MA: Harvard UP.

Cohen-Emerique. (2007). Intercultural Mediators: Bridges of Identities. *InterCulture, 153*, 7-22.

Council of Europe, (2011). *Intercultural Competences in Social Services: Constructing an inclusive institutional culture.* France: Council of Europe Publishing.

Hall, E. (1968). Proxemics. *Current Anthropology, 9*, 83-108.

Hall, E. (1989a). *Beyond Culture.* New York: Anchor Books.

Hall, E. (1989b). *The Dance of Life: The Other Dimension of Time.* New York: Anchor Books.

Hofstede, G. (1980). *Culture's Consequences: International Differences in Work-Related Values.* Beverly Hills, CA: Sage Publications.

Hofstede, G., Hofstede, G., J. and Minkov, M. (2010). *Cultures and Organizations: Software of the Mind* (3rd ed.). McGraw Hill Professional.

Institute of International Mediation. (2010). *Criteria for Approving Programs to Qualify Mediators for IMI Inter-Cultural Certification.* Retrieved 12 29, 2013, from http://imimediation.org/intercultural-certification-criteria

Jabert, M. (1998). Travailler avec un interprete en consultation psychiatrique. *P.R.I.S.M.E., 8*(3), 94-111.

Kalantzis, M. & Cope, W. (2012). *New Learning: Elements of a Science of Education.* New York: Cambridge University Press.

Kalscheuer, B. (2009). Encounters in the Third Space: Links between Intercultural Communication Theories and Postcolonial Approaches. In K. Ikas and G. Wagner (Eds.), *Communicating in the Third Space* (pp. 26-26). New York: Routledge.

Lefebvre, H. (1991). *The Production of Space.* Oxford: Blackwell Publishers.

Miike, Y. (2003). Beyond Eurocentrism in the intercultural field: Searching for an Asiacentric paradigm. In W. J. Starosta and G.-M. Chen (Eds.), *Ferment in the intercultural field: Axiology, Value, Praxis* (pp. 243-276). Thousand Oaks, CA: Sage.

Panikkar, R. (1979). *Myth, Faith and Hermeneutics.* New York: Paulist Press.

Panikkar, R. (1995). *Invisible Harmony. Essays on Contemplation and Responsibility.* Minneapolis: Fortress Press.

Rick, A. (1997). What Space Makes of Us: Thirdspace, Identity Politics, and Multiculturalism. *American Educational Research Association Conference.* Chicago, IL : UCLA.

Riva-Mossman, S. K. (2009). *Conflict Narratives: Mediation Case Studies in an Intercultural Context.* Doctoral Thesis, Universiteit van Tilburg. Retrieved from http://repository.uvt.nl/id/ir-uvt-nl:oai:wo.uvt.nl:3453053

Sampson, E. (2008). *Celebrating the Other. A Dialogical Account of Human Nature.* TAOS Institute.

Six, J. F. (1999). Médiation et Réconciliation. *Lettre aux Communautés, 196*, 11-22.

Skordoulis, C. & Arvanitis, E. (2008). Space conceptualisation in the context of postmodernity: Theorizing spatial representation. *The International Journal of Interdisciplinary Social Sciences, 3*(6), 105-113.

Soja, E. (1996). *Thirdspace: Journeys to Los Angeles and Other Real-and-Imagined Places.* Oxford: Basil Blackwell.

Spivak, G. C. (1990). *The Post-Colonial Critic: Interviews, Strategies, Dialogues.* S., Harasym (Ed.). New York: Routledge.

Stier, J. (2006). Internationalisation, intercultural communication and intercultural competence. *Journal of Intercultural Communication, 11*, 1-11.

Thomas, D. (1996). *Transcultural Space and Transcultural Beings.* Oxford: Westview Press.

Townsend, J. (2002). *The Intercultural Mediator: The nexus of practice and theory.* Retrieved from http://www.agreementswork.com/TheInterculturalMediator.php

Turner, V. (1957). *Schism and Continuity in an African Society. A Study of Ndembu Village Life.* Manchester, UK: Manchester University Press.

Van Gennep, A. (1960). *The Rites of Passage.* London and Henley: Routledge and Kegan Paul.

Verrept, H. (2012). Notes on the employment of intercultural mediators and interpreters in health care. *Facts beyond Figures: Communi-care for Migrants and Ethnic Minorities: 4th Conference on Migrant and Ethnic Minority Health in Europe* (pp. 1-15). Milan, Italy: Universita Bocconi. Retrieved 01 28, 2014, from http://www.unibocconi.eu/wps/wcm/connect/cb9a7985-3ea1-479a-acfb-02ff4525562d/Plenary+3+-+Verrept+(2).pdf?MOD=AJPERES

WikiMediation. (n.d.). *Intercultural Mediation.* Retrieved 12 29, 2013, from http://en.wikimediation.org/index.php?title=Intercultural_mediation.

Chapter 2: Using Interactive Management to Identify the Most Important Competences of Cultural Mediators and Their Interrelationships

Morteza Rezaei-Zadeh and Dermot Coughlan

Introduction

What are the most important Competences that need to be cultivated in cultural mediators? How are these Competences ranked and inter-related in structural models developed by different stakeholder groups? The current study seeks to address these questions using a collective intelligence methodology that facilitates understanding of system interdependencies, specifically, by drawing upon the insights and logic of key stakeholder groups who possess knowledge and experience of cultural mediation.

Cross-cultural mediations are more complex than domestic mediations because of cultural differences (Barkai, 2008). This cross-cultural mediation is examined in the different contexts, such as: tourist (Yu et al., 2002), commercial disputes (Barkai, 2008), social context (Al-Krenawi and Graham, 2001), and students' global perspective (Wilson, 1993). The current study sought to review cultural mediator's competences in the context of immigration issues. To do so, a general understanding of some frameworks which could be used in the cross-cultural studies is useful, providing the possibility of interpreting cultural differences in the national and international levels. One of these frameworks is Hofstede's cultural dimensions theory.

Hofstede's cultural dimensions theory, originally, proposed four dimensions along which cultural values could be analyzed: individualism-collectivism; uncertainty avoidance; power distance and masculinity-femininity. These four dimensions were initially identified through a comparison of the values of employees and managers in sixty-four national subsidiaries of the IBM Corporation. Having written a paper entitled "Cultural Constraints in Management Theories" in 1993, he added the fifth dimension, long-term orientation, to cover another aspect of cultural values not discussed in the original paradigm. Finally, in the third edition of "Cultures and Organizations: Software of the Mind", Hofstede (2010) added the sixth dimension, "indulgence versus self-restraint" to explain why some nations have higher percentage of very happy people. He described these six dimensions as below:

- Power Distance: "The degree of inequality among people which the population of a country considers as normal: from relatively equal (that is, small power distance) to extremely unequal (large power distance). All societies are unequal, but some are more unequal than others".
- Individualism: "The degree to which people in a country prefer to act as individuals rather than as members of groups. The opposite of individualism can be called Collectivism, so collectivism is low individualism".
- Masculinity: "The degree to which tough values like assertiveness, performance, success and competition, which in nearly all societies are associated with the role of men, prevail over tender values like the quality of life, maintaining warm personal relationships, service, care for the weak, and solidarity, which in nearly all societies are more associated with women's roles".
- Uncertainty Avoidance: "The degree to which people in a country prefer structured over unstructured situations. Structured situations are those in which there are clear rules as to how one should behave. These rules can be written down, but they can also be unwritten and imposed by tradition".
- Long-term versus Short-term Orientation: "On the long-term side one finds values oriented towards the future, like thrift (saving) and persistence. On the short-term side one finds values rather oriented towards the past and present, like respect for tradition and fulfilling social obligations".
- Indulgence versus self-restraint: "The extent to which members in society try to control their desires and impulses. Whereas indulgent societies have a tendency to allow relatively free gratification of basic and natural human desires related to enjoying life and having fun, restrained societies have a conviction that such gratification needs to be curbed and regulated by strict norms".

Hofstede website, http://www.geert-hofstede.com is an excellent source devoted to Hofstede's cross-cultural dimension theory. On the website, it is possible to create a table and graph comparing the cultural scores of any three countries in terms of the 6 dimensions above. This information could be well used for interpreting cross-cultural studies and narratives.

The main question which could be addressed by studies in the area of cross-cultural mediation is: who can be profiled as a cultural mediator? This question is responded by the previous studies from two perspectives. The first perspective tries to define a cultural mediator based on his/her role. For instance, previous studies pointed out different roles that could be assumed as the cultural mediators, such as: Bilingual Authors (Jung, 2004), Instructional Leaders (Khazzaka, 1997), translators (Bedeker and Feinauer, 2006), comedians (Mintz, 1985). The second perspective tries to profile cultural mediators in terms of their competences. Some studies such as Barkai (2008) implemented this point of view in defining a cultural mediator. Consistent with the latter perspective, the current study sought to explore competences associated with cultural mediators. Therefore, the research question of this study is: Which competences should be possessed by cultural mediators to equip them better to interact –directly or indirectly - with immigrants in their host countries? This question is more important especially for those people who are indirectly dealing with immigrants, such as: Teachers, General Practitioners (GPs), Police, etc., since we expect that people who are directly working with immigrants usually receive more vocational training before and during their profession.

Methodology

There are some diverse approaches to sourcing a correct answer to the question above. The approach which is being used here is asking people who are working with immigrants and also immigrants themselves questions and also to tell us their stories and experiences and help us to find which competences are more important than others to be possessed by cultural mediators in European countries. Apparently, the qualitative research methods could be best fitted to these objectives. Strauss and Corbin (1990) point out that the qualitative research methods describe and reveal people's experience, behaviors, interactions, and social contexts without the use of quantification. Moreover, Stebbins (2003) points out that given the contemporary growth in popularity of qualitative research, need for a systematic, long-term approach to qualitative exploration has never been more acute.

Participants

Two groups participated in the study. Five Iranian and nine Irish people who had experience of dealing with immigrants were invited to participate in two separate Interactive Management (IM) sessions at the University of Limerick (UL) and Galway County Council, Ireland. All participants were informed about the study procedure and gave their consent at the beginning of the IM sessions.

Interactive Management (IM)

The study sought to investigate the consensus view of the five groups, each of whom worked to build a consensus structural model as to the logical interdependencies between a selected set of cultural mediation competences. Advancing upon previous research in the area, the current study used Interactive Management (IM) to model interdependencies between cultural mediation competences.

Based on John Warfield's (1994) science of generic design, the IM process is a system of facilitation and problem solving that helps groups to develop outcomes that integrate contributions from individuals with diverse views, backgrounds, and perspectives. Established as a formal system of facilitation in 1980 after a developmental phase that started in 1974, IM was designed to assist groups in dealing with complex issues (see Ackoff, 1981; Argyris, 1982; Cleveland, 1973; Deal & Kennedy, 1982; Kemeny, 1980; Rittel & Webber, 1974; Simon, 1960).

IM utilizes a carefully selected set of methodologies, matched to the phase of group interaction and the requirements of the situation. The most common methods and techniques are the Nominal Group Technique (NGT), idea-writing, Interpretive Structural Modelling (ISM), and field and profile representations. The first two methodologies are primarily employed for the purpose of generating ideas that are then structured using one or more of the latter three methods. The current study used both NGT and ISM to identify, clarify, and model a set of cultural mediation competences that were selected as critical competences by five groups of experts in this area.

The *nominal group technique* (NGT; Delbeq et al., 1975) is a method that allows individual ideas to be pooled, and is best used in situations in which uncertainty and disagreements exist about the nature of possible ideas. NGT involves five steps: (a) presentation of a stimulus question to participants; (b) silent generation of ideas in writing by each participant working alone; (c) "round-robin" presentation of ideas by participants, with recording on flipchart by the facilitator of these ideas and posting of the flipchart paper on walls surrounding the group; (d) serial discussion of the listed ideas by participants for sole purpose of clarifying their meaning (i.e. no evaluation of ideas is allowed at this point); and (e) implementation of a closed voting process in which each participant is asked to select and rank five ideas from the list, with the results compiled and displayed for review by the group. A modified version of the standard NGT method was used in the current study, with participants initially working to identify cultural mediation competences from a list of competences made available by the IM facilitation team. However, much like standard NGT, participants were also allowed to generate their own unique items and add to the list of competences derived from the scientific literature.

Interpretive structural modelling (ISM; Warfield, 1994) is a computer-assisted technique that helps a group to identify relationships among ideas and to impose structure on those ideas to help manage the complexity of the issue. Specifically, the ISM software utilizes mathematical algorithms that minimize the number of queries necessary for exploring relationships among a set of ideas (see Warfield, 1976). The five steps of ISM are: (a) identification and clarification of a list of ideas (e.g. using NGT); (b) identification and clarification of a "relational question" for exploring relationships among ideas (e.g. "Does idea A support idea B?," "Is idea A of higher priority than B?," or "Does idea A belong in the same category with idea B?"); (c) development of a structural map by using the relational question to explore connections between pairs of ideas (see below); (d) display and discussion of the map by the group; and (e) amendment to the map by the group, if needed.

In the third step of developing a structural map, questions are generated by the ISM software and are projected onto a screen located in front of the group. The questions take the following form:

"Does idea A relate in X manner to idea B?"

"A" and "B" are pairs of ideas from the list developed by participants in the first step of ISM and the question of whether they "relate in X manner" is the statement identified in the second step.

For example, if a group is developing an influence structure with problem statements, the question might read:

> *"Does problem A significantly aggravate problem B?"*

However, in the current study, given our interest in examining the interdependencies between competences, we focused on enhancement relations, specifically, by asking the following question:

> *"Does cultural mediation competency A significantly enhance cultural mediation competency B?"*

Using the ISM technique and software, groups engaged in discussion about each relational question and a vote was taken to determine the group's judgment about the relationship. A "yes" vote was entered in the ISM software by the computer operator if a majority of the participants judged that there was a significant relationship between the pair of ideas; otherwise, a "no" vote is entered.

To sum up, IM alongside with ISM, and Nominal Group Technique (NGT) are used to identify and rank the most important entrepreneurial competences. Further to this identification and ranking, this study sought to explore the interrelationships between the identified competences. These interrelationships are supposed to help us in better understanding of the cause-effect nature of these competences and also shed some light not only on the scope of the training programs, also on the sequence of those programs as well. Another benefit of implementing IM in this study is enhancing consensus between the expert-groups participated in the study and minimizing the intervention of the research facilitator in conducting the research and concluding the findings.

Findings

Analysis of Two Enhancement Structures across the Two Expert Groups

The output of the two IM sessions held with the experts and immigrants is two Enhancement Structures which illustrate cultural mediators' competences, their ranking, and their interrelationships. These two structures are outlined in Figures 2.1 and 2.2.

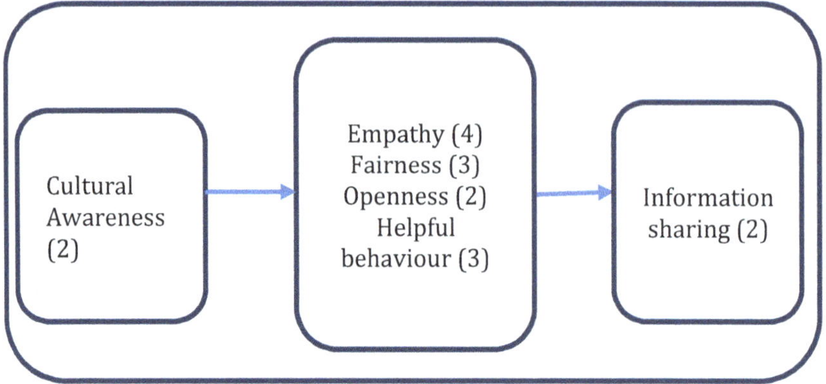

Figure 2.1: The Enhancement Structure of the first IM session: The Cultural Mediators' most important competences and their Interrelationships

The structure is to be read from left to right and the arrows indicate 'significantly enhance'. Values in parenthesis reflect the number of votes the competency received. Items listed together in one box are reciprocally interrelated, with the significant enhancement relation working in both directions. An initial examination of the first enhancement structure (See Figure 2.1) suggests that "Cultural Awareness" is the critical driver of other competences of cultural mediators and significantly enhances a package of competences that are reciprocally interrelated: Empathy, Fairness, Openness, and Helpful Behavior. Information Sharing is placed in the last cycle at stage 3 of the enhancement structure and thus, is viewed as interdependent competency of cultural mediators by the experts in the current study. Information Sharing is a characteristic of the cultural mediators that is driven by a Cultural Awareness, and the cluster of interdependent competences: Empathy, Fairness, Openness, and Helpful Behavior.

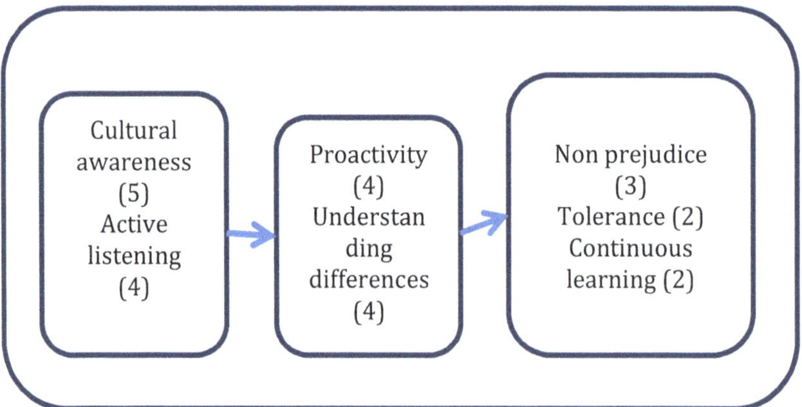

Figure 2.2: The Enhancement Structure of the second IM session: The Cultural Mediators' most important competences and their Interrelationships

Looking more closely at Figure 2.2, it can be seen that similarly to the previous enhancement structure, Cultural Awareness is identified as one of the most important competences of cultural mediators. It is seen as both a highly valued characteristic (with 5 votes) and a key driver of many other skills and dispositions. Both Cultural Awareness and Active Listening significantly enhance two packages of competences that are reciprocally interrelated: Proactivity and Understanding differences are located in the second circle of the structure and Non prejudice, Tolerance, and Continuous learning are located in the last circle of the structure. It means that the latter interrelated package is driven by the previous competences in the first and second circles.

Analyzing and Scoring Selected Competences

Taking into account the two enhancement structures above, Table 1 illustrates the selected competences associated with cultural mediators. As could be seen in Table 2.1, a total of 13 cultural mediation competences were selected when the results of the two expert groups were combined.

Table 2.1: The Cultural Mediation Competences selected by two IM sessions

Expert groups	Selected competences	Number of votes
First IM session : Iranian Experts	Cultural Awareness	2
	Empathy	4
	Fairness	3
	Openness	2
	Helpful behavior	3
	Information sharing	2
Second IM session: Irish experts	Cultural awareness	5
	Active listening	4
	Proactivity	4
	Understanding differences	4
	Non prejudice	3
	Tolerance	2
	Continuous learning	2

But the question here is: do all of these competences get the same importance and priority by the expert groups of this study? The response to this question is no. As can be seen in Table 2.1, these competences got different votes from the participants of the expert groups. Moreover, some of the competences such as cultural awareness were mentioned by both expert groups. More importantly, the location of the competences in the enhancement structures is not same. It means that some of the competences drive more other competences, and therefore, they are more important than the driven competences. Taken into account the different dimensions which can be used in calculating the importance of these competences, an algorithm was designed as below:

The final Score (weight) of each Competency = Commonality + Votes + Level (Reversed) + Succedent interrelations

"Commonality" refers to the number of times each competency appears in the different Enhancement Structures. "Votes" refers to the total number of votes assigned to each competency by the groups. "Level" represents the location of each competency in each enhancement structure. Its score is reversed as competences at level 1 have the highest influence in the enhancement structure, followed by competences at level 2, 3, and so on. For an enhancement structure with 5 levels, those competences located at level 1 receive a score of 5, competences at level 2 receive a score of 4, etc. "Succedent interrelations" indicates the number of competences that are influenced by a competency within the enhancement structure. Table 2.2 shows scores for each of the 37 identified competences. Also, this table ranks competences according to their total score.

Table 2.2: Rank order list of the most important Cultural Mediation Competences from across two IM sessions

Rank	Competency	Score				
		Commonality	Votes	Level (Reversed)	Succedent interrelations	Total Net
1	Cultural Awareness	2	2 + 5	3 + 3	5 + 6	26
2	Active listening	1	4	3	6	14
3	Empathy	1	4	2	4	11
4	Proactivity	1	4	2	4	11
5	Understanding differences	1	4	2	4	11
6	Fairness	1	3	2	4	10
7	Helpful behavior	1	3	2	4	10
8	Openness	1	2	2	4	9
9	Non prejudice	1	3	1	2	7
10	Tolerance	1	2	1	2	6
11	Continuous learning	1	2	1	2	6
12	Information sharing	1	2	1	0	4

As could be seen in Table 2.2, five competences including Cultural Awareness, Active listening, Empathy, Proactivity, and Understanding differences obtained scores greater than 10 and emerged as some of the most influential cultural mediation competences across the two groups. Toward the bottom of Table 2 are competences with lower scores ranging from 4 to 7, including Information sharing, Continuous learning, Tolerance, and Non prejudice. This table clearly illustrates that the cultural mediation competences are not located in the same level of importance and they could be prioritized in terms of their impact on potential cultural mediators.

Conclusion

Over the last decades a number of studies have been conducted to identify the most important cultural mediation competences in different contexts. Different studies have used alternative terms including skills, characteristics, capabilities or expertise to describe different competences. The results of the current study highlight Cultural Awareness as the most influential cultural mediation competency that needs to be cultivated in cultural mediators who want to deal with immigrants. Consistent with the findings of this study, the importance and central position of cultural awareness in cultural mediation is approved by Barkai (2008) who illustrated that cultural awareness and flexibility are two important cultural mediation competences. Wilson (1993) highlighted the impact of getting international experience on increasing students' cultural awareness and finally on their intercultural competence.

Notably, Active listening, Empathy, Proactivity, and Understanding differences were identified as the other main components of cultural mediators by participants in the current study. The role and importance of these competences need to be investigated by the future empirical studies in this area. Furthermore, the training approaches of these competences need to be investigated by the future studies. In this case, the concept maps provided in the enhancement structures generated by this study could be extremely useful. Novak et al. (2008) suggested that the concept maps provided by reviewing interrelationships between a certain set of competences can be enormously useful in curriculum planning by:

- Presenting in a highly concise manner the key concepts and principles to be taught;
- Suggesting more optimal sequencing of instructional material;
- Making the instruction "conceptually transparent" to students.

Therefore, it is recommendable for the future studies, which sought to explore training approaches to enhance cultural mediators' competences, to generate the enhancement structures of the targeted competences or use the enhancement structures generated by this study (see figures 1 and 2).

From the methodological perspective, another contribution of this study is implementing IM method in the context of cultural mediation. To the best of knowledge of this study, it is the first implementation of this method in identifying cultural mediators' competences.

This study was limited to the ideas of expert groups living or working in Ireland. Implementing IM method to identify cultural mediators' competences in other cultural contexts should be useful to have a better understanding of these competences.

References

Ackoff, R. L. (1981). *Creating the corporate future: Plan or be planned for*. New York: John Wiley and Sons.

Al-Krenawi, A., & Graham, J. R. (2001). The cultural mediator: Bridging the gap between a non-western community and professional social work practice. *British Journal of Social Work*, *31*(5), 665-685.

Argyris, C. (1982). *Reasoning, learning, and action: Individual and Organizational*. San Francisco: Jossey-Bass.

Barkai, J. (2008). What's a Cross-Cultural Mediator to Do-A Low-Context Solution for a High-Context Problem. *Cardozo J. Conflict Resol*, *10*, 43.

Bedeker, L., & Feinauer, I. (2006). The translator as cultural mediator. *Southern African linguistics and applied language studies*, *24*(2), 133-141.

Cleveland, H. (1973). *The decision makers*. Center Magazine, 6(5), 9-18.

Deal, T. E., & Kennedy, A. A. (1982). *Corporate cultures: The rites and rituals of corporate life*. Reading, MA: Addison-Wesley.

Delbeq, A. L., Van De Ven, A. H., & Gustafson, D. H. (1975). *Group techniques for program planning: A guide to nominal group and Delphi processes*. Glenview, IL: Scott, Foresman.

Hofstede, Geert. Hofstede, Gert Jan. Minkov, Michael. (2010). *Cultures and Organizations: Software of the Mind* (3rd ed.). McGraw Hill Professional.

Jung, V. (2004). Writing Germany in Exile–the Bilingual author as Cultural Mediator: Klaus Mann, Stefan Heym, Rudolf Arnheim and Hannah Arendt. *Journal of Multilingual and Multicultural Development*, *25*(5-6), 529-546.

Kemeny, J. (1980). Saving American democracy: The lesson of Three Mile Island. *Technology Review*, *83*(7), 64-75.

Khazzaka, J. (1997). The instructional leader as cultural mediator. *The Clearing House: A Journal of Educational Strategies, Issues and Ideas*, *70*(3), 121-124.

Mintz, L. E. (1985). Standup comedy as social and cultural mediation. *American Quarterly*, 71-80.

Novak, J. D., & Cañas, A. J. (2008). *The theory underlying concept maps and how to construct and use them.* Florida Institute for Human and Machine Cognition Pensacola Fl, www. ihmc. us.[http://cmap. ihmc. us/Publications/ResearchPapers/T heoryCmaps/TheoryUnderlyingConceptMaps. htm], 284.

Rittel, H., & Webber, M. (1974). Dilemmas in a general theory of planning. *DMG-DRS Journal*, *8*, 31-39.

Simon, H. A. (1960). *The new science of management decisions*. New York: Harper & Row.

Warfield, J. N. (1994). *A science of generic design: Managing complexity through systems design* (2nd ed.). Salinas, CA: Intersystems.

Wilson, A. H. (1993). Conversation partners: Helping students gain a global perspective through cross-cultural experiences. *Theory into Practice*, *32*(1), 21-26.

Yu, X., Weiler, B., & Ham, S. (2002). Intercultural communication and mediation: A framework for analysing the intercultural competence of Chinese tour guides. *Journal of Vacation Marketing*, *8*(1), 75-87.

Chapter 3: The Ethnographer as Cultural Mediator: Notes on a Case Study and Reflections on Interculturalism

Vasiliki Papageorgiou

Introduction

During the past three decades, questions of multiculturalism and the management of cultural diversity come to the fore more and more often on the political agenda in most European countries like Greece. Discussion of the role, the qualifications, and even the professionalization of the cultural mediator – as it is called – can be placed in this setting, involving a broader concern with the transition of western societies to new forms of co-existence and interaction between natives and the different groups of migrants.

As a consequence, it has been produced a multiplicity of discourses on culture, and related terms like multiculturalism and inter(or cross-) cultural relations. In different fields such as migrant law and policy, education, academic theorization, the politics of NGO and indigenous peoples, actors use conceptualizations of culture that often have certain political and ideological implications. It's important to stress also, that in popular discourse the term tends to be used as a short-hand generalization and, hence, to increase the complexity of the concept of culture.

This paper aims at highlighting some points on this analytical inaccurateness and, especially, contributing to the discussion of cultural mediation. It offers an anthropological perspective on interculturalism, reflecting upon my fieldwork experience working with Albanian migrants in Greece.[1]

I will sketch out an analytical framework for the study of intercultural relations in the context of cultural contact. My main task is to present the actual places where interaction can happen and to trace the cultural processes of this cultural contact. Then I will use an analogy, proposing that cultural mediation shares some common elements with ethnographic work. In particular, I argue that

[1] See my work on Albanian migration in Greece, Papageorgiou 2011.

being a member of the host society, was a very crucial factor in the way migrants perceived what I was doing. In fact, in many cases I was considered some kind of a cultural mediator. I will give some examples, drawing them from my ethnographic material. In the last session, I finally turn to a discussion of some key issues that in my opinion provide critical insights.

Before going further, I should point out one difficulty with the attempt to apply a microlevel methodology which gives an emphasis on politics "from below" in our analysis. What is argued here is that, when we use culture theoretically situated in anthropology, then, the notion of cultural mediator gives prominence and weight to cultural and symbolic processes of everyday interaction. But, we should always bear in mind, that all this rich symbolic work is situated in a broader political and formal framework. At the same time, this framework (e.g. legal framework) regulates cultural mediation as a clear defined task, or profession. So, cultural mediation has a formal aspect too, going beyond the focus of analysis at this point, which I shall turn to later at the conclusion of this chapter.

But in any case, the discussion of cultural mediation may be very productive and has real effects, if it enables us to constitute a new framework for the management of intercultural communication. A point of major importance is the recognition of this fact. We then move one step beyond: it seems that instead of imposing our culture and expect or praise "other's" ability to adapt, as it is supposed in common policies of migration and/or multiculturalism, that still suffer from ethnocentrism or cultural relativism (both implying a fixed conceptualization of culture) we begin to recognize the necessity of "interpretation": this is methodologically close to recent anthropological theory. It seems that cultures are not concrete, fixed entities, as were older views in theory. Moreover, it comes that in a complex world, where sites (or zones) of cultural contact are everywhere, cultural competence may belong to human rights and is not simply a moral discourse, as we will discuss in the following.

Migration Research and the Topic of Cultural Mediation: Tracing a Common Ground for Opening a Discussion

In recent years, theoretical consideration in the field of migration has removed from host societies to the migrants as actors, a condition that brought to prominent issues of experiences, representations and identity formations of the latter. This development was favored by critiques in social science on the relation between culture, place and identity. A static conceptualization of culture has been strongly questioned in the case of movement and border crossings and the dynamics of cultural change and fluidity came to the fore.[2] In the context of this debate, researchers have questioned traditional concepts of fixity, in particular as expressed in symbols like "home" or "homeland". They focus now on the multiple ways people, especially those on the move, create homes and seek forms of belonging and places to anchor their identities, as it has been seen in a rich

[2] For a detailed presentation of this theoretical debate see Gupta and Ferguson 1997.

bibliography on migration studies, including the contribution of many anthropologists.[3] This offers me a good starting point to set my argument.

Interculturalism pertains to this condition of cultural contact and confrontation with new cultural patterns. It is argued that migrants work out new experiences and construct their own worlds on the basis of familiar cultural patterns that creatively rework and locate in new settings. First of all, the fieldwork is actually a place of cultural contact. The ethnographer studies not a fixed community in the ordinary way, but in conditions of cultural contact. Migrants are observed in places of interaction, and patterns of cultural exchange are analyzed. My point is, that to understand migrants' point of view we have to focus on everyday cultural production in contexts of cultural interaction. Interculturalism creates a shifting location where identity and difference are in a constant flow. We may argue that Greeks (the natives) interact and change in the same way, as Albanians (the migrants) do.

At this point, let me introduce the concept of "mediation", and apply it rather loosely and broadly: to put it simply, migrants use (informal) cultural mediation in many – often not explicit – ways: key persons in their communities (e.g. already settled compatriots), or in the host country. This kind of mediation refers not only to useful information and knowledge of coping with routine tasks, difficult to be performed by a newcomer to the country, and problems related to bureaucracy, but also implies a deeper understanding of new cultural patterns.

That was obvious in the case of Albanian migrants. Their orientation towards Greek society, and the patterns through which they organize ways of incorporation, as I'll present in the following, allow and enable them to develop "bridges" with the host country. They aim at creating fields of social relations that include members of the host society. For example, Greek friends, godparents, neighbors, or even employers as well, are considered as persons of great importance by the migrants from Albania, providing ways of intense involvement in the new cultural setting. Consequently, cultural mediation, in this broad sense, reveals the need of the interpretation of cultures in a shifting world of transformations and fluidity, and, hence, increasing interculturalism. Interculturalism implies a condition of exchange and negotiation of meaning. This condition in the case of migrancy, involves the urgent task of understanding and interpreting, depending on the degree of cultural distance, as I analyze in the following.

More particular, cultural exchange is twofold, or organized around two principles:

> Migrants explain and describe the new setting according to their own terms and cultural patterns, while at the same time – or perhaps soon after that – they become familiar with, and are drawn into, new experience and knowledge. If the latter prevails, then we may suppose that more change and transformation of the old ways are produced. Another assumption here is that this process depends on the cultural distance / proximity of the migrants from the natives. The more "open" or "close" the migrant group is towards host society, the more

[3] For a discussion and an analytical framework on this topic see Rapport and Dawson 1998.

importance is given to acquiring knowledge and understanding. Furthermore, it is possible that they seek to share the same "cultural world" with the natives. Consequently, in this theoretical assumption, cultural mediation – informal and formal – is a means of facilitating communication, favoring sameness and not difference.

In the next section, I will focus more closely on the case of Albanian migrants in Greece, and elaborate an anthropological perspective of analysis which aims to offer a critical insight into the issue of interculturalism.

The Case of Albanian Migration in Greece: Cultural Patterns of Incorporation and Discourses of Migratory Experience

I argue that doing ethnographic work on the field of migration is a rather complicated task. The ethnographer has to unravel migrants' point of view, that is in a process of transformation, and hence fluidity. As I've already mentioned, cultural contact, interaction and intercultural communication are extremely important constitutive factors that we have to bear in mind.

Let me start by giving an outline of my ethnographic work on Albanian migration in Greece. Conducted between 2001 and 2006, it was centered on issues of Albanian migrants' settlement and patterns of the organization of their social lives. My aim was to highlight theoretically the transformations of identities and processes of incorporation in a new and sometimes hostile setting. I used an anthropological approach deeply inspired by recent explorations of social theory on the "border" concept.[4] Focusing on how Albanian migrants in Greece meet and exchange with social and cultural "others", in different and hierarchically structured fields of action, I worked on everyday "border crossings" (a trope denoting cultural exchange), seeing them as a cultural practice of involving in the host society.

For the purpose of this analysis, I also use the concept of *incorporation* which I elaborate from an anthropological perspective. In this way, I consider incorporation as a process by which migrants connect to new environments, build new homes, end even alter their worldviews. I mention here that this kind of analysis is also inspired by the work of theorists like Brah or Girloy that has influenced the debate on interculturalism.[5] In the next I will briefly comment on migration as a cultural process and provide selected ethnographic material which in particular focus on the issue of incorporation and explores core symbols and meaning as it is manifested in discourse.

Albanian migration in Greece was an unexpected event in times of fierce crisis and political turmoil in Albania. The first years of illegal entry for the majority, shaped the patterns of this migration flow, historically situated in the condition of the collapsing of communism throughout all Europe. It was a mass movement of families which aimed mostly at permanent settlement in Greece. Especially for the people of south Albania the proximity facilitated the pattern I

---

[4] On the "border" concept and related topics see Alvarez 1995 and Donnan and Wilson 1999.

[5] See for example Brah 1996, Gilroy 2004.

described. From the Greek side, there was also some kind of tolerance that proved to be encouraging. Being one of the most mass population movements in post-war Europe, it is also impressive for one special element: Albanian migrants develop a strong orientation of permanent settlement in Greece and create intense involvement in this social and cultural environment. This is a point that I would like to put some emphasis on.

Albanian migrants are strongly oriented towards new environment. They perceive movement in space – physical movement – as a movement in time. They crossed geographical borders, which were at the same time borders of space and time. They negotiate notions of "western culture" while juxtaposing to the life under Albanian communism. Many informants narrate their encounter with Greece, using the symbolic opposition "old": "modern". This is a crucial point, which I'll try to elaborate.

Since their arrival in Greece, migrants from Albania try to reconstruct their lives, re-interpreting and re- defining basic attitudes and beliefs. This is a process that is performed by contrasting past with present, communism with capitalism and western culture, images of Albania with images of Greece. The new social and cultural environment is perceived through the prism of Western modernity, representing a new, modern lifestyle, a different cultural model, which is described as "culturally rich". I will clarify this point next. To unravel patterns of intercultural communication I argue that we need a deep knowledge of migrants' discourses, especially as expressed in their narratives.

The structure of their narratives, as I suggest, reflects Albanians' migratory experience as a cultural process of relating to place and time. Narratives are structured in the basis of a symbolically powerful dual set of constructing dichotomies, as follows: there (Albania): here(Greece): then: now. This symbolic system of oppositions articulated in practice, however, and in many diverse contexts, is not always fixed, but sometimes ambiguous as well, as it will be discussed in the following.

Among Albanian migrants that had a lived experience of the communist regime, there is a strong tendency to classify and explicitly contrast between things that they do now and things they did then.[6] Place and time are, therefore, interconnected – with the mediation of movement – as place (Greece/Albania) becomes a powerful metaphor for time. The experience of crossing the border (the former strict Greek-Albanian border) alters the conceptualization of time. Albania ("there") belongs to the past, (Albania represents an actual loss of contact with and knowledge of the outside world) and Greece ("here") belongs to the present, the desired world of western modernity. Migrants' new identities (pointing here to the process of identity transformations) tend to orientate towards Greece, "now", the present, rejecting their opposites.

Albanian migrants often state «we were close, we didn't know». This metaphor of a "close people" points to Albanians' supposed ignorance, as opposed to new perceptions of reality, after their movement. «We saw things, we

[6] Most of my informants in my research – during 2001 to 2006 – were between 25 and 65, and have been in Greece at least a period of five years. It is obvious, that the older a migrant is, the more intense memory does he/she keeps from the communist regime. But, even young migrants of 25, that in 1990 were about 10 years old, are considered to have embodied some kind of that ethos.

had our eye opened», is a common metaphor for the experience of coming in Greece for the first time after decades of Albania's isolation. It is suggestive that they underline this situation of "closeness" by appealing to their appearance: for instance, commenting to the "picture" of old- fashioned Albanian women, in sharp contrast with the "modern", "nice" and "seductive" women that they encounter in Greece for the first time.

It is remarkable that they have a deep sense of Albania's distinctiveness, as a state isolated and backward in relation to other European countries. They negotiate new perceptions of places, as they speak about communism and capitalism, Albania and Greece, Europe, America the "West". They construct images of places as they negotiate new experiences and new identities and as they interact with Greeks.

Albania is indissolubly connected to communism, a political system and ideology that is rejected and negatively represented in my informants' discourses. Nevertheless, in addition to this discourse centered on the proximity to modernity, migrants also reconstructed their lives, stressing the cultural idiom of "safety" and "fixity" or "stability" as complementary and often positive elements of life in Albania in their narratives. "Safety" was surrounded by a rich symbolic world and as I suggest, is embedded in a particular political and social organization (communism), became a powerful cultural idiom that informs strongly the current organization of life in Greece.

First, "safety", in my informants' narratives, refers to actual characteristics of social life in Albania. A number of services like work, housing, health care, education were considered public and free. The state provided them to all of the citizens. But "safety" is also symbolized as "fixity", "stability" and "order". "State" is a metaphor for these values. The expression "there is state" is revealing in asserting a political situation where everything is ordered. My informants emphatically refer, for example, to zero criminality, which is reflected on the image of women that could go round freely without the fear of being raped or harmed. The central place of "work" in their system of values has been constituted historically. It is rooted in the dominant ideology of communistic Albania. Employment was one of the main preoccupations of the state, which was obligated to secure jobs for the citizens. Everybody, men and women worked – unemployment as exist in capitalism was unknown.

One of the most impressive narratives refers to Hoxha' s death, as a dramatic event in their lives. From their point of view, Hoxha (the leader of Albania for almost four decades) was a major symbol of stability, orientation and safety. One informant reports «when he died we lamented his loss and wept for days» and explains this reaction by pointing, once again, to Albania's "closeness". «We felt insecure at that time. We didn't know what to do and thought that his death would bring about afflictions and chaos», one woman stresses and explains that Hoxha was like a "father" to Albanian people. In fact, this is a figure that denotes the protective role of the omnipresent state. At the same time they mention the value of family, implying that it was articulated with notions of "safety" and compatible with the dominant ideology. Indeed, they stress a world centered on the idiom of nuclear family, the basic unit used by the state to implement plans, orders and laws.

I now turn to another symbolism of "safety". As it is reflected in their narratives, "safety" connotes a world of immobility, where the potential of changes or improvement was reduced to a minimum. I notice here, that in the countries of the former communist bloc, physical movement was strictly under control and almost totally forbidden travelling abroad. So, crucial to the formations of identities were fixity to a locality and a sense that everything was planned by the state.

Representations of life in Albania, include references of arranged marriages, small chances of fun, simplicity of living, severe work relations, set ways of doing things like shopping and consumption patterns: «you were like a robot», as Albanians say. «You knew what you ought to do». This regularity and routine way of doing things and organize life, constitute a well-known pattern of living.

In addition, they often recall scarcity of goods, times of severe poverty and distress and illustrate their struggle for survival, especially mentioning their mothers' or their grandmothers' efforts: a "picture" of a woman that patched the hole on a cloth is figured in some of my informants narratives. But, what impressed me, is the way that scarcity and poverty are perceived in an ambiguous way and are transformed in these narratives through the acceptable idiom of "simplicity": «A simple, happy life», as one of my informants puts it.

Albanian migrants assert that «in Albania we had households», or «we were householders», in one sense «masters/ mistresses of the house», implying a total integration in this model of domestic world of order. In other words, they refer to a specific ethos of a family- oriented and hard-working individual, ideally the model of the "socialist man" so eagerly fostered by dominant ideology, capable of contributing to the collective social progress. In the context of this analysis, I consider "safety" as a system of orientation and a certain worldview, imbued with values of communist ideology. Ideology of family/ household and work provide the principles for these migrants to rearrange their lives after the rupture of movement. In the place of settlement, life is organized around family (home) and work.

So, life in Albania is reconstructed in ambiguous terms, and this ambiguity underline that meaning is specified by context, as actors are engaged in the politics of representation. Moreover, Albanian migrants develop new discourses in intercultural contexts, where symbols of the past come together and mix with symbols of the present. The concepts and ideology of family/home and work establish a world with stable points of reference and empower them to orientate and re –contextualize in the new social and cultural environment. "Hard work" is a core metaphor to reflect on their lives in Greece. "With hard work you can go on" as they stress. Their overall ideological orientation towards work is in accordance with the basic principles of capitalism. And helps them to adjust to difficult working conditions, by emphasizing not the hierarchical structure of work relationships (especially for those working in the informal sector, like women domestic workers) but the possibility of not being marginalized and improving their position in the host society.

So, work is conceived in terms of "capitalism" and perceived as a more dynamic and more creative force now, as it is linked to individual progress. "Progress" is perceived in terms of material fulfillment: it is connected with accumulation of capital, consumption, and ownership. An important consideration here is the symbolism of western goods and material culture as it is reflected in house making, for example, and how taste and aesthetic standards are articulated with new life in Greece and new perceptions of identities.

This is verbally expressed in the concept of "success". A sense of mobility, in other words, connects with the development of a new sense of individual responsibility. Albanian migrants experience creativity in new ways.

Hence, incorporation is strongly affected by cultural systems already embedded as an ethos and to the transformations occurred in the new setting. It is in this framework that as I suggest our effort to capture interculturalism should be placed.

Strategies of Intercultural Relations and Communication: Migrants from Albania between Acceptance and Rejection—The Issue of Conflict

My thesis is that patterns of incorporation may also include patterns of intercultural relations, and that they are closely interrelating. In social fields of everyday interaction migrants invent strategies of coping with the new setting. They develop strategies of intimacy, of closeness and openness to the "other". They try to interpret new and unknown – at least during the first years of their arrival in Greece – cultural patterns. They also try to take advantage of new knowledge for the fulfillment of their purposes and for their success. Work settings, neighbors, schools, coffee shops (especially for men), are places where migrants and natives are highly interact and communicate. Networks with members of the host society are highly appreciated, as I mentioned earlier. Intercultural communication cannot be separated from social relations that facilitate migrants' involvement in the new setting.

It's worth mentioning here, that Albanians prefer to choose Greeks as godparents, and increase their "social capital" in this way. They also try to empower relations with their Greek employers. They use these relations to their own advance: support (of any kind, including material support, chances for extra work), useful information and advices, learning of Greek language, comprehension of dominant cultural patterns.

Migrants of Albania are well integrated in terms of housing, work, their children's education. It was the first massive wave of migrants from Eastern Europe in Greece and this factor affected positively their settlement in many aspects. On the other hand, they confronted a hostile setting, and they became the target of a strong racist discourse centered on Albania's stereotypical image of inferiority.

Intercultural communication between Greeks and migrants from Albania is strongly affected by negative stereotypes the former express towards the latter. Albanian's identity formation is deeply affected by these processes of powerful discourses of exclusion. The internalization of this negative picture of the inferior, "Albanian other" has render many migrants uncomfortable to express idioms of their Albanian identity freely in public spaces, or, in extreme cases, as in school environment, to hide their origin. In addition they try to stress similarity with Greeks and appeal to the same religion (if they are orthodox), to their common traditions and other cultural elements (e.g. language as in the case of

Northern Hepirotes "Βορειοηπειρώτες- vorioipirotes" – the group of migrants from Albania that considered to be of Greek ethnic identity, the Greek minority in Albania). It has been also recorded that many Albanians prefer the term "vorioipirotis" instead of "Albanian" in settings of self-representation.

The Ethnographer as Mediator

Earlier, I tried to provide a sketch of the intercultural context in the case under scrutiny in this paper. My next task will be rather to present briefly the portrait of a specific relationship, that between me, in the place of fieldwork – the ethnographer, – and my informants. The main points already mentioned in the previous section, form a useful framework of the analysis here.

So, Albanians' encounter with the ethnographer is shaped by the condition of interculturalism and the particular patterns of incorporation already discussed. As I have pointed at the beginning, they perceived in their own terms and "placed" the ethnographer in their worlds. Their general attitude and stance towards me was governed by their understandings and interpretations of the new environment. Hence, it was obvious that, besides being a researcher who was there to observe them, I was also a useful acquaintance, a "mediator" who could facilitate their efforts to cope with the difficulties of adaptation.

I could give useful information, advice, explanations and interpretations on their questions. In this case cultural mediation was also about cultural interpretation: I had to make clear some cultural symbols, patterns, ideas and behaviors embedded in the new setting, and I had the task of, let me argue, transforming the "unknown", the complex understandings and norms of the Greek capitalist, western world, to a "familiar" one. More urgent – let me use the term "instrumental"– mediation may include tasks, such as help them in finding any kind of paid work, which was an issue of major importance. Or to help their children in schooling. Or, to accompany someone to the police, to introduce useful acquaintances like lawyers etc.

But at the same time, they tried to make me "part" of their worlds. They really enjoyed our conversations where they could express their experiences, and reflect on them. They narrated their life stories and continually asked me to comment on them, as they liked to hear my opinion, to exchange and share ideas: they liked to discuss with a member from the host culture as they made bridges of connections. Some of them invited me in special occasions, like weddings and celebrations or asked me to become a godmother for their child.

They addressed me with familiarity and expected sympathy and compassion from me. For them, I was a "good" or a "simple person": this is a label they attached to me, and the way those who already knew me introduced me to their kin. "You are a good person": this statement was repeated emphatically again and again in the place of fieldwork. I was the only one to whom they could express with easiness – and without fear of the consequences – their anger about Greek's racist attitudes towards them. They narrated stories of Greeks bad and insulting behavior. They couldn't tolerate being called by the Greeks "the Albanians" in a negative, stereotypical way, and I was considered as the proper person to open such a discussion with. Because although I am Greek, I was not like the Greeks they met and knew, I was not behaving like Greeks.

Epilogue: The Recognition of Interculturalism: Notes on the Political Implications

A central concern in this paper is to examine a particular way of addressing interculturalism, so as to avoid fixed notions of culture that are embedded in common discourses. My argument is that ethnographic work, and especially in fieldwork places, that are zones where migrant groups and natives are highly interact, may involve some tasks pertinent to those supposed by mediation. What I claimed here, is that, if interculturalism is our main analytical focus, then mediation is more complex than a strict formal and technical description may imply. The brief portrait I sketched here brings out the rich symbolic work involved in this specific intercultural relation.

A word of warning must be entered at this point: as I stressed at the beginning, cultural mediation as a formal task, engaged in official migrant policies, may have some normative aspects, and may, also be informed by more strict and narrow concepts of culture than those prevailed in academic theory. The point I would like to stress, is that political discourses of interculturalism are often normative and simplistic, stressing values like tolerance, acceptance, dialogue or aiming at principles such as cohesion and integration. This kind of discourse, however, may hide the mundane and routine problems of everyday interaction and communication (as it happens in cases of conflict) that can come to the fore in every real place of cultural contact and exchange.

In my opinion the discussion of mediation contributes first to the recognition of interculturalism as a "normal" and not a "marginal" condition in our western societies. The need to mediate also stress, as I argued, that cultural contact is more than a static exchange of cultural identities or the folkloric representation of cultural differences. It's a condition of fluidity and transformation for both the migrants and the natives.

Moreover, the discussion of intercultural mediator brings out some questions of great importance to be answered. One crucial point, in my opinion, is the kind of mediation we wish to offer. Interculturalism, from an ethnographic perspective as it is examined in this paper, is not an ideal, normative condition. It's about the negotiation of meaning, and, hence the issue of cultural interpretation comes to the fore. Like the ethnographer or the anthropologist that produce a text from "the native's point of view" – as the pioneer anthropologist Malinowski has taught as[7] – cultural mediator may carry the same task: of interpretation; and of setting the parameters of the frameworks of communication in each case. To accomplish his/her work on mediation, cultural mediator should be authorized to do so. Some kind of professionalization that includes ethical codes and the empowerment of cultural mediators' identity through their specialization in the domain of culture should be important elements. On the other hand, the formalization of the tasks and the official recognition of cultural mediator as a profession is possible to imply or reflect political discourses of interculturalism that carry particular meanings and express the power of those planning this project (e.g. experts, managers). There also may be the possibility of using cultural expertise to

[7] On this subject see the work of Gefou-Madianou on anthropological theory, Gefou-Madianou 1999.

implement policies of exclusion (for example in the case of illegal migrants that have very few possibilities to organize homes in the host country).

In this chapter, I tried to contribute to the discussion of cultural mediation, reflecting on my experience and specialization in anthropology. I argue that issues of culture are complex and that this is true also in the issue of cultural mediation. I stressed the necessity to make a distinction between common/ popular discourses of interculturalism and analytical ones and to be aware of the political consequences of their various and different uses. Finally, I argue that the legitimization of cultural mediation through its explicit recognition may bring about and form a new discourse of interculturalism, where anthropological accounts may have a large part to play.

References

Alvarez, R. Jr. (1995). The Mexican-Us Border: The Making of an Anthropology of Borderlands. *Annual Review of Anthropology*, *24*: 447-470.

Brah, A. (1996). *Cartographies of diaspora: contesting identities*. London: Routledge.

Donnan, H. and Wilson, T. M. (1999). *Borders, frontiers of identity, nation, state.* Oxford: Berg.

Gefou-Madianou, D. (1999). *Culture and Ethnography, From Ethnographic Realism to Cultural Critique*. Athens: Ellinika Grammata.

Gilroy, P. (2004). *After empire: melancholia or convivial culture*. London: Routledge.

Gupta, A. and Ferguson, J. (Eds.), (1997). *Culture power place: ethnography at the end of the era: explorations in critical Anthropology*. Durham: Duce University Press.

Papageorgiou, V. (2010). Crossing the Greek- Albanian border for the first time: experiences, identities and representations. Anthropological explorations of migration, cultural contact and cultural change. In A. Kalogeresis (Ed.) *The Multifaceted Economic and Political Geographies of Internal and External EU Borders, Proceedings of the European Conference of the Association for Borderland Studies*, Department of Spatial Planning and Development. Aristoteleion University of Thessaloniki, 23-25 September 2010 Veroia – Greece, Association for borderland studies.

Papageorgiou. V. (2011). *From Albania to Greece, Place and Identity, Interculturalism and Incorporation, an Anthropological Perspective on Migration*, Athens: Nissos.

Rapport, N., and A. Dawson (Eds.), (1998). *Migrants of identity, perceptions of home in a world of movement*. London: Berg.

Chapter 4: Mapping the Now Here on Migration Politics: Cartography on the Regional Discourses and Practices on Migration in the 21st Century

Zampeta Papadodima

Introduction

This chapter explores the geopolitical spheres on migration politics in the 21st century, in order to discuss a wider framework for inter-cultural services and programs, as a necessary tool for the public spaces for immigrants in the metropolis nowadays. Therefore, it creates a map of the spheres in migration politics, allowing a better understanding of the interconnected administrative and social fields where these services are destined.

For over twenty years, there can be observed a rather important theoretical production about strategy and policy implementation for human mobility, (Massey Et Al 1993, Castles, 1997, Salomon, 2002) especially in the field of political geography. Today, we can notice remarked advances in addressing these processes and their spatial importance for the current political system. This type of information related to the territories is of increasing interest in migration research and analysis, because of its political and also cultural value for societies. The complexity of migration spheres along with their actors and discourses worldwide, indicate the necessity for studying comparatively regional schemes of politics (Sassen, 1996; Soja 2001; Boisier, 2003; Chambers, 2008). For this purpose, politics are considered all social, political and economic debates and practices both by institutional agents as well as autonomous organizations and networks.

Through a condensed regional identification of the actors, discourses and spatial practices, this paper pretends to present a panorama of the recent transformations and challenges on migration politics. Using a short comparative regional scheming of the most representative actors in migration field during the last decade, and by pointing out the most impacting discourses, we determine a migration map of debates and practices now here (Papadodima, 2011a,b).

Furthermore, we explore the actual transformations in the European region and primarily the socioeconomic restructure in the Mediterranean South. Interesting questions rise not only for the European Union's political agenda but also for the reduced public space for migration within the Nation States of the South.

In order to address this inquiry, this chapter identifies the actual transition in southern Europe's migration politics through a rather representative field for analyzing migration: the spatial practices of mobility. Places and practices of mobility and everyday life as well as all institutions and installations are considered spaces that permit us identify the actual necessities and challenges for inter-cultural services and programs at a regional level.

Spheres of Migration

The complexity in the analysis of migration relies on the fact that since the beginning of 21st century, politics were submitted to vast transformations. Socioeconomic and political fields connected to migration, were difficult to adapt rapidly to this globalized transition. Taking a closer look to the actors of politics we can see how discourses, places and practices on migration have been evolved in the last decade worldwide (Zimmer and Schiller, 2002; Sassen, 2005; Triandafyllidou, 2008). Therefore the actual debate about migration is interconnected, including several spheres of observation, analysis and application,-regional, economical, geographical and humanitarian-, in order not be treated unidirectionally.

Politics on migration is a map of spheres where discourses and practices are produced by all actors involved, institutional and autonomous, contributing to the agenda of the social debate and policies. Consequently for considering the changes in the discourses and practices especially those directly related to the inter-cultural services during the last decade, an interconnected scheme of organizational spheres and actors is to be considered in advance.

Table 4.1: Politics on Migration (2000-2012)

Spheres	Actors	Discourses and Practices
Nation States: National Authorities and Infrastructures	Policy Makers Public Administrators	Asylum
Regional/Inter-National/ Governmental Authorities and Infrastructures Agencies/ Research Companies Various Institutions Autonomous Organisations Networks	Socio-economic/ Political/ Humanitarian Agents Think Tank Academy Migrant-native Collectives Activists	International Relations Environmental Migration Social Development Political Rights

Source: Papadodima Z. and Friedrich E. Mapping the Now Here. (European Cultural Foundation Project, 2012-2014).

Since 2001 and till the actual recession worldwide, the affected spheres of migration faced different challenges within the economic and political processes in different regions (Sassen 2005; Linares 2006; Triandafyllidou, 2010). Nevertheless, for the purposes of the cartography we should only mention the most representative and developed fields for migration during the last decade (Table 4.1). The qualitative definition as representatives is based on the quantity of services, social programs and policies as well as academic and social debate destined to these respective fields.

We are particularly interested in all regional processes that were established or expanded through the last decade and especially processes of regional integration not only for incorporating migration in their agenda but also for their implication in policies and practices at a regional level, in all the above spheres and especially among inter-governmental and non-governmental entities. The regional and therefore national agenda of migration have included numerous issues during the years, depending most on crucial fields such as humanitarian crisis and border management, as well as theorization about human mobility.

In order to comparatively explore politics on migration, we implement a regional analysis by detecting the discourses and practices of the actors. Once more we consider key- regions (Eu.-North/ South America), based on their impact on migration politics in the 21st century. Regional characteristics can be observed in academic, socio-economic, commercial, humanitarian and political fields and services of migration. But most importantly is the administration of security and commerce at a regional level that originated a variety of public policies, institutions, instruments such laws and pacts, social projects and campaigns reflecting the also socio-political transition within the regional processes, during their rather short time development and evolution (Papadodima, 2011a,b).

Map of Migration Politics

In order to define the framework of migration in these key regions, we highlight the most representative fields for politics referred to the above-mentioned actors. By this way we can interconnect the political debates and policies, with the places and practices of human mobility. Depending on the context, the presence of all actors and the implementation of politics in all spheres can be more or less coordinated or opposed. Nevertheless the regional practices are concentrated over two major discourses on migration politics; the necessity for Regional Security and Sovereignty (Ribando Seelke, 2013), and the Human Right for Mobility (Pérez Garcia, 2010).

Table 4.2: Regional Discourses and Practices (Institutions, Social Projects and Programs, Debates, Policies)

Europe **(E.U.)**	North America **(NAFTA)**	South America **(MERCOSUR)**
Trafficking	Terrorism	Social Development and Capital
Illegal Immigration	Organised Crime	Racism and Xenophobia
Border Management	Regional Security	Environmental Migration
Asylum	National Sovereignty	Human Right of Mobility

The production of migration policies in Europe and North of America under the "doctrine of national sovereignty and regional security" (Kingsolver, 2010), has also generated critiques and practices against the constant humanitarian crisis observed in the respective regional administrative zones such as borders and metropolis. For South America though particularities can be observed, such as the recommendation of Mobility as Human Right, and also a more efficient coordination of all migration spheres is assumed by the involved actors (Novick, 2012), consistent demographic changes, political rights, environmental migration, asylum and remittances need yet to be addressed in the most recent transition of the migration flows (Penchaszadeh, 2012). Since the beginning of the 21st century, the above-mentioned regions have transformed in various ways not only the practices of mobility, but also the places. Still, most recent studies (Shah, 2010) reveal social discourses and practices of xenophobia and racism equally in the three most representative regions of the migration map.

During the last decade, as a consequence of the importance granted by each region, theoretical and institutional frameworks as well as practices of mobility - such as inter-cultural programs, services and also policies- have been developed over the above concepts and fields of politics (Table 4.2). Therefore the extended production of discourses and practices indicates the importance that key actors attribute to a regional administration of migration. Intern and outer national and regional borders are implemented along with bilateral pacts as well as networks and projects of research and integration at regional level (Bialasiewicz, 2011).

Nevertheless, recent studies show how these spaces have been transformed radically due to the socio-economic restructure. Especially since 2008 for Europe and North America, the repercussions of the economical restructure to the social fabric consequently have altered not only the social services and policies for immigrants but also the spatial practices of mobility, contributing to the actual vast transformation of the metropolis[1]. In order to identify how the actual regional context on the European South has altered the practices of migration linked to the inter-cultural services and programs, we explore the places of mobility in the metropolis during the social and economic restructure (Soja, 2000).

Spatial Practices of Mobility in Southern Europe

Along the 21st century the metropolis of the European South have experienced a variety of socio-political and economical regional adjustments. Taking into consideration the paces of the regional political and economic processes of the European Union, the Nation States of the South had to adjust their social –legal and economic structure. Consequently for Europe as traditional region - destiny for immigration, the social fabric that already included a dense immigrant population was also altered. Not only the new coming migrant flows were seen affected by this transition but also the previous generations of established and till this point partially integrated migrants as well as the second generation residents (Christou, 2012).

[1] For more information about geopolitical research of migration, see Projects MigMap – Governing Migration. Mapping European Politics on Migration (2004), German Federal Cultural Foundation and The City at a Time of Crisis (2013), Sussex University.

Within this socio-economic context that led to the transition of the services and debates, urban changes and transformation demonstrated ever-shrinking spaces available to immigrants in the city (Filippidis, Dalakoglou, Vradis, 2013). In order to analyze spatially the reduced spaces of the immigrants in the metropolis of the southern Europe there is the necessity to explore migration's places of mobility and everyday life as well as installations and institutions and spaces of influence in the local- national reality.

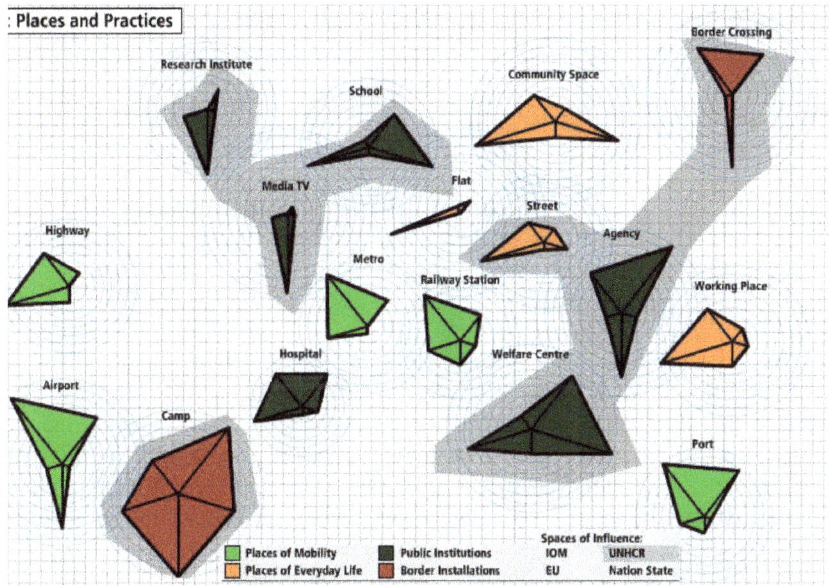

Figure 4.1: Migration Places and Practices in the E. U.
Source: http://www.imap-migration.org. Access December 2013

Additional research is required for a more complete image of the inter-cultural challenges related not only to the above spaces but also to the migration practices in the actual metropolis (Keith, 2005). Nevertheless since 2008 and progressively, not only the services addressing immigrants and inter-cultural fields have been reduced, but also the traditional public services can barely respond to the necessities of the total population. Additionally the physical public space has been suffered alterations and consequently has been limited by the increase of control for the administration of the modern metropolis (Dalakoglou, 2013).

On the other hand, the practices of the immigrants also demonstrate a major social involvement and more visible social participation through mainly their communities and various social and autonomous projects. We should mention that the increase of acts of citizenship by the immigrants is a rather later development of the last decade (Walters, 2008), where an increase of socio-political manifestation of migrants' communities or networks it is also observed, due mainly to extended use of new media technology, starting progressively to build projects and alliances through all European region and beyond.

Likewise, it also reveals a certain necessity for a better understanding how cultural and political identities are constructed in the actual regional context

(Chambers, 2008; Triandafyllidou, 2013; Papadodima & Friedrich, 2013). Nevertheless the remarkable ćulmination of extreme nationalist and xenophobic discourses and practices, challenge the politics of migration in the multicultural metropolis. Mapping of all related public places and spaces of mobility and their transformation, as well as the practices, are yet to be researched and analyzed.

Conclusion

This paper shortly presented the most representative politics in the last century, through a comparative regional analysis, due to the actual socio-political processes that impacted the migration discourses and practices worldwide. Taking into consideration the global, regional and local interconnection of actors, discourses, and spatial practices of migration, we identified the complexity of the spheres related to the migration politics.

During the last decade the actual regional integration processes have also channeled a constant debate, policies and respective programs, services and practices. Comparing representative regions on migration politics enables us to reach to some further conclusions about the transformations and challenges for the actual multicultural metropolis.

Specifically in the actual socio-economic context where the politics of migration present to be clearly affected by the restructure in the places and practices of migration in the metropolis of the European South. During the last years even less spaces for immigrant practices, but more visibility and political involvement along with raised political culture issues have been highlighted in comparison with the beginning of the century, processes directly related with the transition of the European regional integration processes.

By this way we pointed out a primary field for research and comprehension of mobility that yet implies an open field for discussion towards a possibility of extending multicultural social spaces and practices in southern Europe nowadays.

References

Bialasiewicz, L. (2011). "Europe in the Worlds?". In L. Bialasiewicz (Ed.) *Europe in the World: EU Geopolitics and the Making of European Space*. UK: Ashgate.

Boisier S. (2003). Globalización, Geografía política y Fronteras. *Anales de Geografía de la Universidad Complutense*, *23*, 21-39.

Castles S. (1997). Globalización y migración: algunas contradicciones urgentes. *Internacional de Ciencias Sociales*, No September, 165.

Chambers I. (2008). *Mediterranean Crossings: The Politics of an Interrupted Modernity*. London: Routledge.

Christou A. (*2012*). *Immigration in Europe and the Integration of the (European) Second Generation*. UK: Sussex University.

Dalakoglou D., A. Vradis, Ch. Filippidis. (2013). *The City at a Time of Crisis.* UK: Sussex University.

———. *(2013). The City at the time of Crisis: Transformations of Public Spaces in Athens.* UK: Sussex University.

Keith M. (2005).. London: Routledge *After the cosmopolitan? Multicultural cities and the future of racism.*

Kingsolver A. (2010). Talk of 'Broken Borders' and Stone Walls: Anti-immigrant Discourse and Legislation from California to South Carolina. *Southern Anthropologist*, *35*(1), 21-40.

Linares R. (2006). Globalización, Integración Regional, Fronteras y Movimientos Laborales. *Cuadernos sobre Relaciones Internacionales, Regionalismo y Desarrollo*, *1*(1), 45-62.

Massey D., J. Arango, H. Graeme, A. Kouaouci, A. Pellegrino, T. Edward. (1993). Theories of International Migration: A Review and Appraisal. *Population And Development Review*, *19*(3), 431- 466.

Novick S. (2012). La política migratoria argentina a contrapelo de la tendencia mundial. *Voces en el Fénix*, *3*(21), 7-11.

Penchaszadeh A. P. (2012) Migraciones y derechos políticos: Un debate actual. *Voces en el Fénix*, *3*(21), 7-11.

Papadodima Z. (2011). Fronteras Regionales; La Materia De Migraciones en la Geopolítica Contemporánea. *Cuadernos Geográficos, 48*(1), 89-205.

——— (2011). Ο Ρόλος Της Ισπανίας Στην Χάραξη Ευρωπαϊκής Πολιτικής Συντονισμού Για Την Αντιμετώπιση Της Παράτυπης Μετανάστευσης Στη Θαλάσσια Ζώνη Της Μεσόγειου. Ερευνητική Έκθεση, Jean Monnet European Centre of Excellence. Αθήνα: Καποδιστριακό Πανεπιστήμιο.

———, Friedrich, E. (2013). *Mapping images of the uncharted global resistances*. Forthcoming publication.

Pérez G. N. (2009). Seguridad Nacional vs. Seguridad Humana: su impacto en la migración. In Jorge Santibáñez Romellón (Ed.), *Cambiando Perspectivas: de la gestión de flujos hacia la construcción de políticas de migración con enfoque de Desarrollo*. México: Sin Fronteras.

Ribando S. C. (2013). *Mexico's Peña Nieto Administration: Priorities and Key Issues in U.S.- Mexican Relations*. Congressional Research Service.

Salomon M. (2001). La teoría de las Relaciones Internacionales en los albores del siglo XXI: diálogo, disidencia, aproximaciones. *Cidob d'afers internacionals*, 56, p. 7-52.

Sassen S. (1996). Analytic borderlands: race, gender and representation in the new city. In A.D King (Ed.), *Re-presenting the city: ethnicity, capital, and culture in the 21st-century metropolis*. New York: New York University Press.

——— *(2001). The global city. New York, London, Tokyo.* Princeton: University Press.

——— (2005). Regulating Immigration in a Global Age: A New Policy Landscape. *Parallax*, *11*(1), 35-45.

Shah A. (2010). *Racism Global Issues.* International Amnesty.

Soja E. W. (2000). *Postmetropolis: Critical Studies of Cities and Regions.* Oxford: Basil Blackwell.

Triandafyllidou A. (2008). The Governance of International Migration in Europe and North America. Looking at the Interaction between Migrants' Plans and Migration Policies. *Journal of Immigrant and Refugee Studies*, *6*(3), 281-297.

———, Recchi Et. (2010). Crossing Over, Heading West and South: Mobility, Citizenship and Employment in the Enlarged Europe. In G. Menz and A. Caviedes (Ed.), *The Changing Face of Labour Migration in Europe*. London: Palgrave.

——— (2013). National Identity and Diversity: Towards Plural Nationalism. In J. Dobbernack and T. Modood (Eds.), *Tolerance, Intolerance and Respect. Hard to Accept?*. London: Palgrave.

Walters W. (2008). Acts of Demonstration: Mapping the Territory of (Non-) Citizenship. In E. Isin and G. Neilson (Eds.), *Acts of Citizenship*. London: Zed Books.

Chapter 5: Guiding Migrants to their Highest Potential: Training Course for Employment Counsellors and Guidance Staff of Returning Migrants and Unemployed

Charikleia Manavi

Guiding Migrants to their Highest Potential

As European society becomes multi-cultural, the need to advance our understanding of migration processes grows. Migration is continuously changing, so we should devise approaches that respond to new realities. Individuals make rational migration decisions expecting to optimize their personal and family's expected wellbeing or 'utility' (de Haas, 2009). Migrants hope developed countries will become a "Promised Land" the "Cargo Cult"[1], a bestowing of material wealth and freedom and vice versa; developed countries have come to rely on migrant labor to fulfill their labor needs (de Haas, 2009; Canadian Council for Refugees, 2009). Despite high unemployment across most of the continent, too many employers lack the workers they need. Aging populations and low fertility rates in developed European countries have resulted in a decline in "replacement workers" entering the workforce and in greater demand for service-sector jobs and low-skill employment. There is a lack not only for engineers, doctors and nurses but also in farmhands and health professionals. The paradox is that while the vitality and the ability of developed countries to innovate and compete is in danger, migrants' background in Europe indicates

[1] The concept cargo implies a totality of material, organizational and spiritual welfare collectively desired as a replacement for current inadequacy and projected into the imminent future as a coming "salvation". Modern-day Cargo cults are those "activities" arising from the expectation of abundant, supernaturally generated, Western-style cargo. Examples of modern-day cargo cult behavior can be found in migration where we can see what happens when some societies interact with other societies, giving pictures-Cargo (Trompf, 1990).

poor employment prospects, difficulty in using prior learning in the host country labor market, barriers to official recognition of qualifications attained abroad, unskilled employment despite having qualifications, mono-culturally oriented vocational training programs, non-recognition of informal qualifications and skills; difficulty for potential employers to assess professional skills without formal certificates (IOM, 2004; EWSI, 2013; Zarifis, 2012; European Commission Directorate – General for Education and Culture Lifelong Learning 2011). Generally the work situation of migrant and refugee declines on arriving in a new country irrespective of their prior learning (Council of Europe, 2012).

The above situation indicates that it is difficult for developed countries to find a *way* to take a more *positive view* of migration. Some researchers are trying to explain how capabilities to migrate increase during early phases of development when relatively modest increases in development enable many more people to migrate by lifting them over a hypothetical threshold level of capabilities. Also, they claim that this migration-accelerating effect tends to be reinforced by the creation of social capital in the form of migrant networks, which tend to decrease the costs and risks of migration. As a result, under higher levels of development most people will be already capable to migrate. So a very good path for the conceptualization of migration by developed countries should not be the usual way of just a problem to be "solved" but it should be faced as an integral part of broader development processes (De Haas, 2009, p. 39). Nowadays, global structural changes are fundamentally shifting migration flows. The most important transformation is the need for new poles of attraction. Entrepreneurs, migrants with PhDs, and those simply with a desire to improve their lives are flocking to places such as Brazil, South Africa, Indonesia, Mexico, China, and India. In the coming decade, most of the growth in migration will take place in the global south (Commission of the European Communities, 2005). So we can't wonder *for whom the bell tolls*[2] when we speak about migration. In the middle of a huge global economic recession nothing is guaranteed and no job is safe (OECD, 2008; UN, 2006; UNESCO, 2012).

Migration as a transition has three stages: the *ending*, at which a person breaks from their life as they know it, the *neutral zone*; in which one's familiar sense of being in the world is absent while nothing means quite what it did before, and the *new beginning*; when persons regain a sense of being skilled in matters of living (Bridges, 1991, p.4; White, 1997). Although considerable attention is given only to these three stages, the truth is that persons understand that turning back remains a distinct possibility. There are ways of understanding this turning back, and preparing for this, that don't construct it as punishment or as failure. It can be understood that all attempts at migrations contribute to the development of knowledge and the skills for the future (Berry, 1997). A brief review of the literature reveals that researchers have included return migration as a sub-component of their analytical approaches to migration, being the center of the debate on international migration management. Both, migration and return are not permanent situations, but they can be reversed at any time (OECD, 2008 & Cassarino, 2004). Repatriation laws have been created in many countries to

---

[2] John Donne, Meditation 17, Devotions upon Emergent Occasions. 86-87 Anthony Raspa, Ed., 1975.

enable migrants to return to their origin countries which in some cases, incorporate the counseling services needed before migrants' decision to return. Skilled returning migrants are important as they can help build global networks, further links between host and origin countries and generally contribute to development policies. The impact on the home countries results from the combination of the human, financial and social capital they transfer and their intercultural know-how that can offer more than a set of economically viable skills (Pöllmann, 2007 & 2009; Gresham, & Reschly, 1987; Durkheim, 1968). A very hopeful achievement nowadays is that a number of initiatives are being implemented to influence the factors that affect the development potential of returning migrants trying to match returnees' skills with their home country's development priorities, end using the benefits that may bring their embodied intercultural capital (EWSI, 2013; Crasovan & Sava, 2013a, pp. 64-65; Werkuin, 2010; International Association for Educational and Vocational Guidance 2009; European Accreditation Scheme for Careers Guidance Practitioners, 2012).

Training of Cultural Mediators to Identify Prior Learning of Migrants

In the above mentioned framework, competences are going to be a key concept in so called international migration management. Validation of prior learning, knowledge, skills and competences is increasingly becoming a solution towards certification and formalizing the real existing competences being an alternative to the formal path of education and certification (Crasovan & Sava, 2013a, p. 9). Every migrant or returning migrant possesses a set of competences (which are a combination of professional, social and personal skills needed to carry out given tasks in specific situations) and resources, -sometimes unknown to themselves. Especially for the unemployed, the detection of competences and skills, the selection of those that can be transferred to a working environment, their conversion to career goals and their development, reduce the distance and time of transition from unemployment back to work and increase the employability of individuals (CEDEFOP, 2009b; EWSI, 2013). So we could say that the challenge in migration and return migration is integrating them into the society and the workforce, making use of these competences (EWSI, 2013; Crasovan & Sava, 2013a, pp. 13-15; European Parliament Council, 2008).

Cultural mediators as professionals, assist individuals, organizations or communities to ensure that issues of culture, identity and power are well represented in the mediation process so as to result to mutually satisfying agreements *(Law, 2009). Careful planning and design of mediation training and support programs help to produce sustainable cultural sensitive mediation practices. Mediation trainers need teaching and training tools that aim to increasing self-awareness and self-development through reflective processes and lifelong learning principles (Law, 2009).* Professions must be practiced within a set of required parameters. Aspects of culture and mediation have been included in part of the new mediation accreditation process. In Greece several interpreters developed special knowledge focused both in advisory-occupational guidance and interpretership technical matters, through training courses in mediation. This enables them to work as liaisons between the citizens who are in the process of integration and the local labor market. Employment counseling is one of the main services that a registered cultural mediator can provide in Greece. In this context, it is very important for cultural mediators to be able to support people of vulnerable social groups, to identify and take advantage of their skills and competences acquired through work and their social roles in order to create their further career plan and be capable of identifying their own working culture with respect to the values and perspectives of other cultures (host country) in order to obtain greater tolerance and understanding (Launikari & Puukari, 2005).

"Back to Work" Training Course

Subsequently, the main purpose of this presentation is to suggest a course made for counselors and social workers on training themselves on how they can help a person to recollect "his life" in a proper way and synthesize it in an organized portfolio. The theoretical background of the *"Back to Work"* training course comprises theorizations like experiential learning theory, the humanist theory, the holistic development theory, or the constructivist one. The *"Back to Work"* instrument for consultation which is used when working with migrants, returning migrants and unemployed, can help counselors assess and validate experiences in the field of social activities, family life, hobbies, voluntary sector and work while it generally provides a framework for understanding the past events of one's life and for planning the future. Through narrative based communication, main focus is given in the process of reflection, internal mental conceptualization related to the experiential learning, confidence building, empowerment and critical consciousness. In the instrument there is a part which helps counselors and social workers to evaluate themselves and see if they have basic skills for consulting this group of people. The levels of training and qualification for careers counselors across Europe varies dramatically (as evidenced in the Countries Report) and at present in many countries there is no single recognized minimum professional standard for delivery of counseling and advice. With this disparity in mind, the instrument is aimed to counselors with sufficient experience to be able to deliver a good quality service and support migrants in their goal of entering the European workforce (Crasovan & Sava, 2013a, pp. 10-12 & 2013b, p.10).

"Back to Work" project carried out between 2011until 2013 by a group of partner organizations from Romania, Germany, Greece, United Kingdom, Denmark and Bulgaria. The concept of this instrument was built on previous developments, regarding the steps of the validation process: Vinepac project – *Validation of Informal and Non-Formal Psycho-Pedagogical Competences of Adult Educators* (2006-2008), FamCompass project – *Family Competences Portfolio*, 2007-2009 and Acced project – *Continuing Education Designed for Counsellors Working in Adult Education* (2005-2007) (Crasovan & Sava, 2013a, p. 8; Dewispelaere et all, 2011).

The First Step in using the instrument is to assess the professional skills and knowledge of the Counselor who will facilitate the Recognition and Validation Process with the Client. This process consists of two stages. Firstly, the instrument presents a matrix of *Basic Competences* which are considered to be important requirements for all adult career guidance counselors. Counselors should use the *Self Evaluation Checklist* to determine if they possess the required skills and knowledge to be able to support the client through the process in a competent manner; they should assess and reflect on their own knowledge, skills and practice and consider whether they are suitably experienced in order to guide their client through the process (Crasovan & Sava, 2013b, p.14). Afterwards there is a further matrix dealing with competences which are directly related to *Recognition of Prior Learning*. The matrix is intended for the counselor's use to assess their level of skill, knowledge and competence. There are three Parts in the *Self-Assessment Matrix*. Each part asks counsellor to consider their practice in terms of their level of knowledge, skills and competence in each of these areas. Each *Self-Assessment Matrix* consists of three steps a. *Self-Evaluation* whereas the counselor must look at each Competence and assess whether in the course of their work with clients they have knowledge and skills in this area of work, b. *Specify* whereas counselors must draw on some examples of how they do this and c. *Assess* whereas counselors assess whether their knowledge and ability in this area of their work is sufficient or if they need to undertake further training or professional development in this area (Crasovan & Sava, 2013b, pp.15-16). In Table 5.1, you can see the 3 steps of the Self-Evaluation of counsellor competences.

Table 5.1: Three steps Self-Evaluation of Counselor Competences related to Validation of Prior Learning (VPL), EQF level 6

Step 1: Reflect			Step 2: Specify	Step 3: Assess		
	EQF level 6 Knowledge	**Do I have advanced knowledge in the field of recognition and validation of prior learning, and a critical understanding of theories and principles?**	**Check and/or specify <u>knowledge</u> you may have acquired from e.g.:** *(the examples below may work as inspiration for you to discover/realize your knowledge)*	**Do I need further training to develop this?** *Yes*	*No*	*I do not know*
Specific competences required for conducting a RPL process — 1	Present clear and accurate information on the service to be provided, and agree on course of action (creating the contract).	▪ Theories and methods of formal, non formal and informal learning. ▪ Theories of and methods for recognition, documentation and validation of competences. ▪ Knowledge of national and international lifelong learning strategies and laws. ▪ Knowledge of educational system and labor market.	☐ Keeping up with laws and regulations concerning educational and labor market policy. ☐ Attending relevant study circles. ☐ Attending relevant (Open University) courses. ☐ Attending relevant conferences. ☐ Keeping up with relevant articles and literature. ☐ Attending supervision at my work. ☐ Participating in relevant developmental work. ☐ Other/s: Please specify. __________ __________ __________ __________ __________ __________	☐	☐	☐
2	Explain to the client what self-evaluation is and outline its benefits.			☐	☐	☐
3	Encourage the client to express his/her own personal experiences (autobiography) and assist him/her to extract what is relevant in order to reflect upon his/her competences.			☐	☐	☐
4	Understand and explain the evaluation scheme that the client can use to grade his/her competences.			☐	☐	☐
5	Comprehend the significance of assessment and valorization of learning.			☐	☐	☐
6	Demonstrate intercultural awareness.			☐	☐	☐
7	Develop, maintain and update a portfolio for assessment that reflects the total life situation of the client and present it the best possible way.			☐	☐	☐
8	Have a good grasp of specific methods of documentation that is required for recognition of prior learning.			☐	☐	☐
9	Understand of the requirements of an external assessor and ability to explain the recognition process to the client.			☐	☐	☐
10	Ensure that the client has understood and gained ownership of the process.			☐	☐	☐

Step 1: Reflect			Step 2: Specify	Step 3: Assess		
	EQF level 6 **Skills**	**Can I demonstrate advanced skills, mastery and innovation in the field of RPL and solve complex and unpredictable problems?**	**Check and/or specify <u>skills</u> that you may have from experience with e.g.:** *(the examples below may work as inspiration for you to discover/realize your skills)*	**Do I need further training to develop this?** ***Yes***	***No***	***I do not know***
1	Present clear and accurate information on the service to be provided, and agree on course of action (creating the contract).	▪ Skills in using methods and tools for recognition, documentation and validation of prior learning ▪ Skills in communication, facilitation and collaboration with diversified target group	☐ The use of theories of learning, motivation, self-evaluation in teaching and counseling.	☐	☐	☐
2	Explain to the client what self-evaluation is and outline its benefits.		☐ The use of methods of recognition, documentation and validation of prior learning in working with competence development.	☐	☐	☐
3	Encourage the client to express his/her own personal experiences (autobiography) and assist him/her to extract what is relevant in order to reflect upon his/her competences.					
4	Understand and explain the evaluation scheme that the client can use to grade his/her competences.		☐ Adjusting teaching and counseling to specific situations and target groups.	☐	☐	☐
5	Comprehend the significance of assessment and valorization of learning.		☐ Collaborating with different agents, companies and institutions.	☐	☐	☐
6	Demonstrate intercultural awareness.		☐ Other/s: Please specify.	☐	☐	☐
7	Develop, maintain and update a portfolio for assessment that reflects the total life situation of the client and present it the best possible way.		____________	☐	☐	☐
8	Have a good grasp of specific methods of documentation that is required for recognition of prior learning.		____________ ____________ ____________			
9	Understand of the requirements of an external assessor and ability to explain the recognition process to the client.		____________ ____________ ____________	☐	☐	☐
10	Ensure that the client has understood and gained ownership of the process.		____________			

Step 1: Reflect			Step 2: Specify	Step 3: Assess		
EQF level 6 Competences		Can I manage and take responsibility for complex and unpredictable professional activities and take responsibility for managing professional development of RPL strategies?	Check and/or specify situations and examples of <u>professional use of knowledge and skills</u> you came across: *(the examples below may work as inspiration for you to discover/realize your competences)*	Do I need further training to develop this competence?		
				Yes	*No*	*I do not know*
Specific competences required for conducting a RPL process 1	Present clear and accurate information on the service to be provided, and agree on course of action (creating the contract).	▪ Ability to develop own practice concerning RPL in an interplay between theoretical reflection and practice. ▪ Ability to support and interface a client in an open-minded manner. ▪ Ability to act based on professional ethical standards.	☐ Situations that demand professional insight, ability to analyze and overview.	☐	☐	☐
2	Explain to the client what self-evaluation is and outline its benefits.		☐ Examples of collaboration.	☐	☐	☐
3	Encourage the client to express his/her own personal experiences (autobiography) and assist him/her to extract what is relevant in order to reflect upon his/her competences.		☐ Examples of initiatives and developmental work.	☐	☐	☐
4	Understand and explain the evaluation scheme that the client can use to grade his/her competences.		☐ Other/s: Please specify.	☐	☐	☐
5	Comprehend the significance of assessment and valorization of learning.		______	☐	☐	☐
6	Demonstrate intercultural awareness.		______			
7	Develop, maintain and update a portfolio for assessment that reflects the total life situation of the client and present it the best possible way.		______			
8	Have a good grasp of specific methods of documentation that is required for recognition of prior learning.		______	☐	☐	☐
9	Understand of the requirements of an external assessor and ability to explain the recognition process to the client.		______			
10	Ensure that the client has understood and gained ownership of the process.		______	☐	☐	☐

A series of case studies have also been included in the user guide of the instrument and they are intended to provide the counselors with some further guidance as how they may assess their own competences as counselors (Crasovan & Sava, 2013b, p.16). Before the above process there is a series of eighteen (18) different learning activities that are intended for counsellors and clients to develop skills and knowledge that will be useful for embarking on the *"Back to work"* instrument. It is very important counselors to be assured of the client's commitment to the process and ensure that the client remains engaged with it. So it is important for the counselor when planning these activities, counsellor to take into account the availability of the client and the amount of counseling time available (Crasovan & Sava, 2013b, p.38).

Table 5.2: Assessment of Competences

Competences	**Sub-competences**	**Level**			
		1	**2**	**3**	**4**
Communication at work place	I am able to transmit and receive information				
	I am able to involve in group discussion, on professional aspects				
	I am able to argue my own points of view				
	I am able to respect others' opinions				
	I am able to talk openly and honestly				
	I am able to understand instructions				
	I am able to listen in order to clarify information				
	I ask questions to test for clarity and understanding, " explain complex terms ", use concrete examples				
	I am able to communicate with others in the way others like				
	I am able to write in a concise and organized manner				
	I share information with others to help them perform their jobs & seek information from others				
	I listen actively & speak clearly and directly				
	I state my opinion clearly and concisely				
	I demonstrate openness and honesty				
	I ask others for their opinions and feedback				
	I ask questions to ensure understanding				
	Other ability				
Working in a team	I am able to identify the tasks inside a team				
	I am able to involve in a team tasks				
	I am able to communicate with people on all levels informally or formally				
	I am able to share pertinent information with all members of a team				
	I am able to promote a team spirit within and outside a group				
	I am able to respond positively to instructions and procedures				
	I am able to manage own work with others				

The part of the instrument that is used during counseling sessions with the client is: The Recognition of Prior Learning process. This process consists of five sections (General information, Assessment of competences, Reflection file, Portfolio of pieces of evidence, Self-evaluation report/case studies). In *General information* section counselors allow their client to begin to reflect on their past experiences and current situation and to build an overview on their working life to date. In *Assessment of Competences* section the client complete (with the counselor) a series of tables listing competences that are acquired through life. The Assessment Tables cover eighteen (18) areas of competences with their sub-competences (examples are given in Table 5.2)[3]. The clients have to consider each of them carefully and select which level of competence best describes their level of ability.

In the *Reflection File* section the questionnaires provided are used to describe in detail the skills, knowledge, strengths and weaknesses that have been identified as part of the *Assessment process*. The Counselor asks the client to consider and note in his own words how they feel they perform in every area related to social activities, family life, activities done outside of work, voluntary activities and job. The Counselor asks the client to think about each area of their life and referring to the list of competences to choose two or three competences from the list. Afterwards the Counselor asks them to describe how they can demonstrate these through using concrete situations. They complete a reflection for each of the areas described (see Table 5.3). The client has the opportunity to give real life examples from the various areas of life and demonstrate their level of competence. In this way, he forms a social basis for a portfolio which clearly illustrates what they are able to offer to the labor market.

Table 5.3: Reflection File: Discussions: example from Family life

1. Please choose one critical family situation that you are involved in and try to describe it. What happened at that time?
... ...
2. What problem did you solve and how? What was your task?
... ...
3. What were your feelings at that time?
... ...
4. What were the main steps/activities that you followed?
... ...

[3] Communication at workplace, working in a team, planning the activity of a team, diversity of orientation, building relationships, learning and development, creativity, innovation, work commitment, time management, management skills, job knowledge, planning an activity, organizing an activity, decision making, health and security, quality assurance and self-development. As it is obvious from the above table, there is a possibility for the client to add other sub competences not already covered in the list.

5. What do you think now about that situation? Is anything else that you would do in another way? Why? Please explain the reasons!
… …
6. How did you resolve the situation? What were the results of your actions and how do you appreciate them?
… …
7. If the same situation occurred what would you do this time, how would you resolve it in that moment? What would you change about the approach?
… …
8. What did you learn from that situation?
… …
9. Is there anything you would like to learn?
… …
10. Do you use what you learned at that time in another context or situation?
… …

In the Portfolio of Evidence section the client should reflect specifically on learning, experiences which have been acquired in non-formal and informal contexts. In Table 5.4 the client should record the different pieces of evidence that describe their learning experience and answer a series of questions that can help them to remember and describe their experience.

Table 5.4: Portfolio of Evidence a

Activity (learning context)	Periods/years	Competences that you acquired through those activities	Piece of evidence (type) Yes/No

The Table 5.5 helps the client to record their specific competences and evaluate their own level of competence.

Table 5.5: Portfolio of Evidence b

Competence	Subcompetence competences and descriptions	Very well	Well	Well enough	Not well

In the last section *"Self-evaluation report"* section the client will summarize all their competences and experience into a narrative self-evaluation report Crasovan & Sava, 2013a).

Epilogue

Conclusively, the key role in combating migrants and return migrants unemployment is undoubtedly played by the functional and meaningful integration process. Incorporating the European experience, thus enriching theoretical knowledge with its true, practical use is the essential challenge. As long as projects like this do not rise above their project status, the recognition of their results will be undermined. I hope you will find "*Back to Work*" instruments and the SONETOR training platform useful for you to support migrants into their struggle to improve their access to the labor market and to obtain the best possible quality of life.

References

Berry, J.W. (*1997*). *Immigration*, Acculturation, and Adaptation. *Applied Psychology,* 46 (1), 5-34.

Bridges, W. (1991). *Managing Transitions: Making the most of change.* Cambridge, MA: Perseus Books.

Canadian Council for Refugees. (2009). *Talking About Refugees and Immigrants: A Glossary of Terms.* Retrieved from

Cassarino, J.P. (2004). Theorizing Return Migration: The Conceptual Approach to Return Migrants Revisited. *International Journal on Multicultural Societies*, *6 (*2), 253-279.

CEDEFOP. (2009b). *European guidelines for validating non-formal and informal learning.* Retrieved from:

Commission of the European communities. (2005*). Communication from the Commission to the Council and the European Parliament Establishing a Framework Program on Solidarity and the Management of Migration Flows for the period 2007-2013.* COM/2005/0123/FINAL.

Council of Europe. (2012). *Proposal for a Council Recommendation on the validation of non-formal and informal learning.* Brussels. COM(2012) 485. Retrieved from:

Crasovan, M. & Sava, S. (2013a) *Validation of Competences as part of career counselling.* Timisoara: Mirton Printingouse. Retrieved from http://www.irea.ro/ro/images/publicatii/b2w_instrument.pdf

Crasovan, M. & Sava, S. (2013b) *Validation of Competences as part of career counselling. User Guide.* Timisoara: Mirton Printingouse. Retrieved from http://www.irea.ro/ro/images/publicatii/b2w_instrument.pdf

de Haas, H. (2010). *Migration Transitions: a theoretical and empirical inquiry into the developmental drivers of international migration.* IMI – Working Papers 24.

Dewispelaere, J., G. Jennes, L. Schuhegger, B. Thiessen. (2011). Family competences portofolio. Validating competences acquired in family life. *Jurnal of Educational Sciences* 1(13), 99-106. Retrieved from http://connection.ebscohost.com/c/articles/70473232/family-competences-portfolio-validating-competences-acquired-family-life

Durkheim, E. (1968). *The Elementary Forms of Religious Life.* Paris, PUF, p.48.

European Accreditation Scheme for Careers Guidance Practitioners (EAS). (10th July 2012). Retrieved from: http://www.corep.it/eas/uk/

European Commission Directorate – General for Education and Culture Lifelong Learning. (2011). *Report on the EU-wide public consultation concerning the promotion and validation of non-formal and informal learning. Horizontal policy issues and 2020 strategy. Skills and Qualifications.* Retrieved from

European Parliament Council. (2008). *Recommendation of the European Parliament and of the Council of 23 April 2008 on the establishment of the European Qualifications Framework for lifelong learning* (2008/C 111/01).

European Web Site on Integration (EWSI) (2013). *Integration Dossier: Recognition of Qualification and Competences. Retrieved from*

Gresham, F. M., & Reschly, D. J. (1987). Dimensions of social competence: Method factors in the assessment of adaptive behavior, social skills, and peer acceptance, *Journal of School Psychology*, 25, 367-381.

http://ec.europa.eu/dgs/education_culture/consult/vnfil/report_en.pdf

http://eurex.europa.eu/LexUriServ/LexUriServ.do?uri=COM:2012:0485:FIN:en:PDF

http://www.ccrweb.ca/glossary.htm.

http://www.cedefop.europa.eu/EN/Files/4054_en.pdf

http://www.migpolgroup.com/wp_mpg/wp-content/uploads

International association for Educational and Vocational Guidance (IAEVG). (2009). *Application for Educational and Vocational Guidance Practitioner EVGP offered by International Association for Educational and Vocational Guidance (IAEVG);* Retrieved from http:// www.cce-global.org/Downloads/EVGP/app-en.pdf

International Organization for Migration (IOM), (2004). *International Migration Law: Glossary on Migration.* Geneva: IOM.

Launikari, M. & Puukari, S. (2005). The European context for multicultural counselling. In M. Launikari & S. Puukari (Eds.) Multicultural guidance and counselling. Theoretical foundations and best practices in Europe. Helsinki: Centre for International Mobility CIMO; Jyväskylä: Institute for Educational Research, 15-26. Retrieved from:

Law, S.F. (2009). Culturally Sensitive Mediation: the importance of culture in mediation accreditation, *Australian Dispute Resolution Journal, 20*(3), 162-171.

OECD. (2008). *Return Migration: A New Perspective. In International Migration Outlook: SOPEMI 2008.* Paris: OECD.

Pöllmann A. *(2009).* Formal education and intercultural capital: Towards attachment beyond narrow ethno-national boundaries. *Educational Studies, 35, 537-545*

Pöllmann, A. (2007). National and European identities: notions of reconcilability and inclusiveness in a case study of German trainee teachers, *Compare: A Journal of Comparative and International Education*, *37*(1), 89-104, DOI: 10.1080/03057920601061844

Trompf, W. (1990). Introduction to G.W.,Tropmf (ed.), Cargo cults and millenarian movements: *Religion and Society*, 29, Berlin and New York: Mouton de Gruyter, 1-15

UNESCO Institute for Lifelong Learning (2012). *UNESCO GUIDELINES for the Recognition, Validation and Accreditation of the Outcomes of Non-formal and Informal Learning.* Retrieved from www.unesco.org/uil

United Nations. Department of Economic & Social Affairs, Population Division (2009). *International Migration Report 2006.* A Global Assessment.

Werkuin, P. (2010). *Recognition of non-formal and informal learning: outcomes, policies and practices*. OECD. Retrieved from www.oecd.org/edu/recognition

White, M. (1997). *Challenging the culture of consumption: Rites of passage and communities of acknowledgement, 2 & 3 (special edition)* Dulwich Centre Newsletter*: New perspectives on addiction. Adelaide: Dulwich Centre Publications.*
www.cimo.fi/dman/Document.phx/~public/Julkaisut+ja+tilastot/English/multiculturalguidanceandcounselling.pdf
www.oecd.org/edu/recognition

Zarifis, G. K. (2012). A comparative overview of the status and the main characteristics of vocational education and training (VET) trainers in south-eastern Europe. *Journal of the Institute for Educational Research.* 44 (1), 24-41.

Chapter 6: Intercultural Mediation Moves Two Steps Forward: Educational Facilitation and the Intercultural Mediators Registry

Akrivi-Irene Panagiotopoulou and Andrica Rozi

According to the Greek Council for Refugees (GCR), the first step for the successful integration of immigrants into the host society is to provide them with access to reliable information on issues of their concern (Νικολακοπούλου-Στεφάνου, 2008). Legalization procedures, employment, language, dealing with public services, housing, education, and health issues are the first, and often the most persistent, problems migrants have to deal with.

Obviously, these matters are addressed by different policy sectors and various institutions involved in the integration process (government bodies, profit private entities, NGOs), which causes difficulties in coordinating the interventions implemented in favor of the migrant population (Νικολακοπούλου-Στεφάνου, 2008). The host society is another important factor affecting the integration process, given that prevalent attitudes towards immigrants, levels of tolerance and the ability to understand and communicate with the different others, are determinant for the social inclusion of immigrants.

In recognition of these facts, the European Union actively promotes multi-faceted interventions for the improvement of national integration policies, the sensitization of host societies, and the personal empowerment of immigrants. Tools and strategies are being developed to facilitate communication in both directions, as well as immigrant access to public and social goods. One of numerous such interventions was launched in 2009, under the *Lifelong Learning Program* of the European Commission, in order to improve access to lifelong learning for immigrants. Another innovative project, financed by the Greek Ministry of Interior and the European Fund for the Integration of Third Country Nationals in Greece, aimed at fostering intercultural mediation in Greece by creating a register of trained intercultural mediators and providing them with an electronic platform for networking and informing the public, immigrants and stakeholders on the services they render. A brief description of these projects is provided here, followed by the outcomes achieved and the insights gained through implementation.

Learning Community—Migrants as Educational Multipliers Pave the Way for Migrants to Access Lifelong Learning

The EU Grundtvig "Learning Community (LC) – Migrants as Education Multipliers Pave the Way for Migrants to Access Lifelong Learning" project operated in the field of promoting equal opportunities for disadvantaged groups, in particular the improvement of migrant access to adult education[1]. In the LC project, partner organizations from Austria, the Czech Republic, Germany, Greece and the Netherlands came together, under the coordination of the BGZ Berlin International Cooperation Agency. The project started in October 1st, 2009, and lasted 36 months, until October 2012.

The diversity of the chosen countries and partners facilitated the exploration of different migrant populations and perspectives within the EU. Inadequate migrant access to adult education is attributed to structural, institutional and individual factors, which certainly vary from country to country, but nevertheless lead to serious personal, social, and economic disadvantages for many immigrants. Therefore, all three levels were addressed by the interventions implemented during the project, adapted to the specific conditions prevailing in the countries involved.

On the *structural* and *institutional* level much attention was given to raising the stakeholders' awareness on issues of equal opportunities and migrant access to lifelong learning. Public relations, networking and intercultural opening were used to initiate changes in adult education institutions in order to better meet the needs of diverse target groups. Staff development, teaching methods and organizational questions were all crucial to the adaptation process.

On the *individual* level a peer-to-peer multiplier approach was used for reducing barriers to migrant adult education. Persons who were migrants themselves and had good access to the target group were trained and have been afterwards active as multipliers for several months; in the project they were called "Education Ambassadors". The role of Education Ambassadors was to offer low-threshold educational guidance (give information and advice, connect people with offers, etc.), build bridges between the migrant target groups and institutions, as well as to accompany migrants on their paths to integration.

Education Ambassadors as Door Openers

In Germany, Greece and the Netherlands, twenty eight immigrants were trained to volunteer as Education Ambassadors, or multipliers, connecting migrants with adult education institutions and social services. The key-skills asked for were strong communication skills, intercultural competence, in-depth knowledge about

[1] All information on the project is derived from the publication Opening Doors to Adult Education for Migrants: Guidelines for working with Education Ambassadors – Grundtvig "Learning Community" Project, Helga Moser (Ed.), Graz 2012, available at www.learning-community.eu.

the structure of educational and social offers, as well as a reflective approach to the role of a multiplier. On average, a 25-hour course of theoretical and practical training was provided, after which all the participants received a certificate with reference to the European Qualification Framework (EQF).

After their training the Education Ambassadors voluntarily engaged in a number of activities aiming both at facilitating migrants and at networking. *Facilitation activities* included systematic information of migrants on educational offers and related procedures, mediation activities for the facilitation of communication, personal mentoring, social and psychological support of migrants in order to increase knowledge of self-help strategies and the benefits of networking, aid for understanding the cultural norms of the local society etc.

Extensive *networking activities* were an essential part of the multipliers' work. Formal and informal networks within the target group had to be established in order to maximize the multipliers' access to migrants and the effectiveness of their interventions. Cooperation with other multiplier structures and networks, as well as collaboration with mainstream institutions was necessary for the achievement of synergy effects and intercultural opening. Last but not least, the Education Ambassadors themselves had to stay close with each other, so as to enhance visibility in the target group, get mutual support and share their experiences.

The Learning Community Project in Greece

Since the early 1990s Greece has become a major migrant destination country. The migrant population is concentrated in the capital Athens as well as in areas with significant agricultural and/or tourist activity. The LC project was implemented by Olympic Training in the Ilia Prefecture, where agriculture and tourism attract large numbers of immigrants.

Twelve migrant women were trained as Education Ambassadors, gaining insight into structural aspects of educational and social processes, communication procedures and information flows between training institutions and local stakeholders. 6 of these women participated for the following eleven months in pilot activities, in order to adapt what they had learned to the specific needs and living conditions of the local migrant population. Growing professional or family obligations, repatriation or a move to another city for further education were the causes of non-participation for the rest of trainees.

In the frame of the pilot activities six Education Ambassadors acted as mediators, i.e. promoters of lifelong learning opportunities and supporters of other migrants. Educational institutions and stakeholders from the government as well as migrant organizations were actively involved. A multilingual flyer, personal formal and informal contacts with local officials, education institution representatives and influential people (local and migrants), meetings with migrants, and participation in festivals and migrant social events were among the methods and tools used by the Education Ambassadors. In all contacts, the aim was mainly the presentation of the project and its potential benefits for each participant.

The implementation of the LC project coincided with the onset of the economic crisis in Greece. This had a detrimental impact on potential outcomes, given the aggravation of barriers on a structural and individual level. Many adult education structures have postponed their activities and formal/non-formal training opportunities accessible to migrants have become rare. A far from negligible number of migrants decided to leave the area because of unemployment. Due to the economic crisis, a sense of security is no longer taken for granted and survival has become the utmost priority.

In such a context, the persistence of the Education Ambassadors was striking, and so was their attitude towards the financial and social situation. The following comments concisely depict the conclusions they reached from all their efforts:

> It is not a question of motivating migrants to participate in educational opportunities but instead to help the local community and public officials to understand how they could benefit from enhancing the connection between migrants and available educational opportunities [Education Ambassador Alla].

> We strongly believe that the current economic crisis can be seen as an opportunity to redefine one's priorities and choices through communication with other people [Education Ambassadors Pon and Elif].

A major positive outcome during the last months of the pilot activities was the agreement for permanent cooperation between facilitators and three institutions (a municipal library, a municipal support office for vulnerable groups and the Employment & Career Information Hub of a Technological Educational Institute). At the completion of the LC project the form of collaboration had yet to be decided upon.

Migrant mobility and the lack of continuity in the provision of adult education opportunities in Greece, characterized by still evolving adult education structures and an indeterminate administrative system, turned out to be the biggest obstacles for the access of migrants to lifelong learning opportunities. However, through the LC project the need for this kind of mediation services was recognized by educational institutions and stakeholders. There is a high potential for successful and sustainable educational and cultural mediation in Greece, as long as systematic and institutional steps are taken towards this direction.

Conclusions and Recommendations from the Learning Community Project

The Learning Community project was an enriching experience for all those involved. Skills were developed and enhanced, new insights were gained and positive attitudes towards interculturalism were promoted. The employability and the social integration of the participants were strengthened and an innovative methodological consulting approach was developed for the empowerment of migrants. Perhaps the most valuable legacy of this project was the understanding obtained on how intercultural communication and mediation can be best promoted in the participant countries.

We would like to highlight in this article those conclusions that have actually contributed to the further development of multiplier structures and cultural mediation in Greece and still serve as a guide for the next steps to be taken. First, since multiplier structures rely on networking and cooperation, significant time is needed for building up trusting and cooperative relationships. Volunteers need advice and guidance in the realization of their activities; therefore long-term support systems for volunteers are essential. In order to maintain the multipliers' motivation, recognition of their accomplishments and efforts is crucial. In the same time, to be able to take part as a volunteer, an adequate level of income needs to be ensured; otherwise migrants should be given the opportunity to get professionally involved in intermediation activities.

Second, adult education providers should survey and include in their planning the specific educational and training needs of migrants, in order to adapt already existing offers and introduce tailor-made courses. Accessibility would also be enhanced by providing migrant-friendly information (e.g. user-friendly web pages, information material in different languages, clear description of the courses etc.) and counseling services for the personal orientation of interested immigrants. The need for socially embedded information became once again obvious, emphasizing the importance of the role of migrant multipliers. This could also be achieved by employing staff with a migration background, lowering thus access barriers and establishing a better representation of minorities among employees of social and education services. In this regard, intercultural competences are important for all the staff of adult education institutions.

Registering and Networking Trained Intercultural Mediators through an Electronic Platform

Olympic Training and the *Hellenic Open University* worked together for the creation of the first register of trained intercultural mediators that live and work in Greece. The project was implemented from January till June 2013 and was financed by the *Greek Ministry of Interior* and the *European Fund for the Integration of Third Country Nationals in Greece (EIF-Greece)*.

An electronic platform was created (www.intermedation.gr) that covers multiple needs in the field of intercultural mediation. The Intercultural Mediators Platform is the first register in Greece that lists intercultural mediators operating in the country, making their services publicly accessible. It enables third-country migrants and local stakeholders to seek for an intercultural mediator in the area, language or service they are interested in. Valid information about intercultural mediation, and services that facilitate the access of third country nationals to public services and goods, is made available. In addition, the Intercultural Mediators Platform permits mediators to network with each other and provides them with resources that not only facilitate their work, but also promote the further development of their skills.

There are 132 registered mediators till today, whereas the platform content is available in four linguistic versions (Greek, English, Albanian and Arabic).

Why Were the Platform and the Registry Necessary?

The increasing influx of immigrants to Greece during the past decades has naturally resulted in severe linguistic and cultural barriers, which had a direct impact on the processing of basic transactions with public services and the social integration of migrants. In order to deal with the new multicultural reality, intercultural mediation has been recently introduced to Greece through a number of interventions designed by the EIF-Greece and the EU. In these interventions bilingual/multilingual migrants or locals were trained for mediating in specific sectors (health care, education, legal matters etc.) and were given the opportunity to render their services in corresponding institutions for a limited period of time.

The courses designed for the training of intercultural mediators (IM) varied heavily in content, duration, scope, and quality. In addition, no central records of these courses and the IM trained were held that would allow for the monitoring of the activity, the availability, and the geographical distribution of IM in Greece. As a result, the services offered by IM remained widely unknown and little, if any, information was available on their qualifications and contact details. This was exacerbated by the increased mobility of migrant IM, which rendered many of them virtually invisible and inaccessible. No provisions for networking all these trained IM were ever made.

In order to fill this void, the Intercultural Mediators Platform was designed to:

- *Provide migrants and local stakeholders with information* on the role and utility of intercultural mediation services.
- *Register all trained IM* who desired to be accessible and remain active as mediators.
- *Make information available on contact details, qualifications, languages, fields, and areas of intervention* of the registered IM.
- *Offer networking tools* to the registered IM for the better flow of information and dissemination of good practices.
- *Offer resources to IM for improving knowledge* on issues related to mediation.

Creating the Registry

After thorough research it was established that 586 people had been trained as IM in the course of the past seven years. Several of them had participated in more than one training program.

Repeated efforts were made to contact the trained IM through a variety of means (telephone, personal and group email, letters, sms). Only 417 IM could be contacted, since no correct contact information was available for 169 persons. The mediators were informed about the purpose of the registry and its potential contribution to the gradual establishment of mediation as a choice par excellence. As soon as the infrastructure for the registry was developed, all IM were encouraged to register before the end of the project. As it turned out, of the 417 persons contacted, 36 were no longer active as IM.

In order to assure that the structure of the registry and the platform would suit the needs of all possible users, questionnaires were administered to IM, migrants and stakeholders. From the 27 responses received, as well as from the structure of IM registries in other countries, the final decision was made on the information the registry should provide and would appear as the public IM profile. The *Public Profile* was created in order to ensure that future users of the registry would have adequate data on the qualifications of the IM to make an informed choice when employing their services. In Figure 6.1 the fields of the public profile of the registered IM can be seen.

Public Profile
Name:
Surname:
Gender:
Email:
Mobile phone number:
Nationality:
Intermediation languages:
Direct Service Areas:
Service areas upon agreement:
Provided Services:
Working hours:
Educational Level:
Teaching experience in intercultural mediation:
Computer skills:
Professional experience in intercultural mediation:
Would you like to add additional details for your professional experience?

Figure 6.1: The fields of the public IM profile in the registry. *www.intermediation.gr*

Registered IM can be found with the use of two complementary services: The *Intermediator Search Service* and the *Mediators List*. Choosing the *Intermediator Search Service* the user can specify in a form the name and the gender of the IM he is looking for, the area(s) and language(s) of intervention desired, and the services asked for. Only those languages appear in the form for which there is at least one mediator registered. After submitting the form, all entries matching the search criteria appear in a list, giving the user the opportunity to access the public profile of the IM of his choice.

Upon opening the *Mediators List* all names of the registered IM appear in alphabetic order (entries in Latin precede those in Greek). 10 entries appear per page, facilitating the search. Through the list the mediator profile can be directly accessed.

Registration is only possible for mediators who reside lawfully in the country and have received some training in intercultural mediation. The code of conduct of the platform has also to be agreed upon before registering. As far as these preconditions are met, new registrations are possible regardless of the completion time of the project. Until the time this article was written, 132 trained IM had registered speaking a total of 27 languages besides Greek.

Complementary Features of the Platform

Given that in Greece the awareness of issues regarding intercultural mediation is very limited, the registry of IM would be of little use if no supplementary information was provided on what one can expect from a mediator. For this reason, the Intercultural Mediators Platform provides answers on how a migrant or an institution can benefit from collaborating with an IM, what criteria apply when choosing a mediator, and what is the role of IM. A *FAQ* section provides easy-to-understand answers on additional questions.

A special effort was made to present key information in the main languages of the migrant population. So besides a full English version of the platform (which was foreseen by the initial planning), an adapted Albanian and Arabic version were created thanks to volunteering mediators. The limited implementation time of the project did not allow for more linguistic versions to be offered.

All IM and other users can profit from useful links, information on legislation regarding migration issues and extensive training material. The use of networking tools such as the forum is restricted to registered mediators only.

First Reactions to the Registry

Generally speaking, the news about the IM registry came as a pleasant surprise to the mediators themselves and possible future users of the registry alike. The need for it was acknowledged by the vast majority, and wishes were expressed from all directions that the registry may lead to a systematic use of intercultural mediation services in Greece.

Despite the favorable reactions, there were also some practical difficulties. As far as the mediators were concerned, some of them did not have internet access, while others had very limited or no computer skills. Although assistance was provided in our offices for the registration process, it is evident that these IM can profit very little from the services the platform provides. Moreover, the discontinuity between the training programs, the ambiguity of their employment status and the frustration from the inability to use their training in the previous years, were, according to the IM themselves, the main reasons that prevented them from an immediate registration to the platform and inclined them to treat the process with reserve. Personal reasons, such as working full-time in a different field, family responsibilities, time constraints or other undefined reasons, were also mentioned as causes that prevented some IM from registering.

Through an extensive publicity campaign large numbers of public and private institutions providing services to immigrants all over the country, NGOs, representatives of the migrant community and the press were informed on the IM registry and the platform (see Table 1-1). A vivid interest was expressed, mostly from health care providers and organizations committed to human rights protection. The institutional ambiguity of the mediator employment status was the main concern expressed by stakeholders, as they consider it a significant bureaucratic obstacle that might block their efforts to make full use of the IM services.

Conclusions

The importance of socially embedded information when targeting the migrant population was manifested through the implementation of both the *Learning Community* project and the creation of the IM registry/platform.

Table 6.1: Institutions and Stakeholders Informed on the Intercultural Mediators Registry and Platform.

Type of Entity	Number of Entities Informed
Greek Newspapers	8
Immigrant Newspapers	8
Immigrant Communities	49
NGOs Working with Migrants	64
Hospitals (Public and Private)	127
Social Insurance Institutes (Providers of Health Care)	86
Courts	59
Police Directorates	53
Other Institutions Involved in EIF-Greece Projects	3
Branches of International Organizations	6
Total	**463**

Migrants acting as facilitators, multipliers or mediators proved to be very effective "living bridges" between cultures, connecting the migrant population to the host society. Their understanding of two different cultures, social systems and languages, as well as their personal migration experience, was very helpful in building trust in the target groups and communicating the real issues to stakeholders of the host country.

Notwithstanding the training, the persistence, and the voluntary spirit of such multipliers, it emerged clearly from both projects that little can be accomplished on the long term if structural and institutional changes are not introduced. Migrant access to adult education is much more connected to the accessibility and the appropriateness of the services offered, than to personal preferences or initiative. The establishment of intercultural mediation services in the public and social sector cannot be achieved without institutional support. The complexity of integration issues stresses the need for the State to be vigilant for the constant improvement of the social integration services provided, the impact on local host societies and the proper use of invested national and European resources (Νικολακοπούλου-Στεφάνου, 2008). It also requires a central coordination and certification of bodies acting as policy makers in issues of social integration (Νικολακοπούλου-Στεφάνου, 2008).

The cases of Switzerland and Belgium, being multicultural societies for many years now, show how the institutionalization of mediation services can facilitate the administration of public services and immigrants as well. In Belgium as early as 1991 an Intercultural Mediation Program was started by the Centre for Health and Ethnic Minorities (CEMG). Since 1999, Belgian hospitals can apply for funding for the employment of intercultural mediators from the Federal Public Service of Public Health, Food Chain Security and Environment (Verrept, 2008). Intercultural mediators have to fulfill certain requirements to be eligible for funding. Research evidence suggests that the work of the intercultural mediator may result in an important improvement in the quality of care delivered to ethnic minority patients, if adequate use is made of their services, and it may contribute to the elimination of health care disparities (Verrept, 2008).

In Switzerland, INTERPRET[2] acts as a nationally recognized organization, promoting the development of intercultural interpreting and mediating. A qualification procedure for intercultural mediators and interpreters has been developed that consists of two levels: The Swiss INTERPRET Certificate and the Chartered Certificate for Intercultural Translation. A user-friendly registry with thousands of qualified interpreters functions as a central professional register, thus providing official recognition to its members and ensuring their employability and accessibility.

In conclusion, the Learning Community project and the Intercultural Mediators Registry, combined with other related interventions, have an accumulative effect, revealing the real needs, setting the wheels of institutional and structural change in motion, paving the way for more targeted future interventions, and constantly raising public awareness. Thus, these projects have contributed to taking intercultural mediation in Greece two steps forward.

References

Dinçelek-Lettinga, J., Moser, H., Prange, C., Papagiannopoulou, T., Schaepkens, L. and Winterstein, V. (2012). *Opening Doors to Adult Education for Migrants. Guidelines for Working with Education Ambassadors.* Grundtvig *Learning Community* Project. Graz.

Verrept, H. (2008). Intercultural Mediation: an Answer to Health Care Disparities? In C. Valero-Garcés, & A. Martin (Eds.) *Crossing borders in community interpreting. Definitions and dilemmas.* Amsterdam/Philadelpia: Benjamins.

Νικολακοπούλου-Στεφάνου, Η. (2008). Αντί Προλόγου. Στο Κ. Σκλάβου (Επιμ.), *Οδηγός Διαπολιτισμικής Συμβουλευτικής* (Ελληνικό Συμβούλιο για τους Πρόσφυγες) (σσ. 11-17). Αθήνα: Εκδόσεις Παπαζήση.

[2] All information about INTERPRET is from www.inter-pret.ch

Part II: The SONETOR Project: Forging Peer-Learning Synergies through Social Networking

Chapter 7: Facilitating the Peer Learning of Cultural Mediators with the Help of Social Computing Tools: the SONETOR Project[1]

Achilles Kameas and Konstantina Polymeropoulou

Introduction

Cultural Mediators (CM) are professionals who are trained to facilitate relations between local and foreign citizens, and to promote reciprocal knowledge and comprehension aimed at favoring a positive relationship between persons of different cultural backgrounds. They can be considered as specialized mediators. The main characterizing elements of Cultural Mediators are communicative competence, empathy, active listening and good knowledge of both the hosting country and country of origin (culture, laws, traditions, etc.).

In Webster online, the term "mediation" is defined as the act or process of mediating, and more specifically, as the intervention between conflicting parties to promote reconciliation, settlement, or compromise. The term "mediate" is defined as (1) to bring accord out of by action as an intermediary or to effect by action as an intermediary, (2) to act as intermediary agent in bringing, effecting, or communicating or to transmit as intermediate mechanism or agency, (3) to interpose between parties in order to reconcile them or to reconcile differences. A mediator is a person who mediates. However, no definition of Cultural Mediator can be found.

To meet the requirements of their role, Cultural Mediators must possess a combination of formal and non-formal skills and competences that can only be developed with a combination of formal training, practical experience and personal up skilling. In addition, Cultural Mediators are in need of continuous on the job support, as they are often engaged in tangled up situations that require immediate action, and can greatly benefit from the experience of their peers, who have in the past dealt (or failed to deal) with similar situations.

---

[1] The research presented in this chapter has been conducted in the context of SONETOR project (518736-LLP-1-2011-1-GR-LEONARDO-LMP) funded by EU in the context of the Leonardo da Vinci strand of the Life Long Learning program. The author wishes to thank fellow researchers and end users who participate in the project.

Information and communication technologies (ICT) systems and platforms could provide support to these specific needs. Modern technologies, such as multimedia content, online platforms and repositories, mobile technologies and communication tools can become valuable aids to the Cultural Mediators' tasks, provided that they are offered in a comprehensive and easy to access way. Especially social networking applications after having gained widespread use in lay situations, are now increasingly penetrating educational and training settings, leading to the development of new training practices, which realize modern theories of learning (i.e. social constructivism, peer learning etc.) in contemporary networked and mobile environments.

The SONETOR project (www.SONETOR-project.eu) produced a training platform that integrates a plethora of social networking applications with peer education methodologies and specially produced content and services, in order to assist Cultural Mediators in developing formal and non-formal skills and competences and in applying them during their work with immigrants.

In this chapter we present the main outcomes of this very interesting project and comment on the interest it generated among the CM communities of the participating countries. The rest of the chapter is organized as follows. In the next section, we briefly present the project's main outcomes. Then we describe the actions we took in order to organize the user community that would participate and benefit from the project. Based on the outcome of an initial study, a draft profile of Cultural Mediators has been developed; this is described in section "Profiling the Cultural Mediator". Then the SONETOR platform, the main outcome of the project is presented, followed by a description of the way peer learning is realized with it, and the interest this approach generated in the CM community. Some conclusions are presented in the last section, together with the project's impact.

Overview of Project Outcomes

The project achieved the following concrete objectives:

- Description of the competences and skills that professional Cultural Mediators must possess, after conducting a detailed comparative user needs analysis in the fields of legislation, training, collaboration and skills definition;
- Development of a project portal serving as a focal communication point for European Cultural Mediators and other stakeholders. The portal contains a training platform composed of social networking tools, which can be used to support networking and peer learning of Cultural Mediators; and
- Creation of guided and unguided (peer) learning scenarios on topics related to the everyday practice of Cultural Mediators, such as Health, Education, Public services, etc., which are delivered via the training platform

To successfully achieve the above objectives as well as to ensure the sustainability of project outcomes, it was essential to involve Cultural Mediators as end users from the start of the project, and to maintain collaboration with them by organizing various training sessions per participating country.

Organizing the Learning Community

One of the most important aims of the project was to help establish a European learning community of Cultural Mediators who will be using the SONETOR platform to exchange experience, advice and best practice. The whole idea is based on the way open source user community's function. A staged process was put in place.

In the first stage, Core User Groups (CUG) were formed. CUG members served as the "core" group for promoting platform usage in each country. They were selected based on their qualifications and experience with immigrants, the domain of their activity and the interest they showed in using the platform. Their tasks included contribution to platform specification and deign of training scenarios, platform testing, development and uploading of training content and invitation of more users. One person from this group was nominated as National Moderator; her tasks involved the training and supervision of the Core Users, the planning and supervision of the training sessions of the end users, the moderation of the platform content and the evaluation of its functionality.

At a later stage, each member of CUG invited at least 10 new members to join the community. Thus, an initial learning community of at least 250 CM across Europe was formed in the course of the project. The members of this community defined the areas of CM activity and subscribed to the ones they were interested in. In this context, and by collaborating from a distance, the platform users, under the guidance of the National Moderator and the Core Users, uploaded episodes of their experience, digital content, blog posts, etc., while commenting on the content uploaded by their CM peers.

Profiling the Cultural Mediator

In order to compile the CM profile, three domains were studied: everyday practice, collaboration needs and training needs. A combination of desk and field research techniques was applied on the members of the Core Users group.

Respondents pointed the following desirable qualifications when working with immigrants: immigration law, psychology, family studies, education, social policy, sociology, cultural studies, linguistics, political science, philology, international relations, international law, social science or cultural mediation.

Regarding the appropriate skills, they distinguish the following: knowledge of immigrants' languages and way of thinking, knowledge of immigrant culture, ability to remain calm, administrative and psychological skills.

Abilities that would be useful include: communication skills, curiosity, openness, tolerance, empathy, creativity, understanding, accuracy, self-organization, respect, self-control, resistance, power, accuracy, solidarity, sociability, self-confidence, honesty.

Diagnosing and solving various problems related to the process of adaptation of immigrants to the social, cultural and civilizational conditions of the host country requires that the person filling the role of cultural mediator has a knowledge of anthropological and sociological type. On the one hand, the CM should have knowledge about the cultural and civilizational diversity of the world, and knowledge about how this diversity is reflected in the diversity of styles and ways of thinking of people coming from different cultures and civilizations. On the other hand, the CM should have knowledge about the principles and mode of operation of the social system in the host country.

To put it more precisely, the area / block type of anthropological knowledge should include basic knowledge in the field of intercultural communication, with particular emphasis on knowledge of factors posing the most common barriers and problems in interpersonal communication resulting from the variety and diversity of cultural and civilizational contexts, elementary knowledge of proxemics (branch of science that studies anthropological differences in perceptions and evaluation of physical and symbolic space, reported in people from different cultural and civilizational), and of course elementary knowledge on ethnic map of the world.

The area / block type of sociological knowledge should include knowledge of the social network of the host country, with a particular focus on the areas of knowledge and competence of the institutions included in the system of institutions providing social assistance. In addition, cultural mediators should have basic knowledge of the legal system of the host country, with particular emphasis on legal regulations concerning foreigners and immigrants. Almost everyone who took part in the survey emphasized that the main difficulties they encounter in their professional work is the complexity of laws and regulations that regulate areas such as health care, education, and the labor market.

To effectively carry out their responsibilities, CM should also have a specific set of practical skills that enable them to effectively fulfill the role of an intermediary between immigrants and the reality of the host country. This set would include working knowledge of foreign languages and a predisposition to learning foreign languages, skills related to "completing administrative matters" and ability to efficiently interact with the system of institutions in the host country. The importance of knowledge of computer usage and social media is increasing.

During our analysis, it became evident that CM come from divergent backgrounds and occupations, while many of them originate from the communities they are mediating for. Thus, we defined two types of CM profiles. The first one described cultural mediation as a complete and autonomous occupation; the other defined it as a qualifications module that is added on top of existing qualifications (i.e. a qualified caretaker who also acts as cultural mediator). Some of the key responsibilities of both CM types include:

- Maintain and develop a communicational basis between the mediator, the client and the institution.
- Plan and carry out spare time activities to get the migrants involved more directly in the new culture.
- Develop ideas and create offers for the clients to think about the different cultural habits.
- Respond to the questions of the clients and provide them a professional guidance through bureaucracy. Follow up talks through telephone and

personal visits to make sure they understood rituals and habits as well as the relevant legal framework.

- Maintain and develop existing and new relationships to migrants through planned individual support (personal visits etc.).
- Monitor and report on activities and provide relevant information to the responsible management.
- Carry out researches, concerning specific questions and problems of the clients.
- Liaise and attend meetings with other companies/institutions in order to find shortcuts and synergies. So the necessary functions to perform duties and aid cultural consulting can be better developed.
- Provide the public also with information about positive examples of integration.
- Attend training and to develop relevant knowledge and skills (ICT and language…).

Based on this analysis we described the CM job profile in a way compatible to European Qualifications Framework (EQF) using knowledge, skills and competences. We focused on EQF levels 5-7 and divided the qualifications into four categories, of the eight that every individual in the knowledge-based society of the 21st century should aspire to develop, as defined in the European Framework for Key Competences for Lifelong Learning. These are Social and civic competences (SCC), Sense of initiative and entrepreneurship (SIE), Cultural awareness and expression (CAE), and Digital competences (DC). A sample of the listed KSC per level and category follows:

- Using the technical terminology related to social and civic skills (SSC, Level 5 and above)
- Being able to introduce and instruct apprentices/ peers and immigrants in different steps of socialization processes (SSC, Level 5 and above)
- Being able to place him/herself into the position of the immigrants – to show empathy (SSC, Level 5 and above)
- Being able to monitor and direct operations in hazardous situations concerning personnel environment until – other – authoritative assistance arrives (SSC, Level 7)
- Being able to use information from various sources – handbooks, reports, internet etc. (SIE, Level 5 and above)
- Helping colleagues to find necessary details (SIE, Level 5 and above)
- Being able to realize the valid laws for working time (SIE, Level 7)
- Being able to make prompt important decisions (SIE, Level 7)
- Knowing well how to communicate freely using the cultural related terminology, abbreviations, nomenclature and similar (CAE, Level 5 and above)
- Knowing the characteristics and understand behavior related to different cultures and ethnic minorities (CAE, Level 5 and above)

- Knows how to use interactive platforms, social media tools for interaction with the target groups of immigrants (DC, Level 5 and above)
- Being able to complete forms, certificates, reports and other written templates for special software programs used in the daily work (DC, Level 6 and above)

The complete CM profile is publicly available in the SONETOR platform.

The SONETOR Platform

The main achievement of the project is the SONETOR platform; a web based portal supporting learning and social networking, which is accessible at the address www.culturalmediators.eu. The platform has been built by integrating open source tools, such as Joomla, Moodle and BigBlueButton. For the moment, access to the platform requires registration of the user. The user can use his/her login credentials, or request for an account to be created, in a very straightforward manner. For those requiring assistance, a FAQ tab is available upfront.

After entering the platform, the user (that is, the Cultural Mediator) can access a range of services, all of them planned to enhance his skills and knowledge and to bring him/her in contact with peers (Figure 7.1).

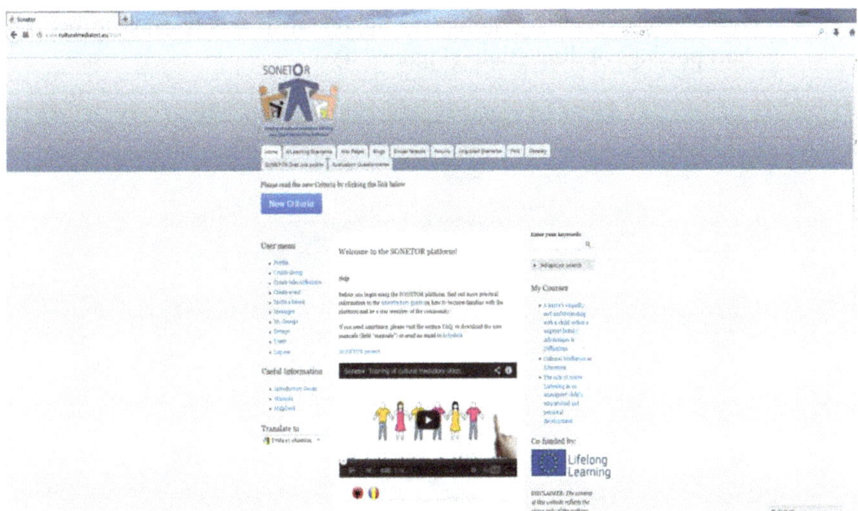

Figure 7.1: The Main Screen of the SONETOR Platform after Logon

By using the items on the left, the user can customize his profile and participation in the community, invite friends to join, see pending personal messages or start a teleconferencing session. The middle section provides announcements, events and information on recent activity on the courses the user has joined. The right column provides a tag based search facility, which allows the user horizontal access to the content of the platform, using the keywords he/she enters as filter.

The topmost bar lists the main services offered by the platform. These include:

- Guided training scenarios: these comprise a series of sequentially ordered steps that end users must follow in order to receive a certificate. Each step contains text and multimedia content that must be studied, as well as a set of questions and exercises that must be answered in order to proceed to the next step (Figure 7.2) Guided scenarios are currently designed by the project partners with help by the national moderators. They are based on episodes described in the context of unguided scenarios enhanced with multimedia content modules and quizzes
- Wikis: users can create wikis for any topic related to cultural mediation. Wikis are used in order to generate a body of knowledge on a specific topic in a collaborative manner. Currently, a wiki of terms related to cultural mediation is available
- Blogs: this service allows users to post articles declaring individual opinions on perspectives on matters related to cultural mediation (Figure 7.3). Other users may comment or provide their own point of view. It may also be used as an announcement / news service
- Social media: this service integrates links to the popular social media, as well as facilities that allow a user to maintain a list of contacts among the platform users
- Forums: this service is similar to blogs, but it is advisable to use for short postings or discussions (Figure 7.4)

Figure7.2: Excerpt from the Guided Scenarios offered at the SONETOR Platform

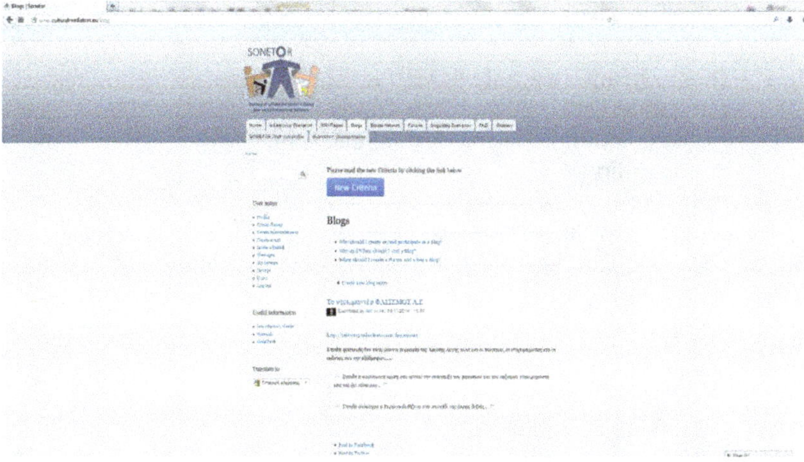

Figure 7.3: The Blogs tab of the SONETOR Platform

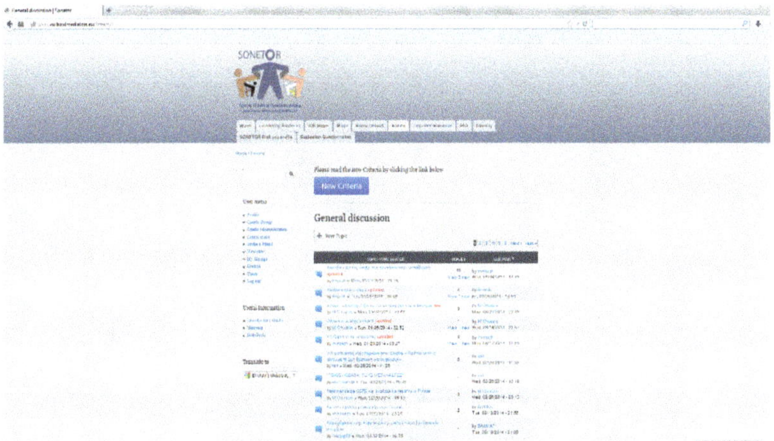

Figure 7.4: Forum Tab of the SONETOR Platform

- It is very helpful for building community spirit among users. All users are requested to present themselves in a special "getting to know each other" forum; discussions on other topics (among them one that attempts to detail the competences of cultural mediator) are ongoing, as well
- Unguided (peer) learning scenarios: they constitute the main learning service offered to end users; in fact, they are developed by end users themselves! Specific areas of cultural mediators' activity have been selected and end users are asked either to upload related episodes or comment on episodes uploaded by their peers, based on their experience (see Figure 7.5)
- FAQ: contains comprehensive information on how to use the platform, as well as on which social networking service should be used for a specific task. We decided this would be a useful addition, as many

cultural mediators were not experienced with the capabilities of social networking tools

- Glossary: this is a wiki-based "official" glossary of terms related to cultural mediation (Figure 7.6). Currently, it is maintained by the project partners, but in the future, cultural mediators themselves should assume responsibility

As one can see from the screenshots, each service is offered in a separate tab. This enhances platform modularity and allows for easy additions or deletions of services in the future.

Figure 7.5: Excerpt from the Unguided (peer) learning Scenarios offered at the SONETOR Platform

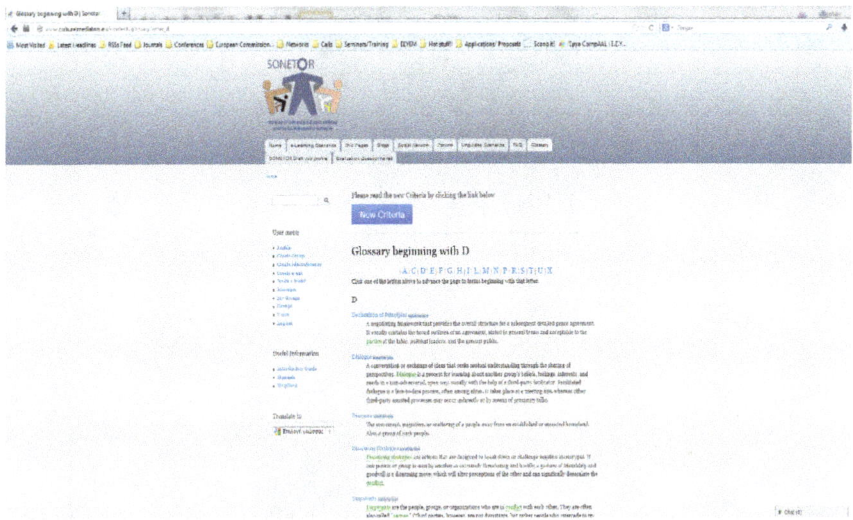

Figure 7.6: The wiki-based Glossary tab of the SONETOR Platform

A specific problem that arose during platform development was support of multilingualism. Not only major European languages should be supported, but also participating CM must be able to upload content in their own language. This issue appears at two levels: user interface and content. The interface of the platform is available in all partner languages; each user, at registration time, must select his/her language of preference.

Regarding content, we dealt with this issue in two ways. Firstly, we have embedded in the platform the publicly available Google translator service. With it, users can get a decent but not accurate translation of any content module in any language. Secondly, we ask end users to officially translate important content modules first in English and then in any other language they wish.

In this way, we overcome at a low cost the problem of supporting end users' native languages, thus removing the most important obstacle in communication, that of now knowing the language of the hosting society.

Training Cultural Mediators

As mentioned in the previous section, the platform offers two types of training opportunities, via guided or unguided training scenarios.

Guided training scenarios consist of a sequence of training steps that each user must complete. Each scenario is associated with knowledge, skills and competences identified in the profile of cultural mediators; thus, when a user completes a specific scenario, he/she is awarded a certification for a specific qualifications module. Access to guided scenarios is free to any registered user platform.

Figure 7.7: Unguided Training Scenarios accompanied by Multimedia Content

Unguided training scenarios constitute the essence of the peer learning service offered by the platform (Figure 7.7). Currently, four areas of cultural mediators' activity have been selected, based on the preference of end users: education, health, housing and law. Within each of these, end users can upload episodes of cultural mediation, based on their individual experience. Each episode contains a description of a situation where the intervention of a cultural mediator was necessary, the actions he/she took and the results; it may also be accompanied with questions regarding the situation or the actions, or documentation justifying the approach. Other end users are expected to comment on the approach taken, supply similar situations and the actions they took provide response to questions raised by their peers or even upload supporting documentation.

Multimedia content, such as videos and podcasts, has been incorporated as part of the peer learning scenarios in order to enhance the CM learning experience. Most of the material was submitted or even prepared by the end users, and it is based on their own mediation experiences. The concept and the initial purpose of each video was to motivate learners to visualize a possible situation that they might face as Cultural Mediators. Each video produced by the project members comes with subtitles in several languages and is available to every trainer for commenting and further discussion. In this way, we facilitated collaboration among members of the European community of Cultural Mediators. The exchange of experience eventually leads to the specification of best practices, which can be up taken by members of the community. In addition, community members can overcome the cultural differences among themselves, and benefit from each other's experience.

By the end of the project 491 users had successfully registered to the platform, collectively submitting 1466 pieces of learning content (325 episodes of cultural mediation experience, 703 blog postings, 148 forum postings and 290 events related to cultural mediation). The number of uploaded episodes is impressive, indicating the rich repository of experiences that the CM community members hold. The collective number of blogs and forum postings reaches almost 1000, indicating the liveliness of the community and the active engagement in the exchange of experience. These figures are also an indicator that the platform meets usability requirements of the CM community members and increase on a daily basis, as the platform is still being used by the CM community. A set of achievement indicators were agreed among project partners and were published in the platform, leading to the awarding of a certificate to the users who achieved them.

Conclusion

SONETOR was realized as a transnational cooperation project aiming to improve the competences and skills of any professional who formally or informally interacts with immigrants by promoting innovation in vocational training of Cultural Mediators through the use of a social networking training platform. The main products of the project (CM job profile, training content and scenarios, social networking platform) can be used to provide continuous support and competence up skilling to the members of the European CM community.

The pedagogical methodology combines peer learning and adult education principles for lifelong learning. Learning services are deployed via a special social networking platform, using digital content developed by the consortium and the emerging community of Cultural Mediators, ensuring transfer of knowledge, culture, best practice and experience at a European level. Ultimately, the project supports the exchange of working experience and real life situations among the members of Cultural Mediators communities within the context of training scenarios, which act as apprenticeship pathways.

The project generated much impact in the participating countries, amassing, during the few months that the platform was publicly open, more than 200 CM users who continue to use the platform beyond the end of the project. These Cultural Mediators participate in a European learning community, achieving personal development and sustainability beyond the lifetime of the project.

The project aligns with a set of European policies. The basic ideas behind SONETOR are compatible with the European Employment Strategy – Mutual Learning Programme (MLP) (http://ec.europa.eu/social/main.jsp?catId=1047). By enhancing and updating CM qualifications the project can increase their employability potential, being thus consistent to the scope of European strategy "Europe 2000" (http://ec.europa.eu/europe2020/index_en.htm) and more specifically, Digital Jobs and New Skills for New Jobs, specifically in bridging the gap between the worlds of education and work. SONETOR is also in accordance with one of the three axis of EaSI (EU Programme for Employment and Social Innovation) (http://ec.europa.eu/social/main.jsp?catId%20=1081) and in particular the PROGRESS axis supporting the modernization of employment and social policies. Last but not least, the project contributes to the policy for fighting poverty and social exclusion (http://www.eppgroup.eu/topic/Fighting-youth-unemployment-and--social-exclusion) especially in the social Investment Pact, which includes measures to help disadvantaged groups and enhance social inclusion.

The platform has already been linked to the Greek National Registry of trained Cultural Mediators and the CM profile has been submitted for consultation to the National Organisation for the Certification of Qualifications and Vocational Guidance in Greece. We are currently trying to transfer the platform to countries that did not participate in the project (i.e. Italy), while we are developing a new, upgraded platform version, which will also support traditional online training.

Chapter 8: Peer-learning and Beyond

Krzysztof Gurba

Introduction

The training of cultural mediators utilizing new network social software is the subject of an international project SONETOR, carried out in the framework of the European Development of Innovation Program. In response to the need for training and retraining of people working in immigrant communities, a platform for e-learning was created, in which educational scenarios are offered. A characteristic feature of the platform is the manifold opportunity for users to participate in learning content production.

Scenarios are created partly in the unguided way, which induces a far-reaching interactivity and mutual co-stimulation of the training materials authors on the web. The structure of the scenario is built around a simple story based on real cases involving immigrants. Creation and development of educational content is open and thus allows and even forces the process of content updating by the users themselves, cooperating in the network and using the tools of social media. The methodology brings interesting experiences indicating additional cognitive advantages of e-learning within proposed innovative approach.

Cultural Mediation—Profession or Mission?

Because not in all of the partner countries of the project, and thus not in every European country there are institutionally established rules for the profession of cultural mediator, the beneficiaries of the project can be two categories of potential users. In the first category are those employed in the profession of cultural mediator who perform their duties and are paid for that. To this group were can include also those who plan such employment. For such persons, the proposed training scenarios would be supportive of their existing vocational training. The second category are those that do not have professional status of a cultural mediators, but fulfill at least some of their roles, for example, social workers, counselors, educators, health assistants, police officers and border guards. For such users educational scenarios are to provide procedural knowledge and skills extending their competence in the specific area of contact with the problems of immigrants.

The importance of such retraining, often informal, underline the authors of the study conducted in the framework of the project SONETOR: "A person as a mediator of culture definitely should not be an official dealing with the immigrant within working hours". The essence of the profession of cultural mediator, according to the participants of research is rather a continuous accompaniment given to an immigrant in a new and different reality and being a guide to the complexities of immigrant life in the host country, explaining these complexities and differences, and practically solving them.

According to our experts cultural mediators should be: understanding, patient, open to otherness and "should like what he does" (Baradziej, Kisiel and Kisiel, 2012, p. 19-20). Besides, most experts in the field of intercultural mediation emphasize the importance of personal characteristics of the mediator in the effective implementation of this function, or even mission (Reynolds & Valentine, 2004; Bochner, 1981).

At the end of the reports prepared by the project several important conclusions were formulated: Firstly, the establishment of position or profession cultural mediator should be regarded as an important complement to the existing "institutional" support in the adaptation processes of immigrants. Cultural mediator is a person who should have a good understanding of institutions and organizations, both of the state and local government and NGOs dealing with immigrants to skillfully use the existing network of institutions and organizations to take their own actions to support the process of adaptation of immigrants into the host country. Position or the profession of cultural mediator does not have to be created from scratch. Some employees of various aid institutions, after proper training can successfully act as a cultural mediator. Secondly, the effective fulfillment of the mission of the cultural mediator requires the ability to combine the thought and action of the different segments of social life of the host country. The need for communication and co-operation and exchange of experience among cultural mediators causes that the tool similar to that used in the project SONETOR can serve as a platform of cooperation and communication of cultural mediators. Thirdly, one has to distinguish between the roles of mediator in dealing with immigrants with regulated and non-regulated status. In the first case, its role is smaller, because their problems at least in part can be successfully solved by social workers implementing integration programs. Cultural mediator should deal also with undocumented immigrants or illegal immigrants who cannot count on any help from aid institutions, or are even afraid to use their help. Fourthly, cultural mediators, especially in the first period of an immigrant stay in the host country should be in constant and intense contact with him/her. Mediation requires a lot more of time and activity, than the ordinary kind of support. The mediator of culture is both a professional, proficient in diagnosing and solving problems of adaptation of immigrants, equipped with the knowledge and skills for the social sciences, and a person equipped with certain type of personality (being sensitive, patient, and empathetic).

Set of Competences

SONETOR project idea was to extract a set of competences, in particular the communication skills necessary in solving typical and atypical conflict and crisis situations in the environments of immigrants. Set of competences prepared on the basis of wide-ranging sociological research not only helped to create a comprehensive professional profile of cultural mediator, but also gave rise to the separation of learning outcomes that should be achieved in a modular training conducted for social workers, public service officials and volunteers involved in contact with immigrants (Baradziej, Kisiel and Kisiel, 2012).

For the purpose of further stages of the project a hierarchy of expected competence cultural mediator was established. Five core competences are the following:

- Anthropological-sociological knowledge
- Communicative and linguistic competence
- Patience
- Openness and tolerance
- Pragmatic skills

On the basis of a set of required communicational competences educational scenarios were created for the specially established e-learning platform of the SONETOR project. The design structure of educational scenarios is created around the story of the typical problems of conflicts and problems in contact with immigrants. Created proposals for educational paths are of two types: moderated and non-moderated. Moderated scenarios have rigid structure and order of the stages of learning, and quizzes and tests included the course must be dealt with sequentially. The ability to communicate with a moderator and between each other is open, but limited to the exchange of opinions and consultations within forum topics and blog posts created around educational scenarios on the learning platform. There are advantages of this kind of story-based learning scenarios, including more regular use of the learning content, strict control of the learner's progress and clear learning path to follow by each course participant.

The Idea of Non-moderated Scenarios

Quite different is the method of learning with non-moderated scenarios. Here on the basis of the outlined starting conditions for a crisis situation in an intercultural environment (generally taken from real life, in the form of described case) trainees build their own proposals for solutions, discuss them in forums, chats and blogs, to modify the path solutions, evaluate them and re-build[1]. Learner's activity motivates him/herself and other users at the same time. The course itself becomes in fact open-ended, because anyone can add new cases, new episodes and topics for discussion. Participant of the course can be anyone who logs on to the website of the project and get his/her profile on the platform. In this sense, the

[1] The idea of common shaping of educational content and mutual evaluation of the educational outcomes is called peer-to-peer learning and peer-to-peer assessment.

training resources of the project are open, which corresponds to the current trend to provide universal and free educational resources[2].

In the testing phase platform users were so called core-users (at minimum five persons from each participant country in the project) and subsequently the end-users (further 50 people more or less involved in the mediation in a multicultural environment). Each group went short initial training of the rules on the use of educational resources on the network. Most users also participated in research on the analysis of training needs of this professional group. After completion of the project, access to educational platform on the Internet and the use of educational resources was open to all users.

In parallel with the educational platform, users contact within the areas of educational scenarios on social networks, like Facebook, LinkedIn, and Twitter. Procedure of self-learning is not inspected by a moderator or a tutor. The person using the script can freely choose the sequence of individual steps that although woven into the story of history, however, are relatively closed unit, which are both assigned to the expected learning outcomes, as well as a large portion of general knowledge, databases, keywords, glossaries of terms, links to further readings, useful suggestions and documentation, decision points, quizzes, self-checking and testing.

For each step the multimedia illustrations and links to forum discussions on-line or off-line with the users of the platform are added.

Cognitive Value of the Method

Distance learning system used in a project SONETOR had to be maximally flexible, to allow live interaction, active involvement of users in the process of modules and content (learning objects) production, to exchange experiences and to influence the course of the training process. Of course one can imagine the flexibility reaching further, towards even improving the functional structure of the platform by the users themselves. However, for the authors of the project it seems that a golden mean was found, in which the field of content creation by users (user-generated content) is sufficient.

The activity of key users and users of the second stage is noticeable. Certainly the further into the later stages of the project the greater extent not only the internal forums, blogs and chat rooms was active, and also widely used popular social media which are even more straightforwardly placed within the philosophy and spirit of the Web 2.0 and Web 3.0 ideas. From the up to date observations follows that users have a mutual exchange of information between them, usually within the same e-learning platform while maintaining a more formal way of communication and the official language of communication.

In parallel, the interaction takes place with the use of social networking sites and instant messaging is less formal, more alive and run in everyday, colloquial language. Along with greater familiarizing with the functions and options of the platform releases own creativity of individual users. They start to communicate, and by commenting and discussing they blur this distinction and bring the

[2] The idea of open-source educational content is now known under the name of Open Educational Resources (OER). We will come back to this idea later in this chapter.

informal language to contacts inside the platform too. This new quality of exchange and support brings about positive effect. Users more often feel co-creators of educational content and therefore persons jointly responsible for its quality and affordability.

The additional advantage of courses proposed on the platform is launching the activity of scholars on the social media platforms in areas associated with the content of the courses and furthermore – real life involvement in cultural mediation.

Beyond Peer-learning

Looking at further possibilities of SONETOR platform development one can imagine and plan more elaborated functionalities enabling modification of the structure of offered courses and their topic of interest. However, more interesting from the methodological point of view would be to attract the interest in taking part in the courses of larger audience. This can be done in many ways.

The first possibility is the use so called chunking of the learning content, which means reasonable modulation of subsets of learning objects. The process of chunking helps both the courses authors – in dividing the content into smaller portions, and courses users – in more efficient knowledge acquisition.

The seecond possibility is connected with the idea of Massive Open Online Courses (MOOCs), courses with huge enrolment and elaborated multimedia structure, wide network of interconnected users and wise moderation of competent instructors. First MOOC was established in 2008 by the University of Manitoba in Canada and was attended by two thousand students. Average number of participants of nowadays MOOCs is 50 thousand. In fact the structure and methodology offered by MOOCs providers is quite similar to the one used on the SONETOR platform.

There is a set of the most popular start-ups offering the highest quality of courses:

- edX – a consortium of top American universities (Harvard, MIT and Berkeley University) specializing in computer science, Artificial Intelligence and electronics courses of the highest possible quality.
- Coursera – also a consortium of universities and colleges (like Stanford University, Princeton University, John Hopkins University) with wide offer of courses in both science and humanities or even arts.
- Udacity – company (partner companies include Facebook and Google) which specializes in robotics and computer science. It offers some basic courses for beginners but also advanced programs in engineering and programming.
- Udemy – company inviting many top and the most famous experts and celebrities to attract future users with both content and form of lectures and workshops.
- Khan Academy – non-profit organization based in India with a mission to offer high quality lectures from many subjects free of charge.

Some of the MOOCs providers may offer, usually paid, certificates of attendance of the course after passing the final exams. Sometimes the certificates are equivalent to the college credits and are recognized by several universities.
Similar idea of educational badges is based on this new trend in online learning underlining the individual path and pace of learning, usually outside classrooms and university campuses, and social media use in enforcing the effectiveness of knowledge achievement. Badges, like the most popular Mozilla Badges, are offered openly, to the wide audience, and are interchangeable between many existing learning platforms.

The third possibility of the further development of SONETOR learning platform is the use of so called tinkering attitude to the learning process (Libow-Martinez & Stager, 2013). Placed within the constructionist framework the method means learning by making. Course users are invited to cope with provided tools and basic ideas to find their own way of resolving problems. It was proved that this practical attitude in many instances is more effective than traditional teaching and gives the learners opportunity to be more creative and innovative. Learning outcomes from this process of self-learning are also more sustainable than usually.

References

Baradziej, J., Kisiel, P. and Kisiel, B. (2012). *Report from the survey done within the Sonetor project*. Kraków.

Bochner, S. (ed.) (1981). *The Mediating Person: Bridges between Cultures.* Cambridge Mass: Schenkman Publishing Company.

Libow-Martinez, S. and Stager, G. (2013). *Invent to Learn: Making, Tinkering, and Engineering in the Classroom.* Constructing Modern Knowledge Press.

Reynolds, S. and Valentine, D. (2004). *Guide to Cross-Cultural Communication.* Upper Saddle River, Pearson: Prentice Hall.

Chapter 9: Experience in Managing a Community of Cultural Mediators

Mara Aspioti and Achilles Kameas

Introduction

Cultural Mediators (CMs) are highly skilled professionals who mediate between communities having different cultural backgrounds aiming at establishing reciprocal communication and understanding. Their job demands continuous update of knowledge and acquisition of practical mediation skills. As they are called to solve situational problems, CMs can benefit from the experience of their peers and could make use of on-the-spot assistance. Project SONETOR, funded in the context of EU Lifelong Learning program aims at the establishment of a focal point for the community of CMs in the form of a web-based social networking platform. CMs can use social networking tools to record their experience, comment on the experience of their peers and in general learn from the CM community experience.

During the project, a CM community was established in each of the partner countries consisting of CMs who were trained in using the platform and its services in order to upload and exchange content. In each country, one of the community members has been appointed as a National Moderator (NM) with the mission to manage and facilitate the operation of the community. In this paper, we shall present the experience of the Greek NM in managing the community of Greek CMs.

After a brief introduction to moderation and related issues in the next section, we shall present in section 3 the NM role in the context of SONETOR project. Discussion will focus on the main challenges a National Moderator is faced with, the strategies she has come up with in order to handle difficult situations and to achieve the involvement of trainees, and the educational aspects of her role. Moreover, this section addresses the outcomes of users' engagement with SONETOR project. The paper concludes with a summary of the qualifications a NM should possess in order to be successful in her role.

Moderation and Moderator

According to Merriam-Webster online, the verb "moderate" means:

- to make (something) less harsh, strong, or severe or to become less harsh, strong, or severe
- to guide a discussion or direct a meeting that involves a group of people (i.e. to preside over or act as chairman or to act as a moderator)

Thus, a moderator is someone who leads a discussion in a group and tells each person when to speak; in other words, someone who moderates a meeting or a discussion.

The term Moderator may apply to various fields such as Religion, Government, Politics & Diplomacy, Nuclear Physics, Education and Computer Science. Regarding the latter, the term has found a new application domain, after the proliferation of web sites and online discussion groups. In this context, a moderator is a person who monitors the conversations in an on-line chat room checking, for example, for uses of bad language, inappropriate content, etc. and sometimes having the rights to remove offending content.

Moderators usually follow a set of documented procedures, collectively known as a "moderation system"; this is a quality management system designed to achieve valid, fair and consistent assessment following certain best practices principles that are basically the same to all moderation systems.

Duties and Responsibilities

Duties and responsibilities of the moderator are often described in handbooks of best practice moderation. In countries where the role of moderator is recognized and registered in the Qualifications Authorities lists, role profile and specified skills and competences have been set to form a framework of standards. For instance, in the *Best Practice Moderation and Best Practice in the Assessment of Unit Standards* of the New Zealand Qualifications Authority (2001), the duties and responsibilities of a national moderator read as follows:

- Monitor, evaluate and improve the effectiveness and responsiveness of the moderation system,
- Co-ordinate moderation activities nationally, advising and informing assessors and moderators as necessary,
- Identify examples of assessment activities, methods and materials useful for assessment guides and moderation training in subsequent years,
- Maintain a work log which is submitted, along with work logs collected from all moderators to the project moderator at specified times,
- Develop and maintain appropriate communication systems and working relationships with moderators as required.

Similar best practices principles are met in other documents of Qualifications Authorities worldwide (Competenz, 2011).

Knowledge, Skills and Competences

To be successful in his/her role a National Moderator should be able to show evidence of:

- Experience in
  - the education sector, preferably at tertiary level,
  - designing, implementing and managing quality management systems,
  - the preparation of reports,
  - policy development and implementation,
  - developing and implementing a communications strategy,
- Expert project management skills and relationship management experience,
- Exceptional communication skills, written and verbal,
- Excellent computer skills in using desktop / mobile and office applications.

Moreover, (s)he should

- ✓ be open to ideas, innovation and assessment,
- ✓ view moderation as a method for both compliance and continuous improvement of standards, material and practices,
- ✓ be comfortable in communicating directly and constructively with the project's assessor,
- ✓ make clear and consistent moderation decisions,
- ✓ provide helpful feedback to the users of the moderated environment,
- ✓ follow the principles of moderation best practices

In the context of SONETOR project, a moderator was appointed to monitor and manage platform usage and guide end users at a national scope, so that they were trained and become successful in completing their obligations for obtaining a certification.

Case Study: Role of the National Moderator in SONETOR Project

To better describe the role of National Moderator and answer the questions addressed in the introduction of this paper we study here the case of SONETOR National Moderator of a Community of Cultural Mediators. This case study will help us better understand the specific skills that a National Moderator has to obtain when moderating an extra-sensitive community on social-oriented issues like the CM community in our case.

Specifically, we present the experience of Mrs Mara Aspioti, the Greek NM of SONETOR project. Having in mind that the Greek partner was coordinating the project, the Greek NM also acted as a coordinator of the NMs of the other partners. As a result, her duties were augmented and her role became more critical for the success of the project comparing to the partners' NMs.

The SONETOR Project: Overview

The SONETOR project aims at (i) the creation of a European Community of Cultural Mediators, (ii) the development of a digital platform to be used as a focal point for Cultural Mediators Community to exchange experience and adopt good practices, and (iii) the establishment of an innovative training methodology specially designed to meet the CM needs through peer-learning.

The community supported by the project consists of a mix of experienced CMs, novice CMs and would-be CMs, who collectively aim to exchange knowledge, opinion and experiences in order to improve their CM competences. The project was designed to support two levels of users:

- Core Users (CUs) are experienced CMs, who have previously been intensively trained in using the platform services; CUs serve as mentors for newcomers, initiating them into the idea of peer learning and encouraging them to make optimum usage of the platform services,
- End Users are usually but non restrictively novice CMs or would be CMs who are interested to use the platform services in order to contribute to / benefit from the community experience or update their knowledge, skills and competences.

It is worth mentioning here that the moderation system on which the NMs moderation role was based has been agreed in the first place between NMs of the participating countries and approved by the project partners; mainly it included strategies to motivate the participation of CMs and guidelines on how to use the various social networking tools offered by the platform.
One of the CU was appointed in each country to serve as the National Moderator, having as main mandate to coordinate the CUs and to monitor platform usage. In addition, the NM participated in the dissemination of project outcomes, the invitation and screening of end users and the assessment of the moderation system and user performance.

Tasks of the National Moderator

Having a key role in the moderation system of the project, the NM is required to carry out certain tasks and duties so as to see to all quality management requirements and task schedules are met.

In particular these tasks in SONETOR included:

- ✓ Close collaboration with the national SONETOR partner,
- ✓ Close collaboration with the users of the national community,
- ✓ Moderation of the learning contents uploaded by the national platform users,
- ✓ Contribution to the peer learning episodes uploaded in the platform, either by uploading new episodes or by commenting on the existing ones,
- ✓ Use of the social computing tools (blogs, forums, wikis) offered by the platform,

- ✓ Participation in the evaluation and testing of the platform and the tools it offers,
- ✓ Close collaboration with the other National Moderators,
- ✓ Strengthening the links between Cultural Mediators in all the European Countries participating in the project,
- ✓ Contribution to the National Moderators' forum in the platform,
- ✓ Help in expanding the national community of Cultural Mediators using the platform,
- ✓ Training of the new members using the modules and material developed by the project partners,
- ✓ Monitoring the platform usage and the users' progress and participation,
- ✓ Raising awareness and public recognition about cultural mediation in Europe,
- ✓ Disseminating and promoting SONETOR Project and its outcomes
- ✓ Participating and contributing to discussions about project improvement and sustainability.

Further to the above, the National Moderator also acts as administrator at a national community level regarding management systems, educational tools and assessment processes.

Tools and Strategies

To be able to successfully carry out one's own obligations, the NM adopted Total Quality Management (TQM), a management system that meets the needs of modern management (Χαμπούρη-Ιωαννίδου, 2003). It is a combination of precedent theoretical approaches (such as Scientific Management, Behavioral Management, Operations Research and Systemic Approaches) and the incorporation of end user satisfaction and constant improvement of instruments, tools, services and procedures. By adopting TQM, the National Moderator has got a powerful instrument in hand to help her face the challenges and difficulties that arose during the moderation process. Advantages of TQM consist in setting about: (i) combined effort, (ii) lifelong education and training, (iii) task grouping, (iv) continuous improvement and enhancement, (v) scientific-data- and analysis-based management and finally, (vi) increased qualitative characteristics by diminishing deficiencies and dysfunctions in the system.

On top of it, the National Moderator moved through a structured sequence to correspond to moderation levels [1]. That sequence could be schematized as follows:

[1] Moderation levels in our case are described in section Resources, Methodology and Material in this paper.

Figure 9.1: Moderation Process

In the specific context posed by SONETOR project requirements, and in light of the aforementioned scientific approaches and processes, the Greek National Moderator applied a series of techniques, such as:

- **Establish sound and open connections with the partners and the partners' national moderators**. The establishment of communication channels with the partners' NMs was significantly important in order to achieve methodological harmonization and homogeneity and a consistent follow-up of the users satisfaction and progress in the project. Thus the NMs were communicating when necessary by e-mails, chats and through a forum group created in the platform especially for National Moderators aiming to the exchange of comments, experience and methodological problems concerning their role.
- **Collect and review applications and CVs of candidates to the project**. Dissemination of information about SONETOR project being made either in person by the Core Users or with calls of interest published in the Media soon resulted in an unexpectedly large number of candidates interested in and applying for the project. It was the NM's duty to collect all these applications and CVs, thoroughly review and assess them, and send a proposal to the coordinating partner on the candidates she considered to be more suitable to meet the requirements of the project.
- **Work out good communication with core users and end users**. After the coordinating partner approved NM's proposal, the NM established a permanent communication with the candidates, starting from congratulation e-mails and continuing with regularly updated information, announcements and guidelines. Moreover the Greek NM was open to any communication the end-users would like to have with her in order to ask more information, clarifications or guidance on the project. Communication was even more intense and continuous with the core users, who had the additional duty to coordinate groups of end-users and had to carry out chores of special responsibility thus their close collaboration with and guidance by the NM was absolutely necessary.
- **Assess end-users capabilities, needs and expectations and create educational material and processes that could keep their enthusiasm and interest unabated so that they stayed involved and productive**. Following the needs analysis that took place during the initial phases of SONETOR, the project focused on CMs with education level of at least EQF5. Thus, all end users were university degree and/or master, even doctorate holders. Nevertheless, the fact that they were coming from different educational backgrounds, different professional environments

and different cultures made planning of educational strategies to be used more demanding and needful of inspirational and incentive-offering educational content and activities during training. In order to keep end-users enthusiasm and commitment high, the NM divided trainees into working groups with common characteristics, i.e. depending on profession, studies and interests on cultural mediation; each group was coordinated by one or two core users. Core users in collaboration with and under the guidance of the NM were assigning tasks to the end users of their groups while at the same time they were supporting and helping them with difficulties regarding the use of the platform.

- **Hold and preside over training sessions, private tutoring sessions and teleconferences in order to meet with trainees' specificities.** SONETOR users were dispersed all over Greece, having different academic background and culture and coming from various professional fields. An effort was made to deal with these specificities by trying to accommodate for the individual timetables and supporting asynchronous communication and collaboration when possible. Thus a combination of training techniques were used, starting from plenary face-to-face training sessions and progressively evolving into small group meetings and employment of tele-conferencing and asynchronous collaboration, using the tools supported by the platform.
- **Evaluate and test the platform and its tools**. NM was online most hours of the day in order to monitor the use of the platform by the end users and to respond to any comments, queries or difficulties should they have while performing activities on the platform. In addition, she intervene whenever necessary to guide, direct or consult end users online on the creation of the content in order to have the content created in conform to SONETOR's content standards. In addition, either informed by the end users or by own experience, the NM had to locate software errors, inconsistencies and misses in order to inform the partner responsible for the designing, administration and technical support of the platform on view of the platform's improvement.
- **Work out conflicts or diversities in the community of cultural mediators,** if any, with in person conversation when necessary or by shifting group members between working groups. Conflict resolution and negotiation are among the most important skills of NM; empathy is a required competence. The Greek NM reacted immediately to all situations, informing the Greek partner for serious cases, such as violation of intellectual rights, non-responsiveness of core user, etc.
- **Bring together people with common interests through the creation of theme groups.** Creation and participation in theme groups in the platform soon became a very popular activity among end users. People with common interests such as legislation on migration, cultural mediation at school, etc. brought people closer making them creative, interactive and willing to share experience. Moreover, the content that resulted from this interaction created a multi-disciplinary, highly interesting repository, forming the sound base for future training cycles.

- **Consult, guide, support and encourage users to the creation and uploading of content to the platform, commenting and re-training them when necessary.** Probably the most important task of the NM, it required a combination of methods and activities. Initially, the core users and end users were contacted via e-mail, but then face to face training sessions were organized, always under the supervision of the NM, who sometimes had to travel to different cities for that purpose. Most users were not familiar with the peer learning method and expressed difficulty in using the platform and sometimes reservations regarding the uploading of personal experiences. The NM had to intervene in all cases, providing solutions and, in collaboration with the project partner, resolving the serious matters, such as management of intellectual property, certification, etc.
- **Help create a sound core of enthusiastic users that would care to keep the platform alive and ensure its sustainability**. This was among the most important tasks of the NM. It requires continuous monitoring of platform usage and the establishment of interpersonal communication with those users. Encouragement and sometimes personal involvement in editing the uploaded episodes and managing the end user groups was among the strategies used by the NM when end users felt insecure about a task.
- **Report to the national partner (who was also the project's coordinator) and submit proposals for improvement of the platform and the educational process.** The NM had to work in close collaboration with the national project partners and the coordinator, ensuring that all problems (as already mentioned above) were resolved. In addition, based on the experience she acquired with the platform, as well as because she was in close communication with the end users, the NM prepared a report including suggestions for improvement of the platform services and exploitation of the project outcomes.

Resources, Methodology and Material

Configuration of moderation system and policy-/decision-making were significant-factor-oriented. These significant factors correspond to the moderation levels in the project and are shown and analyzed as follows:

Human Resources

Our human resources consisted in trainees located mainly in Patras (over 100 participants) and in Athens (over 40 participants) and the rest of them were dispersed all over Greece from Macedonia to Crete and from Zakynthos to Mytilene and Rhodes. As already mentioned, apart from geographical dispersion of participants, multiculturalism, multidiscipline background and variety in profession were the most important characteristics of our trainees groups' synthesis.

Platform Moderation, Educational Methodology and Content

Moderation of the platform aimed to guarantee qualitative educational material being uploaded in the platform in the form of unguided scenarios. Other forms of content (i.e. blogs, forums, events, comments etc.) were used supplementary to the educational material and in order to develop interoperability in the cultural mediators' community meeting in the platform. It was the national moderator's duty to assess whether the content uploaded by the users was acceptable in terms of Relevance – Authenticity – Accuracy – Currency – Sufficiency. Qualitative and quantitative control of the content was facilitated by the platform's tools. On each content section one could see quantitative data useful for the assessment process. In addition, the NMs had specific rights that permitted them to view indicators for all users and their activity in the platform thus helping them make informed decisions on how to continue with the training or the moderating process.

The educational methodology used had mainly to do with self-expression, working in groups, development of a sense of belonging in a community so as the users would develop feelings of trust, support of each other, good-fellowship, contribution, interoperability, collaboration, sharing and open-mindedness. To that end, training sessions were held having a consultative character in the first place, but later on they proved to have got a more functional and productive character and they finally turn to be workshops and seminars on good practices on cultural mediation. Special strategies and educational methodologies had to be summoned in order to meet with the emerging needs of the users during the training procedure. Apart from in person training sessions, there were also core users' briefings, special assignments, workshops, task and role games, PowerPoint presentations, handouts, scenarios and content samples etc. to help end users familiarize with the new education methodology of peer learning smoother and to facilitate follow up of the procedure.

Assessment Systems - Evaluation Tools

Not only has a National Moderator to adopt a well-structured quality management system but he/she also has to use the proper assessment system to evaluate the outcomes of moderation any moment. For this purpose, evaluation forms and questionnaires were drawn up and given to the end users to fill in, follow up reports were sent to core users to fill in, focus group questionnaires were discussed and recorded during training sessions, surveys through the Internet were provided, indicators were used etc. Moreover, the results and outcomes of the elaboration of these assessment instruments were reported to the project's partners for further assessment and consideration.

Challenges and Opportunities

Our experience from SONETOR has shown that the National Moderator is a challenging and demanding role. (S)he has to be responsive, inspiring, decisive, open-minded, diplomatic, leading, supportive and creative, able to cope with challenges and at the same time show insight and wit, able to make out opportunities for development and upgrading to the benefit of the project and to the promotion of its mission.

In our case study the main challenges the NM had to cope with are related to the following issues:

Extensive geographical dispersion. Given the geographical dispersion of platform users, we chose to design a flexible training framework, which could be adjusted to the needs of the trainees and the training procedure; trainings were realized using a blended learning approach. In the beginning, regular face-to-face training sessions were held in Athens and Patras so as to train and familiarize the end users firstly to the use of the platform and secondly to the methodology of content creation. For distant users we chose to hold teleconferences using BBB technology in order to be able to tutor them in the platform's environment. Gradually, training sessions shifted to teleconference and support through the tools offered by the platform, thus maximizing user immersion in it.

Users profile. Worth-considering characteristics of the users' profiles include: multiculturalism, multidiscipline background and a wide profession-variety. These characteristics had to be taken into serious consideration on planning educational methodology and training sessions' agenda. Sometimes they could stand as barriers to a smooth educational process while at a different moment the same could be the means that helped the educational process take off.

Reactions and attitudes. Pluralism and particular idiosyncrasy of the trainees (in being specifically sensitive to some notions and practices) would sometimes result in divergence of views or conflicts in the working group and scarcely even to quarrelling or withdrawal.

Commitment. To have all these people get involved and stay involved, the National Moderator had to be friendly and strict at the same time, traditional yet creative, open-minded yet in moderation, conciliatory and in leadership, fair and detached, helpful but not too intimate; the main challenge being to shift public opinion (of the trainees, too) from suspicion for similar projects to trust. Knowledge of educational psychology proved to be very useful.

Communication. Close collaboration and communication amidst the highest levels of the moderation system was crucial. During the training sessions and at the intervals in between them, the National Moderator and core users were in close collaboration both among them and with the end users. Briefings with the core users ensured up-to-dated and guided management on a common line in order to guide and tutor end users to the best of their interest, to responsibly reply to their queries and to help them create state-of-the-art content to be uploaded onto the platform.

Educational material. The National Moderator prepared handy educational material for the users (both core- and end users) such as explanatory notes, content examples, questionnaires, case studies, situation prompts, tests in order to promote self-expression, and she used specifically designed educational techniques to meet their needs such as brainstorming, sharing of experience and productive and creative thinking and writing.

Last but not least, was the challenge of *keeping interoperability in the interior of the moderation system* that is among involved parts: alive, intra-communicative and well-informed.

Results

We could state that the National Moderator contributed to a great extent to the SONETOR project in (a) raising awareness and public recognition about cultural mediation in Europe, (b) helping bring together people with common interest in cultural mediation, (c) helping develop educational methodology and tools to be used in the training of cultural mediators, (d) uncovering the real needs and problems of Cultural Mediators, and (e) contributing to future discussions on the yet little explored landscape of cultural mediation training in Europe. The main outcomes of moderation process in the context of SONETOR project are presented below.

The peer learning methodology used in SONETOR project - based on the creation, upload and educational use of unguided scenarios - worked well for both core users and end users in all partner countries thanks to the well-organized and collaborative moderation of the National Moderators and the excellent collaboration with the partners of the project. By exchanging experiences on cultural mediation, debating on issues arising from Cultural Mediators'' everyday practice and thinking on the best wording of the unguided scenarios in order to be used as educational material, the trainees got fully involved with the SONETOR project in an enthusiastic and creative way.

Numbers in the platform show the dynamics of this methodological approach (Aspioti, 2014): 174 applications – all approved (106 applicants from Patras - 48 applicants from Athens - 18 applicants from other Greek cities - 2 applicants from Europe), 487 registered users in the platform, 184 applied and trained by the Greek partner, 10 Core Users → 17 Core Users → 12 Core Users each one coordinating 14-16 end-users, 6 training sessions in Athens (4-4.5 hours duration each), 4 training sessions in Patras (duration about 2-2.5 hours each), 1 teleconference for the distant users (2 hours duration), 116 unguided scenarios created & 102 comments on Episodes, 64 Forum topics & 99 comments on Forums, 32 articles & 21 comments on articles, 523 Blog entries & 122 comments on Blogs, 224 Events created & 2 comments on Events, 24 Groups, 1 Meeting, 5 Wikis.

Key Competences of National Moderators

Following our experience as a National Moderator of a community of Cultural Mediators, we summarize the key competences a NM should possess in order to successfully fulfill his/her role:

- Sound educational background; studies in Pedagogy, Culture or Educational Psychology is an asset
- Literacy and language competence – knowledge of a number of foreign languages at a very good level and of the associated culture is necessary
- Communication skills – has to have excellent communication skills and be familiar with a number of communication and conflict resolution strategies
- Negotiation skills- these skills are always necessary when managing people in particular when the groups of people managed are from different backgrounds and have different attitudes under certain circumstances.
- Training skills – has to be able to instruct, consult, guide, inspire, and make people commit themselves to the learning process.
- ICT skills- these skills are absolutely necessary since all training is provided in a digital environment, while all communication are performed mainly via digital applications. On top of this more than basic ICT knowledge is necessary in order to be able not only to teach the use of a digital platform but to administer it, evaluate its operability and assess potential errors of the software and be able to propose whatever improvement and enhancement necessary.

Conclusion

In this chapter we described our experience from moderating the user training and usage of a social networking platform aimed at supporting peer learning of Cultural Mediators.

The main challenges in the role of National Moderator of a community of Cultural Mediators stem mainly from the complexity of human resources (s)he has to manage each time. This determines to a great extent the success or not of his/her moderation role.

A National Moderator may sometimes be faced with unfavorable situations during moderation process. In such cases (s)he has to call into his/her specific skills and competences to smooth tenseness out keeping everyone satisfied and still in commitment.

The National Moderator has to find ways to keep trainees interest and spirit alive inspiring them to get and remain involvement in the project. Specific educational methodologies and tools have to be designed and applied each time in order to meet with assessment unit standards and trainees needs.

In a nutshell, the NM role has been determinant to the sustainability and improvement of SONETOR educational process and platform. Our experience has shown that in many cases core and end users have stayed involved giving their best just because they have been inspired and supported by the National Moderator.

References

Aspioti, M. (2014). The role of National Moderator in the SONETOR project. Paper presented at the *ESI-CM 2014 International Conference*, on Jan. 8-9, 2014, in Agora Argyri, Patras, Greece.

Competenz (2011). *Moderator Guide* (1st Ed.) Retrieved from http://www.competenz.org.nz/assets/Downloads/Moderator-Guide.pdf

New Zealand Qualifications Authority and Skill New Zealand, (2001). *Best Practice Moderation. Best Practice in the Assessment of Unit Standards*. New Zealand.

Χαμπούρη-Ιωαννίδου, Αικ., (2003). Στρατηγική διαχείρισης των πολιτιστικών ιδρυμάτων. Στο Μ. Βινιεράτου (και συν.) *Συλλογικός Τόμος Πολιτιστικής Πολιτική και Διοίκηση: Πολιτιστική Διαχείριση*. Πάτρα: Ελληνικό Ανοικτό Πανεπιστήμιο.

Chapter 10: The SONETOR Platform: Functionalities and Services

Jeries Besarat, Catherine Christodoulopoulou, Andreas Koskeris and John Garofalakis

Overall Description

SONETOR Platform Specifications

SONETOR is a social networking platform through which users from different countries will be able to create accounts and communicate with each other. The platform offers different roles and actions per user role. That means that the platform supports three basic roles:

- The authenticated users (or core users),
- The partners' moderators
- The administrators

The authenticated users are the main users of the platform. They can interact with the social tools and perform specific actions that will not negatively affect the main functionalities of the platform. The moderators are users that can perform more actions than the main users such as edit specific content and modify it so as to meet the correct needs. Finally, the administrators have all the permissions to administer and manage the platform and its functionalities. They can manage the user generated content.

SONETOR Platform Architecture

SONETOR is a stand-alone platform that can be installed on a server. It consists of four main components: Drupal, Moodle, Lams and databases. The main architecture of the platform is shown in Figure 10.1. We have developed two different platforms. The first (Drupal) is the main platform called SONETOR while the second (Moodle) is the e-learning platform. The two platforms communicate in such a way that the users can navigate easily from one platform to another. Our aim is to create a social networking platform that will help users to learn how to use the social tools and also learn how to deal with daily and real life issues. For this purpose, we developed the e-learning platform which aims to help users learn from others.

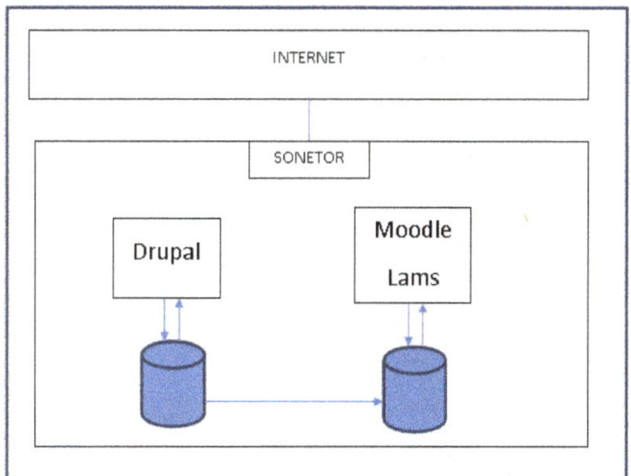

Figure 10.1: Main Architecture of the Platform

SONETOR is developed using Drupal and PHP. Drupal is an open source content management system. The main goal was to create a social networking platform that will enable users to interact with various social tools and learn in a collaborative environment. The platform intergrades with an e-learning management system (Figure 10.2) and uses services in order to communicate. We have developed a web service that is responsible for synchronizing the databases between the two platforms in order to achieve a single sign on. In particular, the service, every 5 minutes, queries the main database of the platform and inserts into the second database only the active users, ignoring the inactive ones. Thus, we use 5 minutes interval in order not to delay a user from signing in, in both platforms from the moment he registered to the main platform.

Our work focuses in creating a social networking platform. Social network applications and services enable users to share and live their social life using just their computers. For the purpose of the project we have to provide all the necessary networking tools such as blogs, forums, wiki pages, messages etc. The platform lets users to engage with each other in a social environment and create friends relationships and share real-time statuses. Furthermore, it enables users to create group-centered online communities, useful for sharing ideas, views and interests. The platform offers real time communication via the chat functionality, where user can talk to each other quickly.

Platform Interface

SONETOR platform offers a simple and easy to use interface. The users can interact with various tools and communicate with each other in several ways. In particular, the user has to join the platform in order to have access in all the functionalities that it offers. Authenticated users can use the social tools of the platform such as create blogs, wikis, communities and forum topics. Furthermore, they can create events and invite people to join the platform. The functions of the system will allow users to register and sign in to the platform, exchange messages public or private with other users, create and share new content, distribute their material in the platform and to other social networks and attend classes. In order to do these actions the user should use any of the known Internet browser software. The Figure 10.2 shows a simple diagram with all the actions a user can do and functionalities the platform offers.

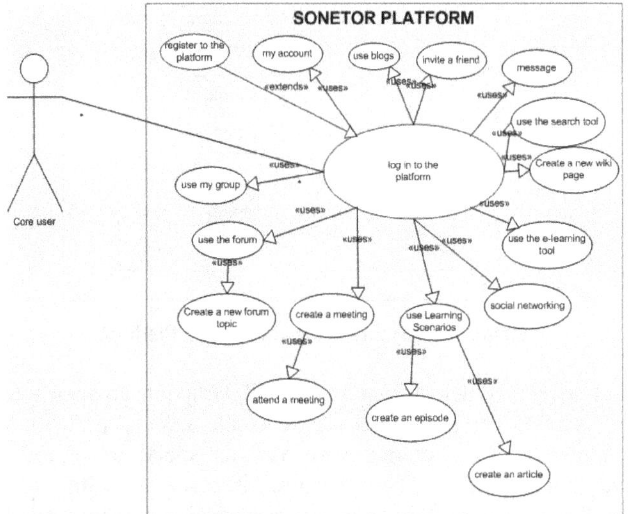

Figure 10.2: SONETOR Platform diagram

The platform is divided in two main sections. Firstly, the main menu where all users can use in order to navigate to the main functionalities and the secondary menu where users can use to navigate to secondary functionalities and personalized pages such as the users profile page. Specifically, the main menu is organized as follows:

Home: The front page of the platform. The platform has dynamic content which is generated automatically when new content is created. The content in the front page is updated according to the actions of the users. In particular, users can seek for new content, view events and their e-learning courses, if any.

E-Learning: User will be redirected to the front page of e-learning platform and they will be logged in automatically. The e-learning platform enables users to take courses and interact with quizzes and questions and learn from real life experiences.

Wiki pages: The wiki section of the platform enable users to read existing wiki pages written by other users and create new pages. In particular, users can generate content in a collaborative way for a specific topic.

Blogs: The Blogs menu item shows the blog entries that users write. The blog section is useful because allows users to seek topics that they are interested and view other people opinions on a topic and comment.

Social Network: Users can share real time statuses, so their friends can see what they are up to. By navigating to the social network section users can interact with their friends or make new ones. Furthermore, users can view the activity of their relations, comment and make social actions such as sharing or like.

Forums: The users can create discussions in topics. Users can ask questions and get information depending on the matter they have.

Unguided Scenarios: The unguided scenarios (Figure 10.3) offer specific scenario topics where users can have access. This section provides a list with the predefined scenarios and the time that they were last updated, so users can easily know which one has updated content. In particular, the main topics are housing, educational, legal and health fields. Each scenario holds episodes related to the title of each one and users can read in their native language if it's translated or translate it using the translation tool offered by the platform. Furthermore, they can create new episodes and share their point of view on real life issues. This section is one of the most important tools as it offers the opportunity to learn in a "free" and collaborative environment.

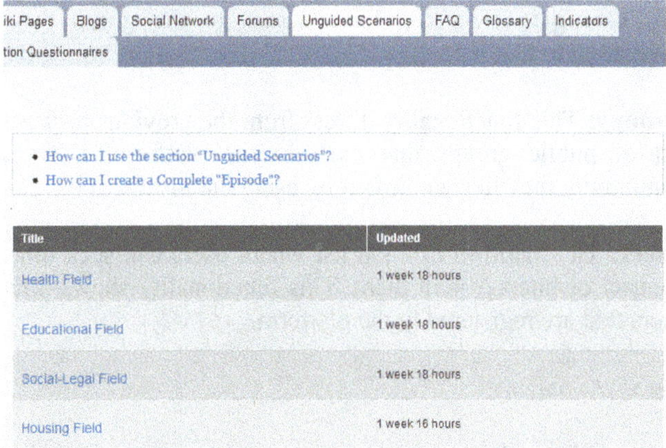

Figure 10.3: Unguided Scenarios Page

The secondary menu consists of links that give access on secondary functionalities of the platform. The secondary menu is visible all the time so the users can have direct access when they want.

This menu is organized as follows:

> **Profile:** The profile page for each user. Users can edit their account and change settings by visiting this page. Furthermore, they can have access to their messages and edit their security settings concerning their social actions (who can view their updates etc.).
>
> **Create group:** This action enables users to create communities and invite other users to join. Group helps users to create workshops and focus on specific topics that the manager of the group wants.
>
> **Create teleconference:** This functionality enables users to create real time teleconference meetings while they are remote from each other. The users can use their cameras and microphones in order to communicate, create presentations etc.
>
> **Create event:** We developed a tool that helps users create events and allows other users to get reminders for an event that they are interested and they don't want to miss. The event can hold dates, that indicate when it will occur and can notify users hours or days before the date specified. Users can view all the upcoming events right in the front page of the platform and they can find all the events in a calendar view which is filtered in monthly, daily, weekly and yearly intervals.
>
> **Invite a friend:** SONETOR platform is a network platform that enables users to invite others in order to grow. By this way, users can invite their friends, right through the platform easily.
>
> **My Groups:** Users can have access to the group they create by navigating to that list.
>
> **Groups:** This functionality differs from the previous because it shows a list of public groups that exist in the platform. Users can find a community they like and join it by using that list.
>
> **Users:** The platform offers a list where users can seek other users and connect or interact with them. This functionality shows a list of all the users that are registered in the platform.

Users Generated Content

The platform enables and encourages users to create content that others can view and comment. Web 2.0 technologies such as blogs, wikis etc. have been dubbed 'social software' because they are perceived as being especially connected, allowing users to develop Web content collaboratively and open to the public (Alexander, 2006).

The purpose of the project is to help users deal with daily concerns and real life events. Thus, users can upload their own experiences and get advisable feedback from users who know how to deal under a similar situation or even write their point of view as an answer. Users' generated data can prove very useful because finding patterns in it can help answer questions about the way the world works. The platform supports all the major types of content that users can create and described later here. The Figure 10.4 show the data types that users can generate in the platform.

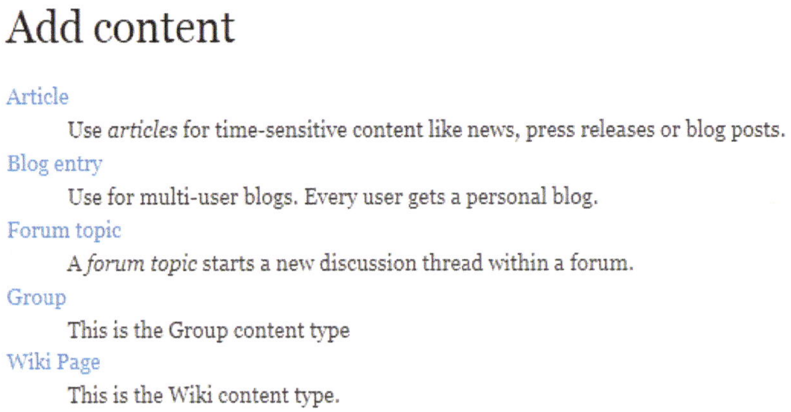

Add content

Article

Use *articles* for time-sensitive content like news, press releases or blog posts.

Blog entry

Use for multi-user blogs. Every user gets a personal blog.

Forum topic

A *forum topic* starts a new discussion thread within a forum.

Group

This is the Group content type

Wiki Page

This is the Wiki content type.

Figure 10.4: *Data Types*

Main Functionalities

Forum

Discussions are very important when people wants to deal with a situation or give solution to a problem. Forum is a digital discussion room where users can talk about specific topics each one organized separately from the other. It has been found that forums have a greater ability to generate empathy among the users. Participants in online discussions are in a sense "performing" for other forum members, and contributions to the forum are often assessed in terms of the participant's ability to educate other members of the community (Baym, 1997).

As Deighton, Romer, and McQueen (1989) have pointed out, forum topics have an ability to draw in and cause the reader to empathize with the feelings of the writer, in effect, creating vicarious experience. The platform supports a multilingual forum which means that users don't have to speak the same language in order to discuss with each other. The user in any forum may create new discussions and either learn from others or provide knowledge. The Figure 10.5 shows the forums that the platform has while Figure 10.6 shows the forum statistics.

Forums

FORUM	TOPICS	POSTS	LAST POST
National Moderators A place for national mediators to exchange knowledge & experiences about the guided & unguided scenarios and about the exploitation of the produced results of the SONETOR project.	4 2 new	5	language... by chri_kin 01/22/2014 - 12:51
Video μεταναστών	0	0	n/a
Εκπαίδευση μεταναστών	0	0	n/a
Μάρθα - Νοσηλεύτρια - Εκπαιδευτικός	0	0	n/a
ρατσισμός	0	0	n/a
Σχολείο μεταναστών	0	0	n/a
General discussion	98 29 new	178	Η μικρού μήκους... by aspant 1 day 6 hours ago

Figure 10.5: Create new Forum Topic

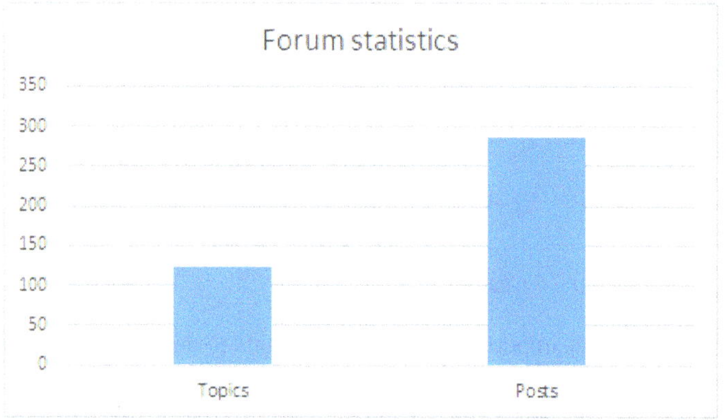

Figure 10.6: Forum Statistics

Wiki

Wiki is one major component of Web 2.0 that can be used to enhance the learning process. A wiki is a web communication and collaboration tool that can be used to engage users in learning with others within a collaborative environment. Collaborative learning becomes even more powerful when it takes place in the context of a community of practice. A community of practice consists of people engaged in collective learning in a shared domain. Thus, learning becomes a collaborative process of a group. Wikis can serve as a knowledge platform for a community of practice where members of the community can share their knowledge with the group, put up interesting pieces of information, work together, discuss issues, etc.

Blog entry

Blogs combine the immediacy of up-to-the-minute posts, latest first, with a strong sense of the author's personality, passions, and point of view. Any user may create blog entries, view other users' entries and make comments to other posts.

The platform supports a notification system where users can be alerted about new posts. Users can upload multimedia content (such as video, image) in their posts.

Group

Users can create communities or request membership to others people groups. They can have a list of groups that they are member of and create articles in those groups. That means, that people with the same interest can meet each other in a group and share opinions or discuss on topics they are interested. Group is an important social tool as it helps users to create social circles and meet new people. The group functionality enables users to create articles and the rest of the members can read and comment. Finally, they can share their point of view by writing a new article. Thus, the community can grow bigger and users can find useful information and advice which can adopt to solve daily issues. Groups are divided to public- where anyone can view and joint- and to private- where only members can view, create and comment on the content.

Episode

As we already stated, users should learn in a collaborative environment and with the help from other users that share their knowledge on specific matters. The episode is the main social tool to achieve this aim. In particular, users are creating episodes using real life examples and inviting other users to share their opinion and comment on how they would deal with such a situation. Furthermore, users can rate each episode and also each comment that is left in order to easily know if that episode is really good and which comment is the best advice or answer that users should eventually follow in such a situation. The episode tool is the main peer to peer learning functionality. Currently, the platform has 231 episodes and more than 240 comments. This is an indicator showing that this offered application is quite popular among users.

Meetings

Users can create teleconference meetings and invite people to join and attend. This tool is useful because it helps users to learn even when they are remote from each other. A user who creates a meeting can moderate it. In particular a moderator of the teleconference can do the following actions:

1. Control how the teleconference will proceed
2. Choose whom of the users that are interested, can attend.
3. End the teleconference
4. Permit to a user that raises hand to speak

The teleconference tool supports chat, presentations and audio. It is helpful because enables users to create classes and make presentations easily without having users to be at the same place.

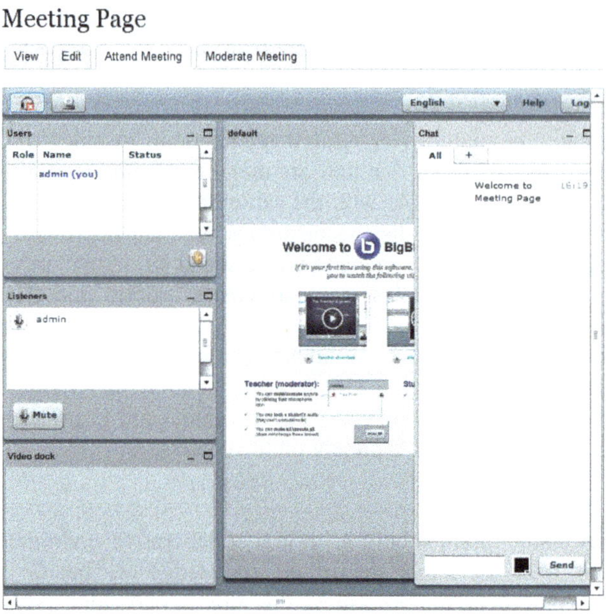

Figure 10.7: SONETOR Platform Meeting Page

Secondary Functionalities

Instant Messages

In instant messaging users can exchange messages in real time and have a conversation. The user enters the application (Figure 10.8) and appears online in order to notify other users that he can accept messages. Users can change their status to busy, away, offline etc.

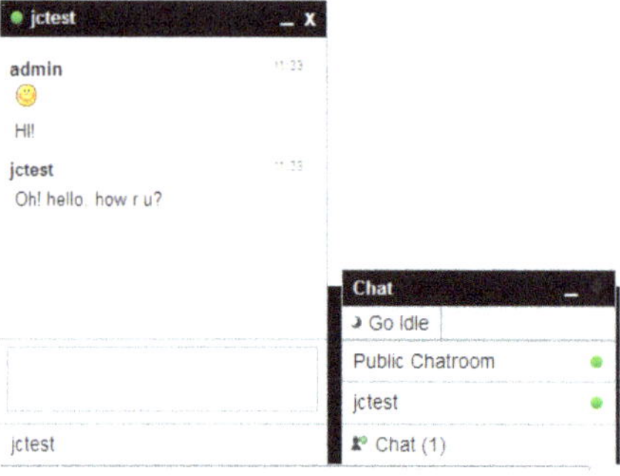

Figure 10.8: Instant Messaging

Folksonomy Tools

The user can contribute in collaborative/social tagging by creating tag cloud. The tag cloud is a visual depiction of user-generated tags, or simply the word content of a site, used typically to describe the content of web sites. Tags are usually single words and are typically listed alphabetically, and the importance of a tag is shown with font size or with a counter next to the word.

The tag cloud application can interact with wiki, blog, articles, e-learning and forum applications. Tag cloud is helpful because categorizes the content in a words and users can easily find the most popular content. The Figure 10.9 shows a tag cloud, as we can see "scenario 4" is a tag that has been used more than once. Thus the font is bigger in order to stand out from the rest.

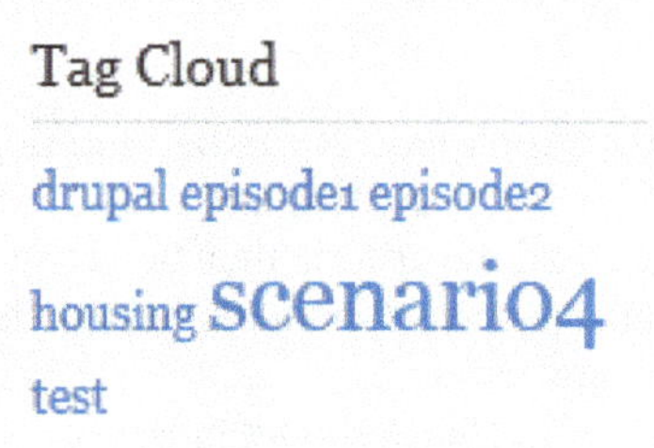

Figure 10.9: *Tag Cloud*

Video Sharing

The video sharing application enables users to upload videos in any of the known video formats and share them with others. Videos can be viewed on line through a graphical interface, while, users can make comments. Users can upload a video as a file from their personal computers or from online web sources such as YouTube. Videos can part of the posts providing better description of a situation.

Messages

This functionality enables users to send private messages to each other. It is useful for community oriented platforms such as SONETOR. Messages link appear under user menu. By navigating to messages section users can view their inbox and send new messages to one or more users simultaneously by separating usernames with commas. Messages is an internal messaging system that can notify the users by email when new messages arriving in their inbox.

Messages

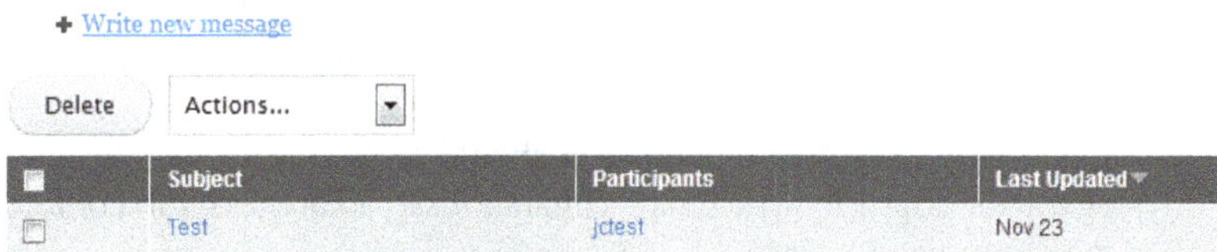

Figure 10.10: *Messages*

Search

The search engine application provides an interface where the user can search for specific information. The user enters a number of keywords and the application returns as a result a list of links to the related content in the platform. Users also have the ability to use the advanced search feature of the platform. In particular, the advance search exposes filters that users can use in order to specify their search and receive more accurate results. The search functionality can be used to seek users or their content and connect.

Indicators

Indicators are the main evaluation tool. It can be used only by the moderators of the platform in order to find users' content and evaluate their contribution in the platform. If a user completes all the criteria then he gets a certification that he has accomplished and used all the main functionalities of the platform and now he can provide knowledge to new users.

In particular, the criteria that users should have are:

1. It is highly suggested that the user has to attach his/her photo to his/her profile field
2. The user has to introduce himself at the relevant Forum "Let's get to know each other" at the link "Let's get to know you..." --> About You..."
3. The user has to create at least four (4) well-structured and complete episodes according to the FAQ instructions
4. The user has to grade at least two (2) topics of the General Forum's topics and make comments either on those two or on other topics
5. The user has to create a Topic in the "General Discussions" Forum
6. The user has to add at least 3 comments in three different scenarios of different authors. (NOTE: A good practice is for the user to read, comment and grade at the same time, something that does not prevent the user from scoring/grading other scenarios)
7. The user has to become a member of at least one group (NOT just a member of his/her own group)
8. It is highly suggested that the user should create a group. (NOTE: In order to do so, the user has to contact the National Mediator of his/her country who will decide whether to approve his/her request and confirm the group's purpose, correctness and functionality). For those who have already created a group, the National Moderator will decide whether to delete it or not.
9. It is highly suggested that the user should create EVENTS relevant to the agenda's concept which will enhance user awareness for conferences, meetings, actions, etc.

References

Bickart, B. and Schindler R.M. (2001). Internet forums as influential sources of consumer information. *Journal of Interactive Marketing*. *15*(3), 31-40.

Bonnie, A. N., Schiano, J. D., Gumbrecht, M. and Swartz, L. (2004). Why we blog, *Communications of the ACM*, *47*, 41-46.

Parker, K. and Chao, J. (2007). Wiki as a Teaching Tool. *Interdisciplinary Journal of E-Learning and Learning Objects*, *3*, 57-72.

Chapter 11: How can New Computing Technologies Support Cultural Mediation?

Achilles Kameas, Mara Aspioti and Georgia Antonelou

Introduction

Cultural mediation is mainly a communication activity, thus any communication means can be of assistance; therefore ICT technologies that rule modern Information Society offering a vast range of digital applications, tools and digital devices can prove to be very important and helpful in cultural mediation. A recent survey that we conducted over a large number of Cultural Mediators (working in Greece) on whether they use ICT in their everyday routine has come up with a high percentage of positive responses indicating that they do. The same sample of respondents has indicated that they use digital applications and social media largely to complete tasks and duties related to cultural mediation. Questions arise though: do these applications meet suitability and appropriateness requirements for being used for cultural mediation? Do they offer Cultural Mediators real support on the field? What characteristics should such ICT applications have? Are there any digital applications especially designed for Cultural Mediators? What way can social media contribute to cultural mediation and community activities? Is the public aware of the benefits from using such technologies?

In view of ICT technologies having rapidly developed and infiltrated almost all kinds of human activity during the recent decades on the one hand and the increasingly significant role cultural mediation plays in Europe of multi-cultural societies on the other hand, this chapter aims to discuss the ways that new Information Society technologies can support cultural mediation. It looks at technologies that can be used in cultural mediation and in particular at digital applications and social media as well as education platforms promoting the scope of cultural mediation. In addition, this chapter presents the main characteristics of the most popular social media tools (chat, forums, blogs, content editing and teleconferences) in order to show how these can be used to promote the values and scope of cultural mediation. On top of that, reference to SONETOR project platform is made, a multilateral European-funded project platform unique in its kind in terms of combining e-learning and peer-learning methodologies with social media tools, all carefully designed to:

- support Cultural Mediators' training needs, promote good practices, exchange of experience, knowledge, skills and competences development and enhancement in a community of Cultural Mediators all over Europe through peer learning and
- help disseminate the importance of Cultural Mediator's role in the contemporary European society that faces the serious implications from the unbalanced integration of migrants in the European countries.

The chapter concludes with discussion on the future of ICT Technologies in cultural mediation.

Emerging ICT

Nowadays the vast amount of available information in conjunction with the fast pace of everyday life and its requirements for communication, cooperation and access to information, make the use of new technologies imperative. The increased demand for instant access to information and communication devices and services contributes to the rapid evolution of the Information and Communication Technology (ICT) field which constitutes one of the main technological achievements in recent years.

At the same time, the evolution and the diffusion of ICT in the Educational System (concerning teaching, learning, training) is also quite remarkable, especially in the last two decades. ICT has penetrated into the formal educational and training settings and has led to the development of new training practices and modern theories of learning (Sharples et al., 2013), e.g. peer-learning, social constructivism, crowd-learning, massive-learning, seamless learning etc. It has been shown that ICT can enhance the effectiveness of education and training by providing users with specific tasks which increase their engagement and motivation, facilitates the acquisitions of basic (formal and non-formal) skills and eventually improve the exchange of information at different levels. According to Jung (2005) ICT can facilitate not only delivery of instruction, but also the learning process itself far from any institutional level. In fact, ICT can promote international collaboration and social networking and also provide a flexible and effective life-long professional development for learners who participate in any formal educational structure.

Nevertheless, increased use of ICT raises issues of effectiveness and efficiency and, furthermore, the need for assessment and evaluation. In addition, it seems to be essential to base ICT applications on appropriate pedagogical frameworks and models guarantying the effective and efficient use of those applications, being at the same time consistent to set codes of conduct, best practices and privacy policies. ICT competences comprise a subset of digital literacy skills necessary for developing a good understanding of ICT tools which in turn will lead to better appreciation of these tools and redefinition of their role in connecting individuals and communities (Leye, 2007; Umrani & Ghadially, 2003). Competences regarding ICT literacy include: a) access, management, integration, creation, communication, information transmission, b) navigation through digital environment, c) searching, locating, retrieving and sieving sets of data, d) classifying, organizing, synthesizing, storing and creatively producing new information according to specified formats and, e) the ability to select how to use specific tools.

Nowadays ICT technologies and the Internet are two notions rarely considered apart; both are evolving by the presence of each other. This bond between them has brought into existence the era of social networking and its applications that have managed to invade people's everyday lives worldwide and change them to a great degree. In fact, all three (ICT, Internet, social networking) have opened new horizons in communication, education, interaction and innovation in the 21st century.

Online Social Networks (OSNs)

According to the original definition in Boyd et al. (2007), an online social network (OSN) is defined as an online platform that (a) provides services for a user to build a public profile and to explicitly declare the connection between his or her profile with those of the other users, (b) enables a user to share information and content with the public or selected users and, (c) supports the development and usage of social applications with which the user can interact and collaborate with either friends or strangers. Social Networking and a wide range of Web 2.0 tools that support social networking are abundant and available for use. Here below we present the most popular social networking services used by millions of people all over the world every day.

Blogging. The main purpose of a blog is the publication of articles or texts that express an attitude or opinion without requiring an extensive commentary on this subject; the learner can submit a brief comment, but not necessarily a documented answer. Also, in a blog the learner can post announcement(s) and/or event(s) as a notification of an interesting content that may be a useful source for other peer-users in the training environment (e.g. in a platform).

Forums. The need of a tool that enhances co-operation, discussion and communication among participants led to the development of the Forum Tool. The user can browse topics whenever he/she wishes without time constraints and commitments. Moreover, the user has the ability to actively participate in a forum any time he/she feels like entering or following a discussion and/or creating his/her own Topic. It is noteworthy that the user can prepare an answer he/she would like to submit in a discussion without having any time constraints

Chatting. It is another means of synchronous communication which helps users to stay tuned. By chatting, the users can discuss by exchanging short and spontaneous messages. This way, the users have the sense of belonging in an active community and feel comfortable to share thoughts and concerns. In many cases, they feel more comfortable to discuss and seek for solutions to issues that might concern them. Either a private or a public e-conversation is more direct from a forum conversation. The fact that the users can receive an answer in real-time makes that tool more useful and effective.

Content editing. Users are able to write their own full context related to a topic, to offer answers to Q&A-like activities, to comment on a blog or forum-like environment, to post a question etc.; in addition, users are supported in collaboratively creating a corpus of knowledge about a specific topic. Generally, the user is in the position to create own artefacts and products of knowledge, which can then be published to a relevant community and receive feedback from peers (e.g. peer-users of a lesson).

Teleconferencing. It is essentially a means for synchronous communication and collaboration. According to Reddi (2004) "Teleconferencing makes it possible to connect the resource persons at one end and the participants gathered at dispersed centers, and to engage them in dialogue, discussions and doing activities with effective learning outcomes." This technology has great potential for distance education and training, especially when participant groups in various settings are involved, because they can be engaged in discussions and, thus, gain more complete view of an issue or problem. The fact that users are present in different locations but can see and hear each other makes communication more effective and meaningful. Also, the use of teleconferencing reduces the sense of isolation and encourages sharing of concerns and ideas. Teleconferencing services include: online oral discussion, presentation using slides or other resources, online sharing of resources (documents, applications, desktop, etc), Q&A sessions, chatting, collaborative document editing, group formation and work, online surveys and expression of opinion, etc.

ICT Technologies and Education

Social media have gained increasingly diffused use and popularity during the last decades worldwide due to the user-friendliness, flexibility, accessibility, interoperability and variability of the tools and applications they use. This can be considered one of the main factors causing social networking tools to have been introduced into the educational process too, resulting in positive impact, as shown in many research papers (Roblyer et al., 2010; Brady et al., 2010; Bergman, 2009; Minocha, 2009.) This phenomenon can be attributed to the new era of Information Society, where populations usually averaging from the age of 5 to 60 years old, are nurturing and growing their knowledge, skills and competences in the newly-developed digital culture. This has resulted in societies of two types of digital citizens, according to Prensky (2001): *Digital Natives* and *Digital Immigrants.*

The new generation of *digital natives* includes the people who learn to communicate, understand and use the "language" of digital technology as a mother tongue being familiar with digital devices and applications (such as TV, mobile phone, PC, i-phone, tablet etc.) since they are born in a "digital" environment. In contrast, people who have been born in previous decades, have not got used to that kind of technology and most of the times find it very difficult to adjust in it; sometimes they even refuse to yield in that kind of evolution although they are obliged to do so in order to meet with requirements and challenges at work or everyday routine. Those people are known as the *digital immigrants*. Nevertheless, when they get to understand the benefits from using this technology, in most cases they cannot but acknowledge too the unique characteristics and easiness it offers. Especially in the realms of communication, information, entertainment, services provided, self-expression and education utilizing technologies, such as the Internet, the options are unlimited.

As far as education is concerned (that is to say learning and training), newly developed web-based technologies offer unique opportunities to evaluate and enhance the factors affecting users' learning capacity which is an important element of successful learning. Web 2.0 technologies have increased accessibility and use of social networks at multiple levels among community members (Lockyer and Patterson, 2008). Recent research and many case studies on the use of Online Social Networking technologies in formal and informal education and training environments have reported remarkable positive learning outcomes. The main purpose of those case studies is to explore the potential of Web 2.0 social networking technologies to enhance formal and informal learning contexts. Another objective of these case studies is to highlight ways and practices on how to effectively use the technologies and applications of social networks in learning and training educational settings.

Social Networking applications help users remain connected and continuously informed about the actions and current status of their peers. It is noteworthy that these applications have the ability to provide situated learning, a feature which has contributed to their wide-spread acceptance and use by all trainers. Situated learning is not just a simple transmission of abstract and decontextualized knowledge from one individual to another, but a social process whereby knowledge is co-constructed by all participants (Lave and Wenger, 1991). Thus learning is situated in a specific context and embedded within a particular social and physical environment. In order to provide situated learning, a typical training (and/or learning) process contains a plethora of applications that are embedded – usually in the form of a training platform- in the learning procedure. In particular, it provides users with the ability to blog, chat, create focus groups, edit content, participate in teleconferencing, work collaboratively etc.

As shown above, an OSN may have communicative, entertaining, educational or informative character. There is a long list of OSNs on the Internet to choose from; however this chapter will only address to those OSNs related to cultural mediation and community activities promoting cultural mediation and education on cultural mediation.

Use of Social Computing in Cultural Mediation

Communication and Networking Needs in Cultural Mediation

Cultural mediation is a reaction-dependent process, thus conditions and situations may affect the strategies adopted during cultural mediating. Moreover, cultural mediation is closely related to developments in political, social and legal fields thus it is important that the Cultural Mediator is being informed on what is new on a constant basis. Last but not least, cultural mediation is a process of interaction meaning that the parts involved and in particular the part playing the bridging role (i.e. the Cultural Mediator) has to possess certain skills and competences such as negotiation skills, crisis management skills, empathy and more that have to be taught and well-exercised beforehand in order to become a

Cultural Mediator's asset. All the above cannot be developed and managed but with the aid of certain environments and educational methodologies, utilizing the facilities offered by ICT and more specifically, the Internet and social media, followed by applications offered by modern digital devices such as PCs, laptops, mobile phones, tablets etc.

Before moving on we summarize the main needs of Cultural Mediators on the field and in general:

- to have immediate access to acknowledged, accurate and updated information on laws, policies and news on immigration and on cultural mediation,
- to be able to communicate either with the parties involved to the conflict to be resolved (individuals and public services) or with other Cultural Mediators and/or organizations (NGOs, professional associations etc.) and generally with everyone that could be useful to the resolution of the conflict,
- to enhance existing knowledge, skills and competences or to obtain new ones through training,
- to use tools and applications that would facilitate their work,
- to search and find supporting structures for themselves and for the immigrants for whom they act as mediators,
- to learn about the best practices and codes of conduct on cultural mediation,
- to promote their role and in general to raise public awareness,
- to connect their profile to the labor market,
- to download literature, statistics and software useful to their work,
- to get informed about conferences, events, actions and training programs related to cultural mediation.
- to keep records on the cases they mediate for, to create, save, publish, browse and share reports and other content, or to download and print forms and other documents useful in their work.

ICT Projects and Applications that can be Used by Cultural Mediators

To be useful, ICT applications have to offer Cultural Mediators real and effective support on the field. Above all they should promote cultural mediation, be easily accessible, user-friendly, offer safety and apply privacy policy rules, operate in a stable and supported digital environment, be carefully and specifically designed to meet the challenges and tasks a Cultural Mediator faces when in contact with immigrants, be updated and informed and conform to a pedagogical framework.

According to responses to a survey we conducted over a sample of 76 Cultural Mediators, 34 of them (53,1%) responded that they are aware of digital applications and tools for cultural mediators and 30 (46,9%) that they know there aren't any or that they don't know if there are any. This shows a lack of information and a certain confusion regarding available computing technologies on cultural mediation. Moreover, there exists no literature on assessment of the suitability and appropriateness of existing digital applications and tools especially designed for cultural mediation.

To complete the picture, we searched for projects and online tools that aim at facilitating the Cultural Mediators' practice and training. Our research was based on the following criteria: (a) communication, (b) training, (c) exchanging of knowledge, experience and information, (d) enhancement of skills and competences, (e) promotion of cultural mediation and (f) connection to the labor market. In the following we present some very interesting findings in Greece.

Our research resulted in a certain number of projects on Cultural Mediators' training offered in European countries and in Greece in particular, which were implemented by municipal authorities and Vocational Training Centers in the context of European-funded projects. However, most of these projects do not meet the criteria we set above. The only projects found to be purely related to Cultural Mediators' training and socializing needs thus fulfilling all our criteria were two European-funded projects: TIPS and SONETOR, which aimed at the creation of social computing applications and tools especially designed to be used in the training and everyday practice of Cultural Mediators. These projects resulted in the development and application of ICT technologies and applications carefully designed for the needs of Cultural Mediators based on a need analysis that was carried out in various European countries.

In particular, project TIPS "Practicing and Enhancing Cultural Mediation in a Pluralistic Europe" was a Leonardo da Vinci project (Multilateral project) that produced a distance learning course that took place from February to August 2009 in five European countries: Italy, Austria, France, Greece, Poland. It combined ICT and t-learning methodology balancing the use of Internet, Television and Mobile devices. It was an innovative pilot project aimed to allow continuous training and in depth case studies for the training of Cultural Mediators. Training was delivered in a three-fold-module: (a) an e-learning platform accessed on the Internet in which carefully designed comprehensive training content and appropriate Learning objects were developed, (b) an m-learning platform using various digital applications for Mobiles and, (c) the ipTV-learning platform with specially designed audiovisual content for educational purposes.

The SONETOR project could practically be considered as the successor of TIPS. Designed on the experience gained from TIPS and taking into consideration the needs of Cultural Mediators in Europe recorded in a recent survey in five European countries (Greece, Austria, Spain, Ireland and Poland) it produced a user-oriented platform addressed to Cultural Mediators and anyone else interested in getting involved with cultural mediation. Its scope is to become the focal point of communication for a European CM community and contribute in many ways to the lifelong education, training and enhancement of CM skills and competences. Since its official opening to the public it has attracted members from Greece, Austria, Germany, Spain, France, Great Britain, Ireland, Italy and Poland. Its members have various backgrounds (mostly Education, Social Sciences, Law School and Linguistics). The SONETOR platform (http://www.culturalmediators.eu/) allows its users to communicate, exchange experiences, knowledge and information on cultural mediation, create content used for educational purposes according to peer learning methodology, and gives the opportunity to benefit by the facilities offered by social networking tools (such as Chat, Blogs, Forums, Socializing, Teleconference, Content Editing,

Comments, Content Evaluation and more), get trained and enhance skills and competences they already possess; it also offers its members the option to attend e-learning courses on cultural mediation. Its operation includes three main functions: (a) focal point for the communication of CM community, (b) digital platform for the lifelong training of Cultural Mediators, and (c) trustworthy repository of updated information and high-quality content; all in a safe and controlled environment carefully designed to meet the needs of Cultural Mediators in Europe.

We also found out that common social networks such as Facebook or LinkedIn can also be used and are used as means of promoting cultural mediation, communication among Cultural Mediators, creation of a CM community, exchange of experience and information by some people; potentials that can be added in their merits. In other words, they respond mostly to our criteria (a) and (c). Examples of it are found in Facebook pages: Εκπαιδευμένοι Διαπολιτισμικοί Μεσολαβητές (Trained Cultural Mediators - [1] the SONETOR project page[2] MEDIATION CULTURELLES[3] Cultural Mediation[4], Cultural Mediation in Greek Hospitals[5] , MEVIT4618 - Mediatization of culture and society[6] ,projet "UNESCO", Ministère de la Culture de Tunisie: MÉDIATION CULTURELLE[7] , or a great number of Facebook pages from NGOs or groups unofficially cultural-mediation-oriented, e.g. PRAKSIS[8] , or Ecosistema Urbano[9].

However, given the sensitive-case character of cultural mediation as it handles sensitive personal data, we would like here to stress some of these media's strongest demerits such as the lack of membership control, the generality and sometimes the complete irrelevance of their content, and the possibility of the user receiving improper comments or even bullying by some people disagreeing with the main principles of cultural mediation. NING[10] is another social network that claims to be the focal point of communication and the leading online platform for the world's organizers, activists and influencers to create social experience that inspire action; from that point of view it could be very useful for the promotion of cultural mediation role, yet it is not exclusively dedicated to cultural mediation.

Regarding the connection of Cultural Mediators with labor market, most NGOs in Greece and in other European countries have created sites where a CM can find out about vacancies every now and then such as PRAKSIS in Greece[11], Emergency in Italy[12], Association Médiation Culturelle (MCA) in France, and more.

---

[1] https://www.facebook.com/groups/ 309026989228482/,
[2] https://www.facebook.com/CulturalMediationSonetor?fref=ts
[3] https://www.facebook.com/pages/M%C3%A9diation-Culturelle/412710618809950
[4] https://www.facebook .com/groups/107789704868/members/
[5] https://www.facebook.com/CulturalMediation,
[6] https://www.facebook.com/groups/664639000241696/
[7] https://www.facebook.com/groups/projetpilote/
[8] https://www.facebook.com/ngopraksis
[9] https://www.facebook.com/ecosistemaurbano?ref=profile
[10] http://www.ning.com/%20cultivating-community/
[11] http://www.praksis.gr/6_1/Career
[12] http://www.emergency.it/work-with-us/cultural-mediator.html,

We have also come across Volunteer4greece.gr [13] an online platform in Greece permitting NGOs and other voluntarism organizations to post vacancies for volunteers on the one hand and on the other hand, volunteers to search vacancies per region and organization category. In addition, there is the Registry of Trained Cultural Mediators[14] where Cultural Mediators can upload their CV and fields where they would care to offer their cultural mediation services; then organizations and public servants can search to find those candidates that best meet their needs.

It is noteworthy that some of the tools developed for TIPS have not been exploited as much as they should to the benefit of CM work, such as phrasebook, IPTV, e-books on cultural mediation and more, while some others have been further used, developed more and enhanced in later projects such as SONETOR, yet there are still some that need to be elaborated and tested to reach a state-of-the-art quality so as to be widely used by the CM community.

Using the SONETOR Platform to Support Cultural Mediators

The SONETOR platform is specifically designed to correspond to CM needs for training and information combining the theoretic approaches of peer learning (unguided learning) and guided learning utilizing latest ICT developments. It uses some of the most popular and widely used social networking tools such as Blogs, Forums, Chat, Wikis and a number of other digital applications and functions like teleconferences via BigBlueButton (BBB teleconferences), e-mailbox, post ratings, post commenting, social networking by friendship request etc. During the design phase, all the above described aspects were taken into consideration in order to integrate specific ICT applications that meet the trainers' needs, making SONETOR Platform the benchmark for users who want to be educated and trained as Cultural Mediators. As a result, the platform has been developed to support peer learning, learning through collaboration, social constructivism and crowd learning. Web 2.0 applications for learning through collaboration are representative examples helping users-trainers to develop ICT competences; they empower users with a venue for personal expression, sharing, communicating and collaborating with others (Hsu et al., 2014).

The collaborative nature of learning tasks and their authenticity (Bower et al., 2006) require the group to develop and attain shared goals. Only by shared goals will the task promote the kind of interactions that enable collaborative knowledge construction among the participating learners. In SONETOR training, the goal is to harness the knowledge and experience of many people in order to answer questions or address immediate problems and furthermore to collaboratively create content that relates to CM' issues.

Learning through collaboration compromises the spectrum of learning through interactions, including cooperative learning, collaborative learning, and collective learning that emphasize different levels and ways of learning by the group and community. Thus, through interaction with others and through situated involvement in social, cultural of training activities and content, the group

---

[13] http://volunteer 4greece.gr/S/v4g/

[14] http://www.intermediation.gr/

becomes the core of the production of knowledge. The learning platform allows learners to create, to co-construct artefacts together and to build on each other work. (Hsu et al., 2014). Web 2.0 and peer-learning applications provide the means to support knowledge building through multiple modalities for negotiating ideas and creating artefacts, multiple means for quick or thoughtful sharing and multiple channels for exchanging shared and varied perspectives and feedback among the participants wherever they are. In a literature review, Hhu et al. (2014) show that Web 2.0 practices include a) publishing and sharing learning achievements b) supporting collaborative tasks c) making thinking, collaborative processes and products visible d) communicating ideas and disseminating artefacts with multimedia capacity e) social networking in authentic learning environments and f) building communities of practice for learning in authentic and meaningful context.

The SONETOR platform can be considered as unique in its kind, as it offers a set of qualities and tools that support peer learning in order to train and help enhance knowledge, skills and competences of Cultural Mediators. The platform itself is described in a different chapter of this book; below are given some real examples of platform usage that prove its uniqueness and innovative character.

Blogging

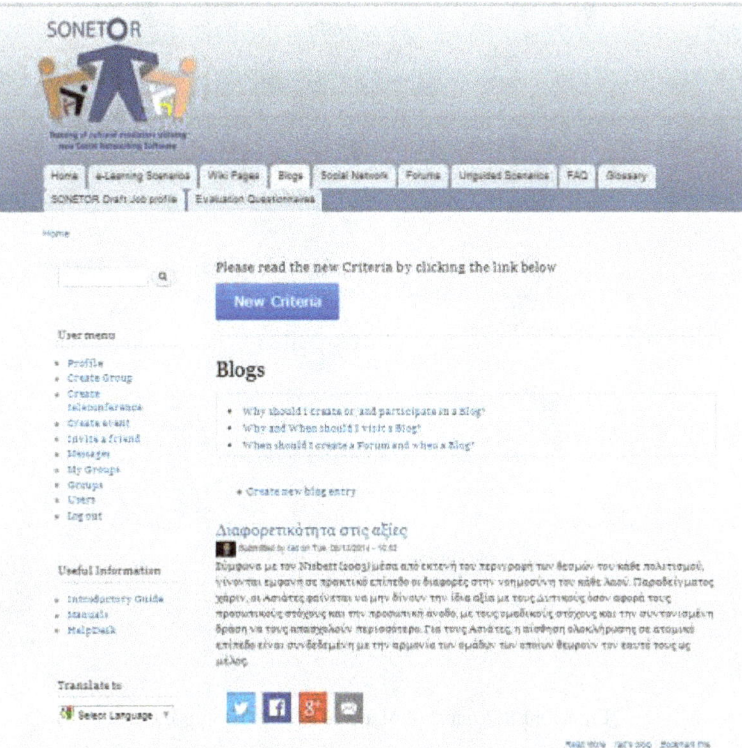

Figure 11.1: The Main Page of the Blog Tool

The need for a space/environment where the CM community can post articles and exchange opinions is covered by the Blog Tool (
Figure 11.1). The main purpose of a blog is the posting of short articles and announcements, which constitute the content of the blog (Figure 11.2). Also brief comments on postings could be submitted, but not long and documented answers or views; for this purpose, a new blog entry should be made, or the Forum Tool could be used. In addition, rating by the readers of a blog posting content is supported. Moreover, the ability to use TAGS and CLOUDS TAGS helps the users to quickly search with keywords for a topic they are interested in and would like to find information about.

In Figure 11.2 we show a Blog posting in Polish regarding a video that was developed in the project "The kids and hip-hop against violence". Users can follow the link to watch the video, can post comments, or can even subscribe to this page to receive updates concerning this specific posting. Moreover, they can translate the content using the Google translate tool, bookmark this page, or search for related postings. Finally, they can go to the blogger's own page.

Figure 11.2: Snapshot of a SONETOR Blog posting

Discussing

The Forum Tool enhances cooperation, discussion and communication among participants (Figure 11.3). Each user can create his/her own discussion topic, or participate in the discussion on a specific topic by giving informed answers (replies) to it. The user can browse the topics freely without time constraints and commitments and has the ability to actively participate in one or more forums at any time he/she feels that he/she wants to write something or just read a discussion.

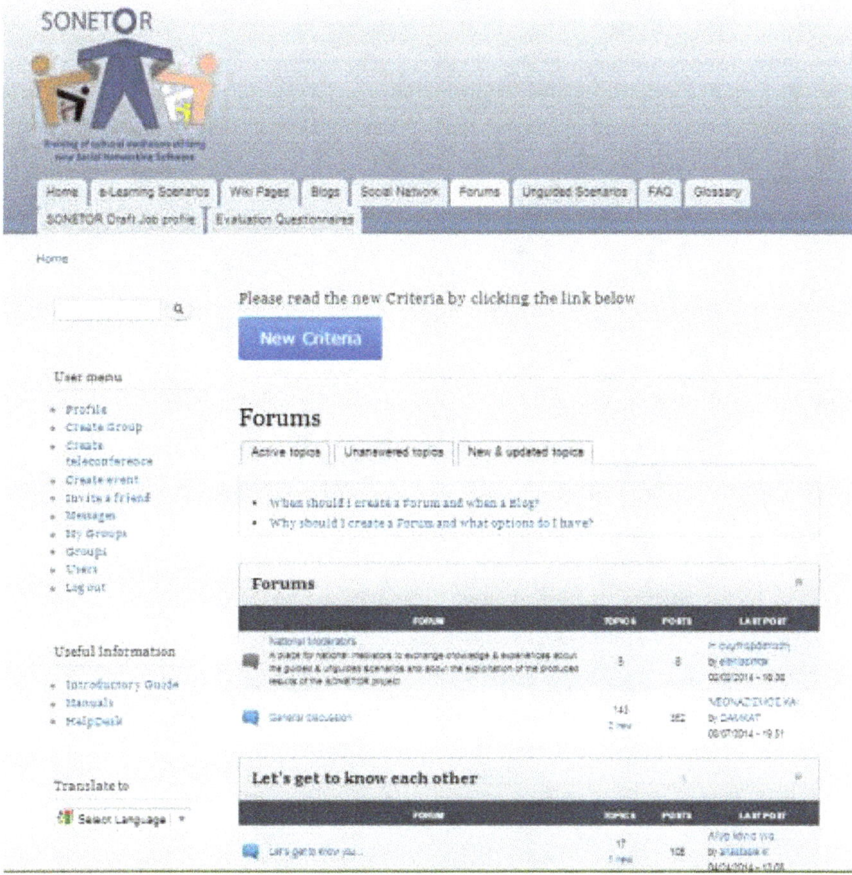

Figure 11.3: The Main Page of the Forum Tool

In the context of the project, we created:

- a forum that would allow platform users to get to know each other,
- a forum to include general purpose discussions, and
- a forum for National Moderators

In Figure 11.4, we show a discussion about a book lending library for immigrants. Users can follow links to obtain more information, can post their comment or reply, can subscribe or bookmark the page, can quote it in their own posting, etc. In Figure 11.5, we show a subset of the postings in the forum where users post information about themselves.

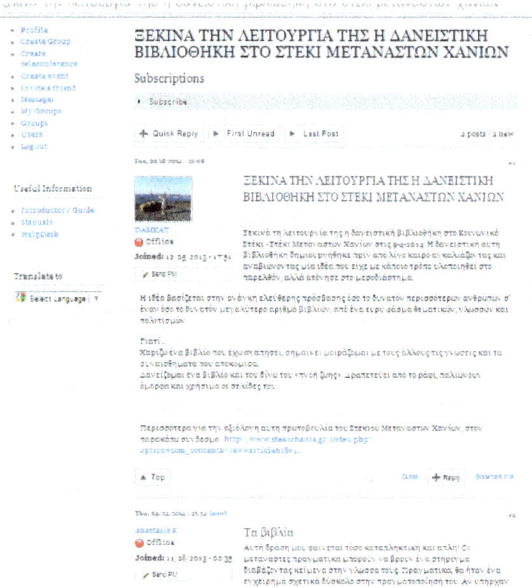

Figure 11.4: Snapshot of a SONETOR Forum Discussion

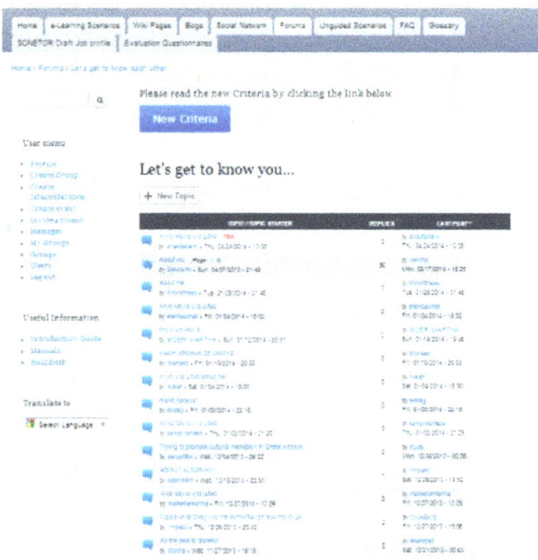

Figure 11.5: The "Let's get to know each other" Page of the Forum Tool

Content Editing

The Wikis pages have been created to meet the needs of a collaborative tool that encourages the joint creation of content by a group of users. For the moment, a set of definitions of terms related to cultural mediation are under development by the CM community (Figure 11.6). As with every wiki, users can edit the content of a page, or add a page of their own. Following the approval of the National Moderator, they can start a wiki on a topic of their own.

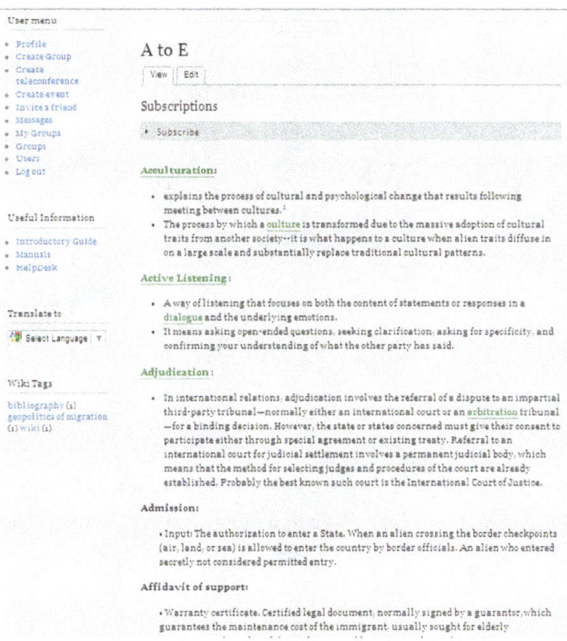

Figure 11.6: Snapshot of the Wiki page on Cultural Mediation Terms

Events – Calendar

The calendar plays the role of a personal agenda or/and a planner for each trainer. The user can be informed about events, conferences, meetings etc. in which might be interested. Also, the user has the opportunity to add events and actions that the CM community might be interested in. It can also be used as a notice board for various announcements and calls of interest (Figure 11.7).

Groups

In order to enhance the user's participation in a community, the platform provides users with the ability of creating focus groups. Each user has the option to create a group and invite other platform users to participate as members, or become a member in another user's focus group. Apart from facilitating communication and exchange of ideas, views and knowledge between people with common interests, this feature of group-creation also provides a private repository for subject content and encourages collective actions on the promotion of and awareness about cultural mediation. In Figure 11.8, we show the home page of group Cylon, which was created in order to facilitate discussion and exchange on legal and asylum related issues in Europe.

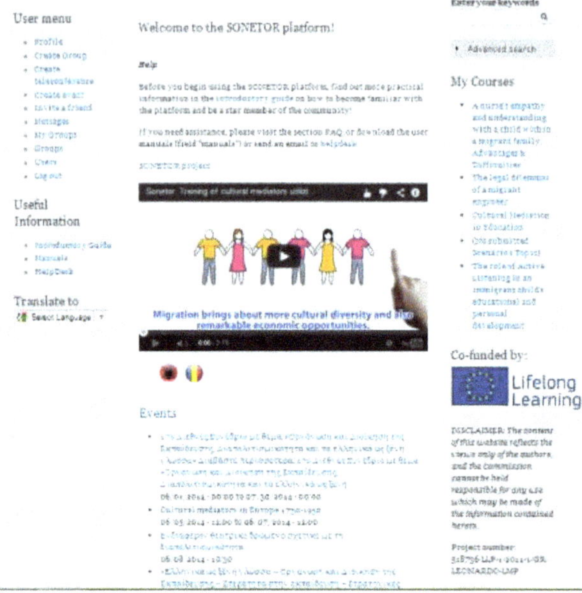

Figure 11.7: Snapshot of the Home Page of the SONETOR Platform, where events are listed

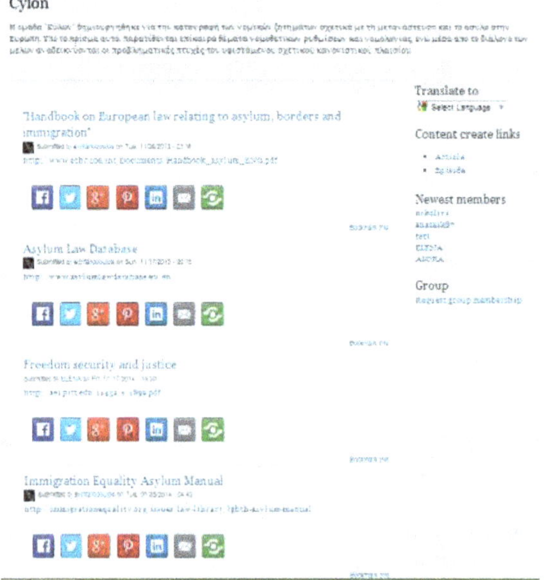

Figure 11.8: The Home Page of group Cylon

Peer Learning

The main purpose of the SONETOR platform is to support peer learning among Cultural Mediators. Members of the CM community are encouraged to submit their experiences from cultural mediation and to comment on the experiences submitted by their peers. We are interested in real life experiences; that is why the platform provides four broad areas which correspond to society sectors where mediation may be required: Education, Health, Housing, and Legal.

Experiences are submitted in the form of episodes (Figure 11.9). An episode has a title and may contain a textual description accompanied by any other media type that enhances understanding and transfer of the experience. In any episode, it is hugely important to highlight the role of the Cultural Mediator, by describing his/her goals in the context of the situation, the actions he/she took towards providing a solution, and an evaluation of the result (all of these can be backed up with multimedia material, as already mentioned). At the end of each episode, we ask the contributors to select the Cultural Mediator skills and competences that were necessary in order to deal with the situation; these can be selected from the Cultural Mediator profile, which is available in the platform (Figure 11.10).

Figure 11.9: An Episode in the Health domain uploaded in the SONETOR Platform

Figure 11.10: An Episode in the Health domain uploaded in the SONETOR Platform (video section)

Then, other members of the community may choose to translate the episode (although Google translator can be used also for informal translation), upload supporting documents, comment on the episode providing their own related experience, or even rate the quality and usefulness of the episode (Figure 11.11). In this way, they become engaged in the situation, learning from the experience of their peers and at the same time contributing their personal view and experience. Moreover, users can promote episodes using social media platforms, like Facebook and Twitter.

Episodes can be uploaded by any platform user in any language; comments too (Figure 11.2 -11.13) A search facility is available for users to seek the episodes that relate to the situation they have to deal with, thus enabling the platform to be used for on-the-job training and assistance.

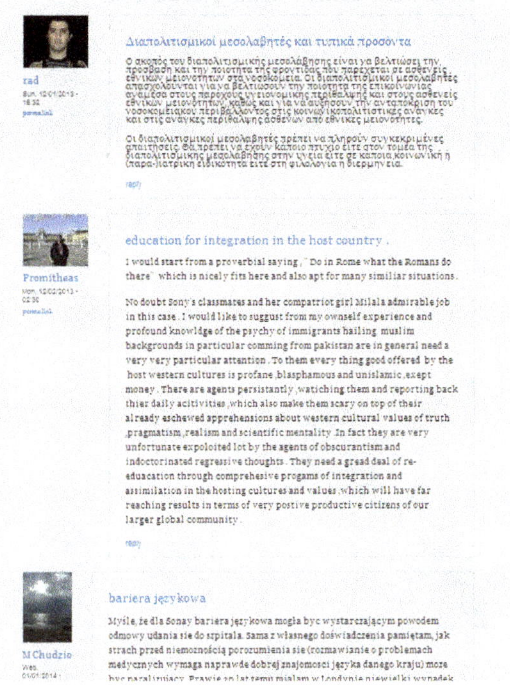

Figure 11.11: An episode in the Health domain uploaded in the SONETOR platform (comments section)

Figure 11.12: An episode in the Education domain written in Spanish

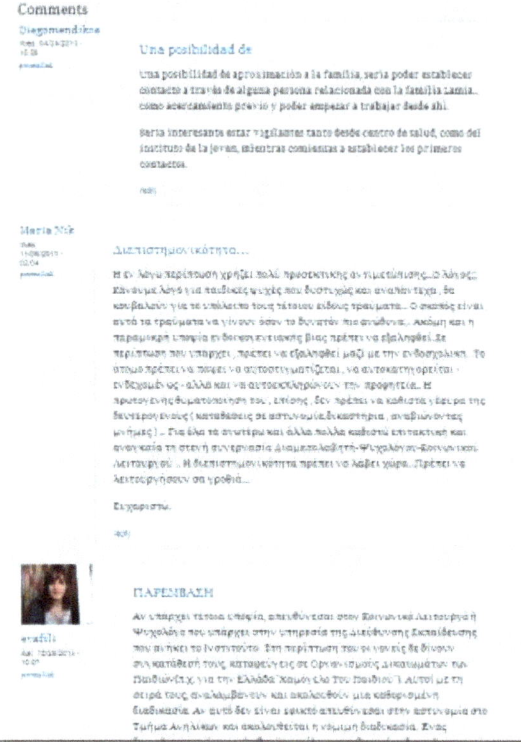

Figure 11.13: Responses to the episode in different languages

All the above constitute some of the basic tools of SONETOR platform available to the users for being trained utilizing social networking software in the context of peer learning. In this way, the SONETOR platform becomes an essential ICT application and tool for the whole community of Cultural Mediators. By combining SONETOR platform's service and other ICT APPs and tools available in the Internet, Cultural Mediators can deliver high effectiveness and quality cultural mediation services.

APPs and Games for Cultural Mediators

A number of games and APPs that foster cultural diversity awareness and cross-cultural understanding are used overseas for the training of school kids, teachers and parents, or even for use within a company or an organization's environment (http://www.sietar.de/SIETARproject/Games&simulations.html). Some of them are available and are being used already since the 70s. Although the list of this kind of games and applications is growing day after day, we consider useful to refer here to the best known of them. These games fall into the following major categories: (i) role play games, (ii) card games, (iii) simulation games, (iv) awareness games and (v) experiential activities games. Their aims are to raise awareness on cultural diversity issues, to train professionals on conflict resolution and to enhance Cultural Mediators' knowledge, skills and competences; these are achieved by the use of certain applications (APPs) specially designed for that purpose. These games and APPs can be found, accessed and/or downloaded via a PC, a tablet or a mobile phone; generally speaking via any device able to connect to the internet.

ECOTONOS [15] is a simulation game focused on problem solving and decision making in heterogeneous groups and teams. The objective of the game is to help the opposite parties come to a decision towards a common goal despite the barriers and obstacles that arise as they conceptualize things and situations differently due to cultural diversity.

Redundancia. [16] is another simulation game that teaches empathy for non-fluent speakers, and cross-cultural listening skills. It has been conducted in English, Spanish, French, German, Japanese, Korean, and many other languages.

DIVERSOPHY® [17] is a card game which compels participants to put themselves in a certain situation and guess the appropriate answer. Also, participants share some of their previous experiences dealing with cultural components and/or within a specific country. After the game, questions and discussion take place. It can be played informally by having each player pick a card, answer it and move to the next person, or it can take a more formal approach by forming small teams and keeping score.

Brief Encounters is a group game aiming to help participants gain skills in observing and describing behaviors and develop an understanding of how our cultural values influence the way we view other groups. [18]

Barnga is a card game that helps participants experience the shock of realizing that despite many similarities, people of differing cultures perceive things differently or play by different rules. Players learn that they must understand and reconcile these differences if they want to function effectively in a cross-cultural group[19].

BaFa BaFa, RaFa RaFa, Guns or Butter and Where Do You Draw the Line? are games especially designed and currently used for the experiential training on cultural awareness, diversity, team building, ethics etc. [20]

Furthermore, there are applications on cultural mediation for Android to download free of charge. Most Android applications on mediation are addressed mainly to Mediators of all fields and to the public, when they need to search for Mediation Professional Services and Options.

Mediation by Specialist Mediators LLP allows the user to select the type of dispute (e.g. Divorce, Boundary dispute etc.) and view UK based mediators who have specialist experience in that field. It also provides a phone button to call and speak directly to a mediator. Similar type APPs are: Mediation by Mike Krause, Mediation Master by Buckhead Mediation, Experte Mediator by Walter A.

---

[15] http://www.ceeintercultural.com/sites/default/files/prilohy/priloha-simulace-ecotonos-en.pdf

[16] http://www.nipporica.com/prod.htm

[17] http://diversophy.com

[18] http://plato.acadiau.ca/courses/educ/reid/games/Game_descriptions/Brief_Encounters.ht

[19] http://plato.acadiau.ca/courses/educ/reid/games/Game_ descriptions/Barnga1.htm

[20] http://www.simulationtrainingsystems.com/

Speidel, and Mediation Mobile by Mediation Mobile, which is mirrored online at www.MediationMobile.com.

Other online mirrored APPs are Mediator by Mediationcenter[21], Mediate2Go (M2G)[22], and IMI Mediator Search[23]

Finally, another interesting online application on Cross-cultural diversity is Culture Compass by ITIM International, ideal to learn and find out about different cultures worldwide.

It is noteworthy that there are more games and APPs that are not merely addressed to Cultural Mediation but to mediation in general, nevertheless they could be adapted in order to serve the needs of Cultural Mediators, such as games on Mediation in general, conflict resolution in general, group motivation and collaboration, learning to identify the signs of body language, cross-cultural communication and understanding etc. Here are some interesting links on such suggestions:

http://corejolts.wordpress.com/2013/05/17/board-games-for-mediators/
http://www.wilderdom.com/games/PeaceEducationExperientialActivities.html
http://users.elite.net/runner/jennifers/
http://www.sfhgroup.com/ca/training/online-training/test-your-skills.php
http://www.thiagi.com/games.html
http://plato.acadiau.ca/courses/educ/reid/games/Game_descriptions/InnerCity.htm

Conclusion

Cultural mediation in Europe can be greatly benefited by the use of computing technologies that will support and facilitate the CM role. ICT can help establish a dense network of highly experienced and informed professionals in cultural mediation in the context of a European CM community facilitating at the same time the exchange of knowledge thus supporting CM continuous training and lifelong learning, at the same time providing them with powerful and effective tools that can make them feel safer and more confident in their daily mediation and decision-making.

Experience from TIPS and SONETOR projects shows that Cultural Mediators are fond of belonging to a community of peers, where they can discuss concerns, create and promote strategies to the public awareness on cultural mediation issues, exchange ideas, experiences and information and meet with people of common interests and vision.

Since the need for trained professionals in Cultural Mediation is pressing nowadays, ICT technologies can offer the most modern and facilitating foundation on which solutions with unlimited capabilities can be developed. Platforms like SONETOR can become affordable, easily accessible, user-friendly, adaptable and appropriate tools able to provide communication, community actions, training, information, interoperability, interactivity, creative

---

[21] https://itunes.apple.com/dk/app/mediator/id595440286?mt=8
[22] https://www.mediate2go.com
[23] http://imimediation.org/mobile/#page2

production of content and dissemination of ideas, views and useful tips on best practices and codes of conduct for cultural mediation.

Moreover, well-structured training web-platforms should be based on the appropriate use of ICT applications and a well-defined framework. In particular, the approach of a well-structured platform at all levels (framework, tools etc.) also helps trainers to develop a set of competences and other skills such as retrieving and effectively using information with different forms of technologies and communication tools. Existing applications and games on cultural mediation are very interesting yet still in their infancy. It would be useful to have experts on both education and cultural mediation suggest the best scenarios for the creation of such applications so that they will be really handy and useful for the training of Cultural Mediators. In the Information Society of our times the easiest, most affordable and fastest way to do this is by utilizing the facilities offered by ICT. Internet and social media could be considered as two of the most popular ICT domains followed by applications used by modern digital devices such as mobile phones, tablets etc.

References

Bergman Elizabeth (2009). *Social Networking Tools in Education*. Stellenbosch University, Department of Modern Foreign Languages, Faculty of Arts. (http://academic.sun.ac.za/forlang_s/ftp/seminar/2009/social_nettools_lb.pdf)

Bower, M., Woo, K., Robert, M. & Watters, P.A (2006). Wiki pedagogy – A tale of two wikis. Paper Presented at *the 7th International Conference on Information Technologies Based Higher Education and Training* (ITHET 06), Sydney, Australia.

Boyd, D., Ellison N.B. (2007). Social network sites: Definition, history, and scholarship. *Journal of Computer-Mediated Communication*, *13*(1–2).

Brady, Kevin P.; Holcomb, Lori B.; Smith, Bethany V. (2010). The Use of Alternative Social Networking Sites in Higher Educational Settings: A Case Study of the E-Learning Benefits of Ning in Education. *Journal of Interactive Online Learning*, 9(2), 151-170. (http://web.a.ebscohost.com/abstract?direct=true&profile=ehost&scope=site&authtype=crawler&jrnl=15414914&AN=52800698&h=WqA6qZ%2fNf1b3b%2b3ygkThspAuFvnmltLyBd1UbFkjO5nNI9nRsxvPmfFqZfLCNV8FNM1J6Iyj9qEHPM0Z5EorTA%3d%3d&crl=c)

Hsu Y.C., Ching, Y.H., & Grabowski, B. L. (2014). Web 2.0 Applications and Practices for Learning Through Collaboration (pp. 747-758). In J.M. Spector et al. (Eds), *Handbook of Research on Educational Communications and Technologies*. New York: Spinger.

Jung, I. (2005). ICT-Pedagogy Integration in Teaching Training: Application Cases Worldwide. *Education Technology & Society*, *8*(2), 94-101

Lave, J. and Wenger, E. (1991). *Situated Learning. Legitimate peripheral participation*. Cambridge: University of Cambridge Press.

Leye, V. (2007). UNESCO, ICT corporations and the passion of ICT for development, modernization resurrected. *Media, Culture and Society*, *29*(6), 972-993.

Lockyer, L., Patterson, J. (2008). Integrating social networking technologies in education: a case study of a formal learning environment, paper presented at the 7th IEEE International Conference on Advanced Learning Technologies (pp. 529-533), Santander, Spain, 1-5 July 2008. Los Alamitos, California: IEEE Computer Society.

Minocha, Sh. (2009). Role of social software tools in education: a literature review. *Education + Training*, *51*(5/6), 353 – 369.

Prensky, M. (2001). Digital Natives, Digital Immigrants. In *On the Horizon*, 9(5). Retrieved on March 2, 2014, from http://www.marcprensky.com/writing/Prensky%20-%20Digital%20Natives, %20Digital%20Immigrants%20-%20Part1.pdf.

Reddi U. V. (2004). *Teleconferencing A Training Kit, New Delhi, India, Commonwealth of Learning.* Commonwealth Educational, Media Centre for Asia. Retrieved December 2013 from http://www.cemca.org.in/ckfinder/userfiles/files/teleconf6.pdf

Roblyer, M.D., McDaniel, M., Webb, M., Herman, J., and Vince Witty, J. (2010). Findings on Facebook in higher education: A comparison of college faculty and student uses and perceptions of social networking sites. *Elsevier, The Internet and Higher Education*, 13(3), 134-140. (http://www.sciencedirect.com/science/article/pii/S1096751610000278).

Sharples, M., McAndrew, P., Weller, M., Ferguson, R., FitzGerald, E., Hirst, T., Gaved, M. (2013). *Innovating Pedagogy 2013: Open University Innovation Report2.* Milton Keynes: The Open University.

Umrani, F., & Ghadially, R. (2003). Empowering women through ICT education: Facilitating computer adoption. *Gender Technology and Development*, (7), 359-377.

UNESCO – Universal declaration on cultural diversity, series no. 1, a document for the World Summit on Sustainable development, Johannesburg, 26 August-4 September 2002.

Chapter 12: Cultural Mediation: The SONETOR Project its Relevance and Impact

Dermot Coughlan and Morteza Rezaei-Zadeh

Introduction

When deciding to become involved in this project or indeed any project the relevance of the work to your individual setting is crucial to gaining the maximum return from the endeavor. In this regard as we review the work and outcomes of the SONETOR Project it is perhaps a good idea to review the current position regarding the extent of migration in Ireland. This is important for two reasons

Firstly to estimate the extent of issues that might arise pertaining to migrants and their integration into Irish society and secondly to attempt to predict or assess the services that they might require and from this the training required by those working with migrants.

Every country and possibly every individual consider themselves to be unique and or different. In terms of migration however Ireland can clearly state that it is unique. It is the only territory, on this planet at any rate, in which the population is smaller today than it was two centuries ago. The cause very simply is migration and in this instance emigration. While we use the word globalization very freely today it must be remembered that the first era of globalization occurred in the 1800's and coincided with Irish great famine in 1848 which saw the population of Ireland go from roughly 8 million to 4 million through death and emigration.

Our uniqueness in terms of outflow is only matched by the inward pattern of migration that Ireland experienced over the last ten to fifteen years which again was unique at least in the European context. From recently published figures

Table 12.1: Population and Migration Estimates - April 2013

	Year ending		
	April 2012	April 2013	
Immigration	52,700	55,900	
Emigration	87,100	89,000	
Net migration	-34,400	-33,100	
of which Irish nationals	-25,900	-35,200	
Natural increase	44,900	40,800	
Population change	10,500	7,700	
Population	4,585,400	4,593,100[1]	

While point in time figures is important what is more important in this case is to review the trend and the figures for the past decade make for interesting study.

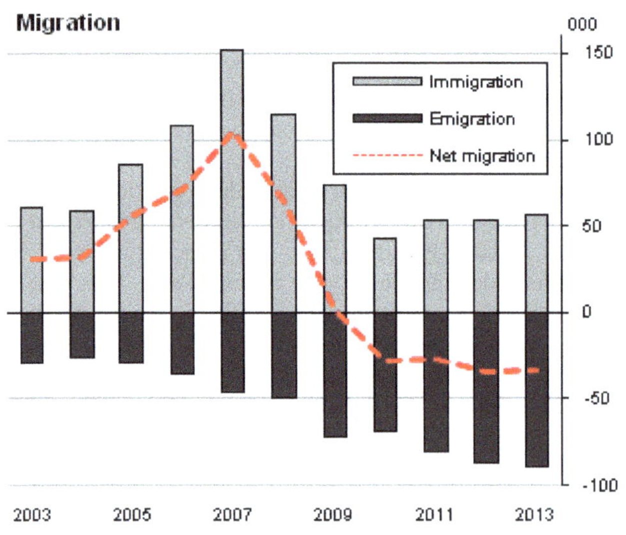

Source: Irish Central Statistics Office

Figure 12.1: Migration Flow

[1] Irish Central Statistics Office

Immigration peaked as the Celtic Tiger Period was in full flow in Ireland but despite the fact that Ireland has been in a deep recession for the past number of years immigration rose again in 2013. A starker figure is that from data gathered through the 2011 census close to one in eight people who were resident in Ireland at the time of the census claim not to be Irish. In the 1990's Ireland was, by European standards the most homogeneous society but based on the statistics from the 2011 census we are now the continent's most heterogeneous with no fewer than 199 nationalities recorded.

With overall unemployment at the time of writing this article running at 12.5% the days of the Celtic Tiger are long gone. A breakdown of this figure identifies the level of unemployment amongst the migrant community is high with some 67,893 non-nationals unemployed.

Table 12.2: Live Register Classified by Nationality Grouping

		Nationality grouping						
		Non-Irish nationals						
		United Kingdom	EU15 excl. IRL & UK	EU15 to EU28[1] States	Other	Non-Irish nationals	Irish nationals	All Persons
2011	November	17,648	3,571	40,788	13,512	75,519	354,048	429,567
	December	17,798	3,605	41,263	13,554	76,220	358,564	434,784
2012	January	17,827	3,648	42,831	13,845	78,151	361,438	439,589
	February	17,783	3,685	43,341	13,946	78,755	360,667	439,422
	March	17,521	3,608	43,025	13,926	78,080	355,974	434,054
	April	17,337	3,558	42,268	13,852	77,015	352,986	430,001
	May	17,447	3,551	41,634	14,151	76,783	356,124	432,907
	June	18,054	3,770	41,360	15,072	78,256	373,718	451,974
	July	18,290	3,756	41,167	15,209	78,422	381,901	460,323
	August	18,143	3,700	40,629	15,277	77,749	378,507	456,256
	September	17,135	3,525	39,335	14,324	74,319	355,016	429,335
	October	16,767	3,477	39,347	13,906	73,497	346,675	420,172
	November	16,695	3,530	39,935	13,588	73,748	343,529	417,277
	December	16,806	3,575	40,491	13,667	74,539	349,194	423,733
2013	January	16,934	3,743	42,004	13,761	76,442	352,954	429,396
	February	16,799	3,853	42,561	13,616	76,829	352,047	428,876
	March	16,555	3,851	42,246	13,194	75,846	349,242	425,088
	April	16,180	3,683	41,635	12,864	74,362	343,231	417,593
	May	16,187	3,663	40,858	13,124	73,832	347,905	421,737
	June	16,706	3,750	40,634	13,520	74,610	360,747	435,357
	July	16,873	3,748	40,136	13,312	74,069	367,907	441,976
	August	16,515	3,679	39,175	13,083	72,452	362,828	435,280

	September	15,543	3,536	37,842	12,320		69,241	339,429	408,670
	October	15,145	3,490	37,275	11,627		67,537	328,975	396,512
	November	15,099	3,660	37,748	11,386		67,893	323,614	391,507
[1]With the addition of Croatia from July 2013, EU15- EU28									

Source: Irish Central Statistics Office

The question that this poses is why people still come to Ireland? One reason being suggested but yet to be proven in any substantial way is the fact that Ireland has a very generous welfare system hence it is still an attractive location especially for those from within the EU. It must also be remembered that legal migration is not measured regularly and with the free movement of people throughout the enlarged EU Ireland has seen very significant numbers of Europeans entering the country. A further point to be borne in mind is the proximity of Ireland to the UK. We obviously share the island with a part of the UK and the mainland is very accessible also. This has led to a very significant increase in "identity swapping". Ireland has introduced fingerprinting for all asylum seekers and since its introduction 30% of those refused entry to Ireland had a recorded history in the UK also.

Irrespective of the reasons Ireland has a significant migrant community and the issues pertaining to this in the context of the training of those dealing with the migrant population made the work of the SONETOR Project very relevant and timely. Let us therefore examine the impact of the project not just in Ireland but across all partner countries.

Overview

This article is a synopsis of the work undertaken as part of the piloting and testing phase of the SONETOR project and details how the impact of the project was measured and assessed. The primary tool used to test the products of the project was 3 online questionnaires which were used to elucidate information of the effectiveness and efficacy of the tools developed. Table one outlines the detail of the questionnaires coupled with the number of responses.

Table 12.3: SONETOR Questionnaires

SONETOR questionnaire	Language	Link	No. of Responses	Total Responses
Short Questionnaire - SONETOR Training Course Evaluation	English	https://www.surveymonkey.com/s/Sonetor0	66	77
	German	-		
	Spanish	https://www.surveymonkey.com/s/Sonetor0Spanish	6	
	Polish	-	5	
	Greek	-		
	Croatian	-		
	French	-		

Questionnaire 1 - Social Networks, Unguided Scenarios & General Information	English	https://www.surveymonkey.com/s/Sonetor1	56	69
	German	https://www.surveymonkey.com/s/sonetor1german	10	
	Spanish	https://www.surveymonkey.com/s/sonetor1spanish	1	
	Polish	-		
	Greek	-		
	Croatian	https://www.surveymonkey.com/s/Sonetor1Croatian	1	
	French	https://www.surveymonkey.com/s/sonetor1french	1	
Questionnaire 2 – E-Learning	English	https://www.surveymonkey.com/s/Sonetor2	30	47
	German	https://www.surveymonkey.com/s/Sonetor2German	5	
	Spanish	https://www.surveymonkey.com/s/Sonetor2Spanish	1	
	Polish	https://www.surveymonkey.com/s/Sonetor2Polish	9	
	Greek	-		
	Croatian	https://www.surveymonkey.com/s/Sonetor2Croatian	1	
	French	https://www.surveymonkey.com/s/Sonetor2French	1	

In addition to the questionnaires other initiatives undertaken to assess the tools were:

- Designing two standard templates for National Report Training of the Core Users Group (CUG) and Training Scenarios Report
- Designing and writing (E-Learning) Scenarios and uploading them in the platform.
- Each partner conducted several workshops in different cities across the different partner countries introducing SONETOR's capabilities, training users, engaging users with the platform, and getting feedback from them
- Designing the e-learning process which could be used in conducting the e-learning courses in the platform
- Analyzing the gathered feedback and Providing some Recommendations for improving the project

Some of these will be discussed in detail in this paper but a very full report on all aspects of this work is available in the final report to the funding agency and will be available on the project website once approved by the agency.

Analytical Report

Methodology

Quantitative Methodology

The methodology which was used in this study was a mixed methodology and consisted of two quantitative and qualitative methods. In the quantitative part of this study a survey method was used. The gathering of data in this survey was conducted through 13 online questionnaires which were translated into 6 languages (See Table 12.1). Table 12.2 illustrates the number of participants who completed the online survey by country. Analyzing the data gathered in this phase was conducted using the descriptive analysis method.

Qualitative Methodology

In the qualitative part of this study, a Content Analysis has been conducted. The resources which were analyzed in this part of the study were:
The answers to the open-ended questions of the 13 online questionnaires above;

The reports of SONETOR partners which have been received in the two templates; The discussions of some of the SONETOR core users in the workshops which were conducted by the authors during their work in Ireland; and A high technical review and report which is written by an expert in the area of Information Technologies (IT) and E-Learning Platforms.

Table 12.4: The Number of Participants of the Online Questionnaires from each Country

Country	Feedback received		
	Short questionnaire	General questionnaire	e-learning questionnaire
Greece	18	18	15
Ireland	23	17	-
Spain	7	1	1
Austria	16	19	16
Poland	8	6	11
Others	-	7	4
Total	72	88	47

Further information regarding the demographic attributes of the participants of the online surveys is presented. Together with Table 12.2, Figure 12.2 illustrates where the participants of this study came from. As can be seen from Figure 12.2, most of the participants in the online surveys came from Greece (32%), Ireland (30%), and Austria (25%).

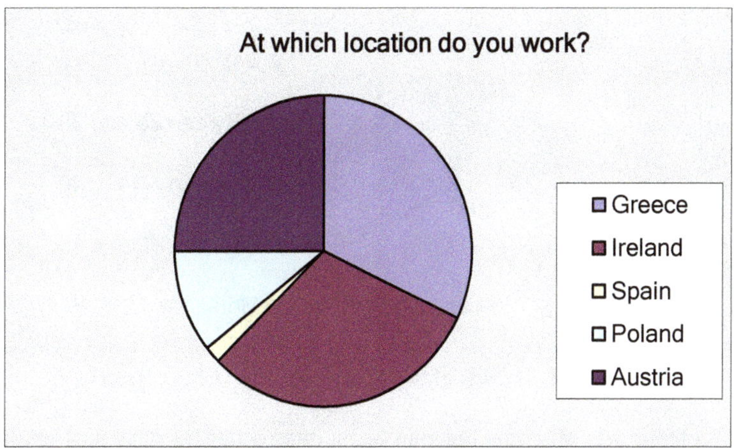

Figure 12.2: The location of the participants of the online surveys

According to Figure 12.3, most of the participants in this study (77%) were female.

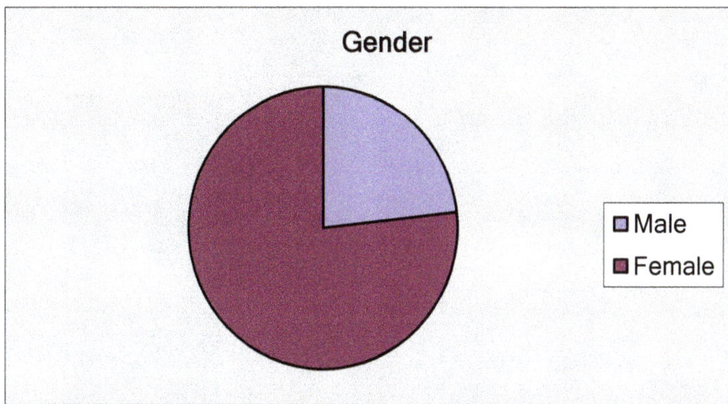

Figure 12.3: The Gender of the Participants

In terms of the participants' age, as can be seen in Figure 12.4, the overwhelming majority of the participants (68%) were over 30 years old. This indicates that the most of the participants in this study had the opportunity to and indeed did, gain some level experience in the field of cultural mediation experience in their everyday life.

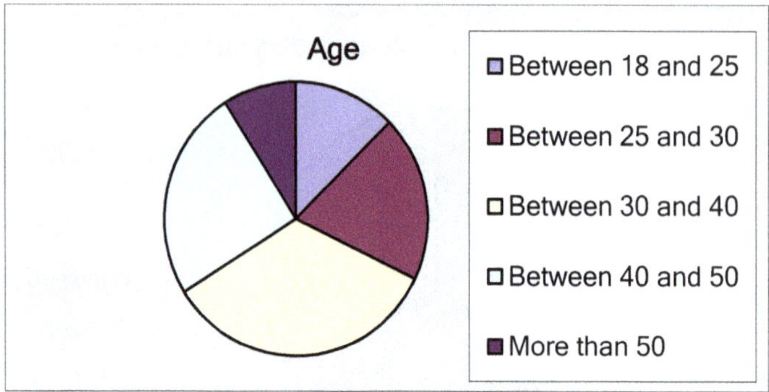

Figure 12.4: The Age of the Participants of the Online Surveys

Both Professionals who are dealing with immigrants as well as immigrants themselves were able to take part in this study. Figure 12.5 illustrates that the majority of the participants in the online surveys (76%) came from the first group and a minority of them (24%) were immigrants themselves.

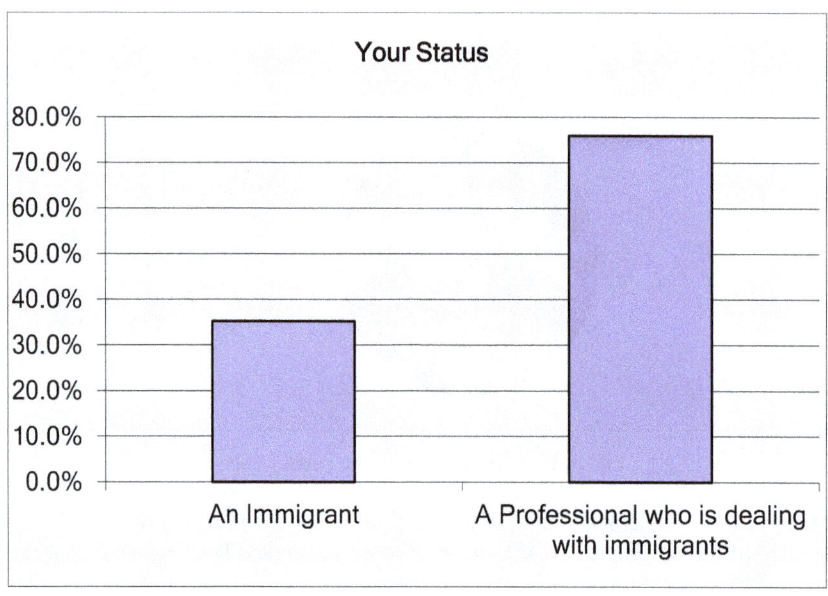

Figure 12.5. The Status of the Participants in the Online Surveys

Regardless of the status of the participants (Professionals who are dealing with immigrants OR immigrants), the area of the participants' activity was diverse. Figure 5 shows that the number of people who showed an interest in this cultural mediation project from Education sector (50%) is even more than experts who come from Immigration Organizations (32%). Figure 12.6 also illustrates that people from the Police and Health sectors by 1.8% and 5.4% participation in this study shows the least interest in this cultural mediation project.

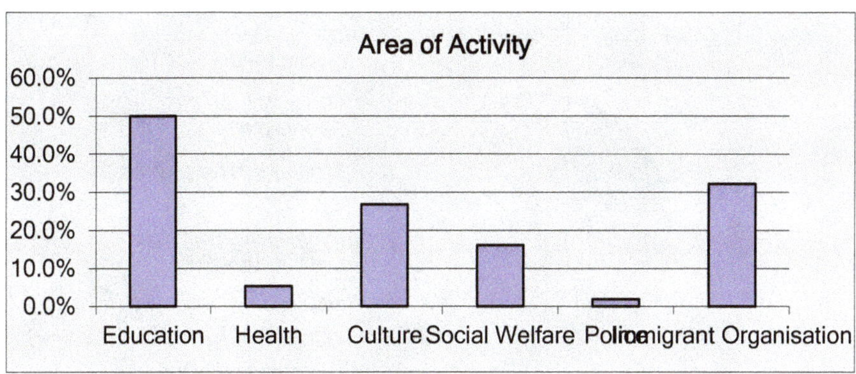

Figure 12.6: The Activity Area of the Participants of the Online Surveys

Figure 12.7 highlights that a majority of the participants have significant experience of dealing with immigration issues. According to that figure, more than 32% of them have more than 70% engagement with immigrants in their day to day work. Also, 41% of them are engaged with immigrants in more than 30% of their daily work. From this we can conclude that the participants in this study have a good level of experience of dealing with immigrants. This experience is a very important indicator for validity and credibility of the results of this study.

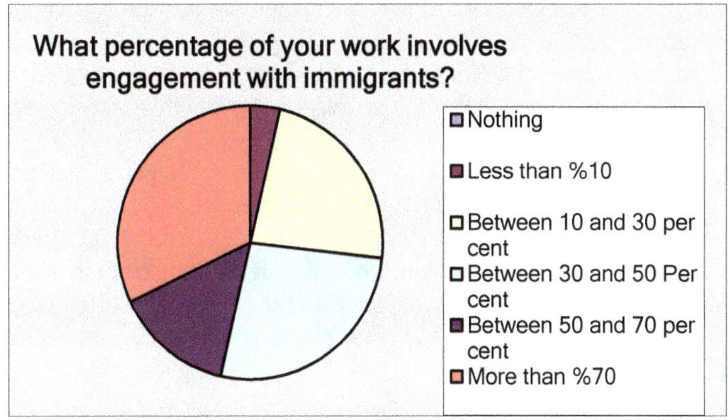

Figure 12.7: The Level of Participants' Engagement with Immigration Issues

The level of education of the participants is another important demographic feature. Studies such as this one can expect more valid and effective results if its participants have a good level of experience and knowledge. According to the previous figures, it is confirmed that participants have a good level of experience. Figure 12.8 shows that they have a reasonably high educational award as well. Half of the participants have a Master degree, 30% of them have a Bachelor, and 4% of them gained a PhD degree. 84% of the participants in the study have a Bachelor or higher qualification.

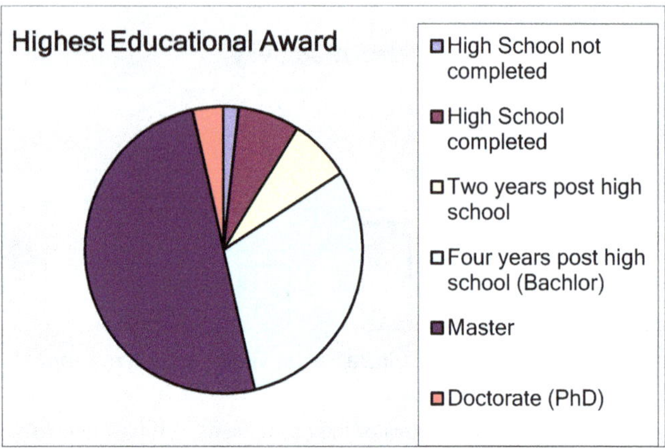

Figure 12.8: The Highest Educational Award of the Participants in the Online Surveys

Qualitative Feedback

This qualitative feedback is divided into three sub-sections. Each sub-section presents the results of analyzing each questionnaire.

SONETOR Training Course Evaluation

The partners of the SONETOR project conducted some training workshops for their core users. At the end of each training workshops, participants were redirected to an online questionnaire, asking them to evaluate their received training in the workshop. All of the responses of this survey were kept anonymously.

One of the questions, which was asked of the participants, addresses their overall evaluation of the SONETOR project. Figure 12.9 shows that more than 75% of all participants evaluated SONETOR as “Excellent” or “Very Good”. There was not even one vote assessing SONETOR as Poor or Fair, a minority of the participants (2%) assessed it as Average and the remainder (30%) evaluated it as Good. Accordingly, it can be concluded that, overall, the training sessions were successful.

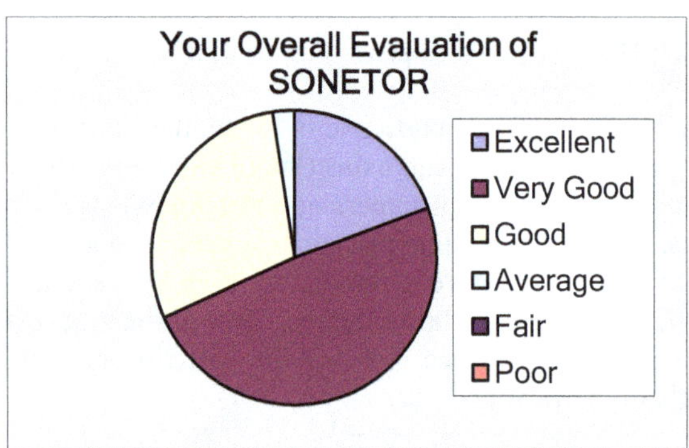

Figure 12.9: The Overall Evaluation of Training Workshops

Figure 12.10 specifically shows that participants in the training workshops were satisfied by the quality of presentations which were delivered to them by the SONETOR partners, with 70% of them evaluating the quality of presentations as Excellent or Very good.

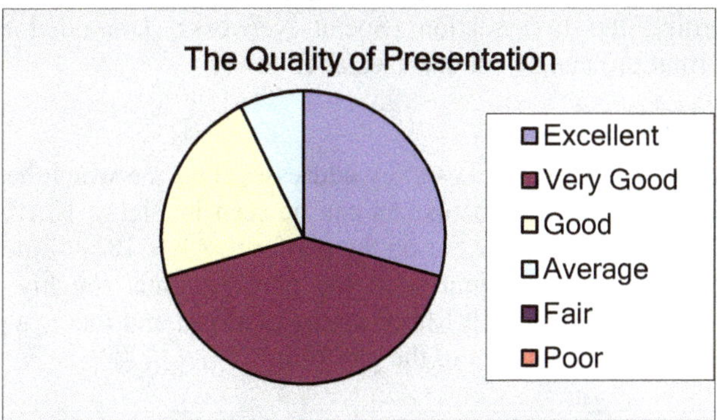

Figure 12.10: The evaluation of Training Workshops

Another question which was asked of the workshop participants was about the usefulness of the platform for them. As can be seen in Figure 12.11, an overwhelming majority of them (89%) believe that SONETOR is highly useful and effective for them. Again, this is another sign of the trainers' success, since they could make a good connection between the participants' requirements and SONETOR platform.

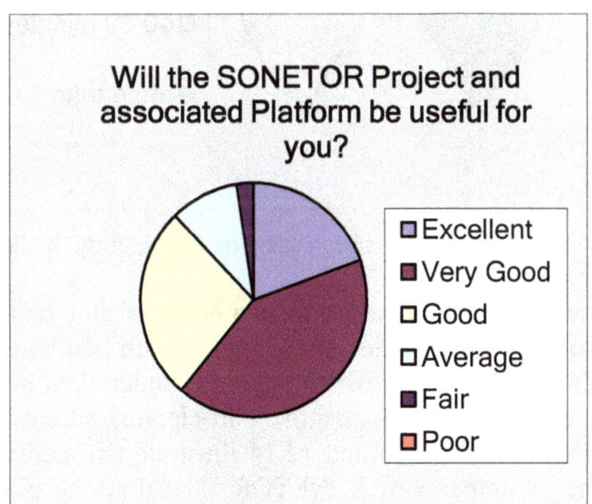

Figure 12.11: The Evaluation of Training Workshops

Social Networks, Unguided Scenarios & General Information

Those of you who have engaged with the project will be familiar with its structures and content. For those of you who may not have interacted with the project the main SONETOR platform consists of two primary sections: Social Networks, Unguided Scenarios & General Information; and E-learning section.

The participants in the survey were to engage with the various elements of the project and work with the different components of the two sections outlined above and then respond to an online questionnaire. This online questionnaire, which was provided in the different languages, enables users to submit their feedback regarding the different aspects of those sections. The results of this survey regarding the first section (Social Networks, Unguided Scenarios & General Information) can be summarized as follows;

General Evaluation

One of the first questions in this survey addresses the time which has been spent on the platform by the participants. As can be seen in Figure 12.12, 41% of the participants spent more than 1 hour on the platform. Also, 18% of the participants spent between 40 and 60 minutes on the platform thus roughly 60% of the participants spent approximately1 hour on the platform and this is a good sign of the usefulness and effectiveness of the platform.

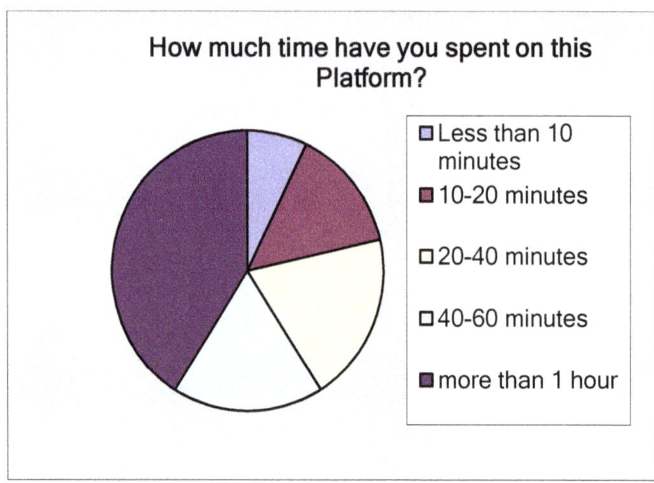

Figure 12.12: The time which has been spent on the platform by the participants

After realizing that participants spent a good amount of time on the platform, it is important to know what activities they engaged on while on the platform. Therefore, the potential activities which could be undertaken by the participants in the platform were used to assess the participants' interest in the various elements available. Figures 12.13 and 12.14 illustrate two activities which were undertaken by the participants of SONETOR. The first one is Reading and the second one is Writing the unguided scenarios. According to the first potential activity, Figure 13 illustrates that 37% of the participants read more than 4 scenarios. On the other hand, just 11% of them did not read even one scenario in the platform. Overall, we can say that participants' interest and tendency to read the unguided scenarios in the platform is relatively high.

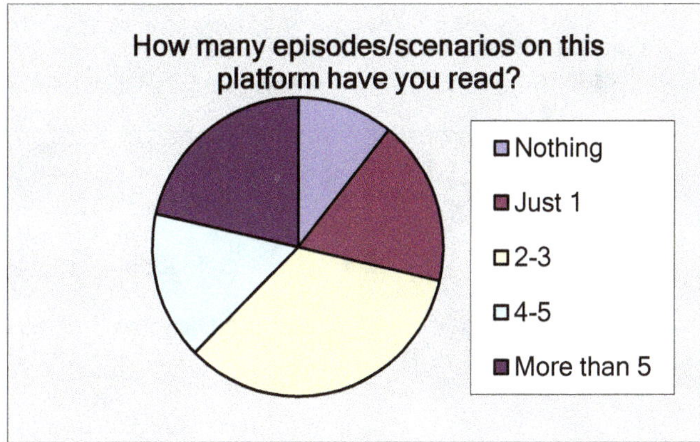

Figure 12.13: The Number of Scenarios which have been read by the Participants

The second expected activity from the participants was writing an unguided scenario. Unlike the previous question, the amount of participants interested in this activity was not considerable. According to Figure 13, while a minority of people (13%) indicated that they wrote more than 4 scenarios, most of them (61%) indicated that they did not submit even one scenario.

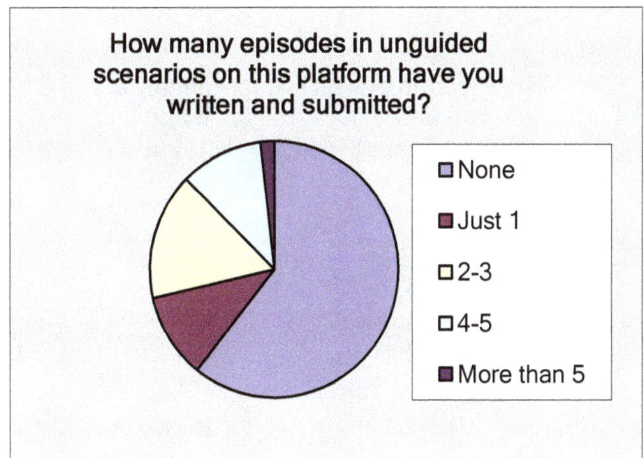

Figure 12.14: The Number of Scenarios which have been written by the Participants

Usability Evaluation

The second issue which was evaluated was the usability of the platform in this section. This usability was assessed by asking different questions and two of them are presented here. The first question, which is illustrated by Figure 12.15, addresses the ease of finding the aim and objectives of the platform. As can be seen there, an overwhelming majority of the participants (96%) were strongly agree and agree that the aim and objectives of launching SONETOR platform is easy to find.

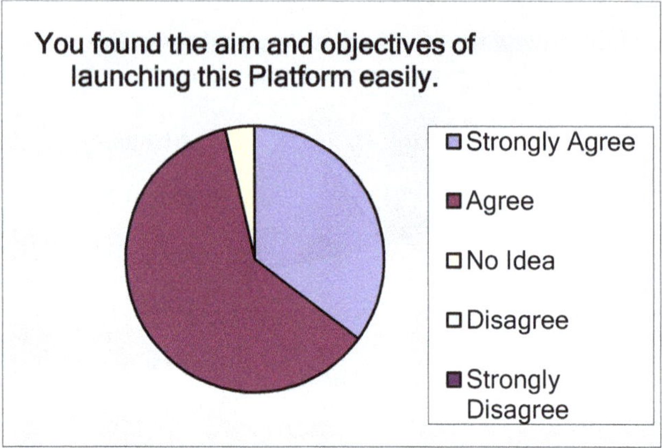

Figure 12.15: The Ease of finding SONETOR's Aim and Objectives by the Users

The next question, focused on the social networks section, and assessed the user-friendliness of the platform. This question wanted to assess if users of the platform could easily track, navigate and find the information in the Platform. According to Figure 12.16, a significant majority of the participants (83%) believe that it is a user-friendly platform, with just a minor population (6%) of the participants disagreeing.

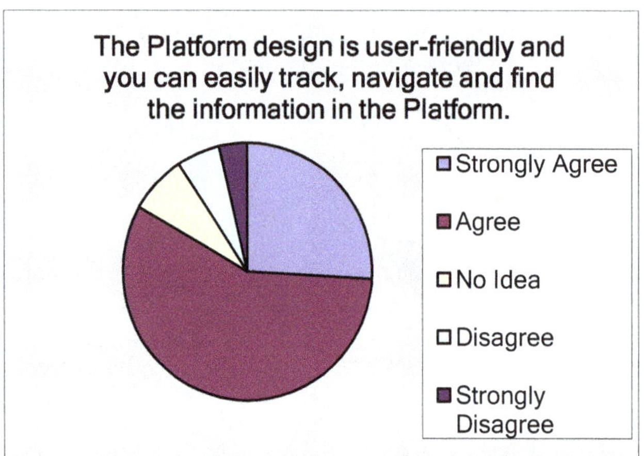

Figure 12.16: The User-friendliness of SONETOR Platform

Content Evaluation

The last component of the social networks and unguided scenarios which is evaluated here is the Content of these sections. While this content is mostly written and provided by the users of the platform; however, it is important to know what is the judgment of other users regarding the effectiveness and usefulness of the content. There are some questions for assessing the content of different components of social networks and unguided scenarios and due to the lack of space, just a few of them are presented here.

The first question tries to directly address the usefulness and effectiveness of the content of the platform in the social networks and unguided scenarios. As could be seen in Figure 12.17, an overwhelming majority of participants (93%) are strongly agree and agree that the content is effective and useful. That's a major success for the platform that the overall evaluation of its users about the content of the platform is in such a good manner.

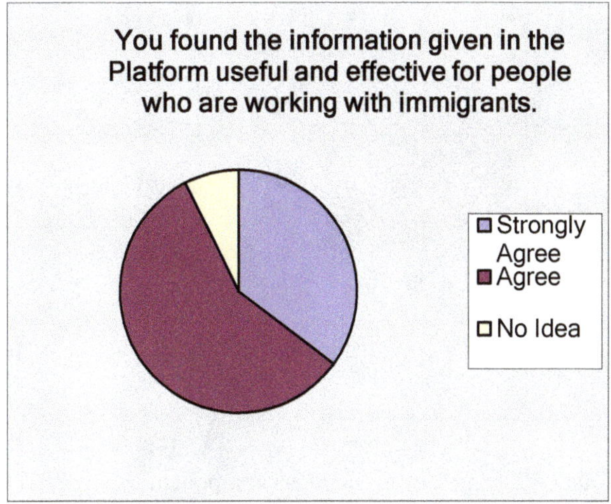

Figure 12.17: The Effectiveness and Usefulness of the Platform's Content

The second question which tries to assess the content of the platform addresses the level of the users' expectations which are met by the content of the platform. According to Figure 12.18, while 6% of the participants were disagree that their expectations are met by the platform, 80% of the core users were strongly agree or agree that their expectations were met by the platform content. That would be another major success for SONETOR platform in terms of providing the reliable and effective content by the users themselves.

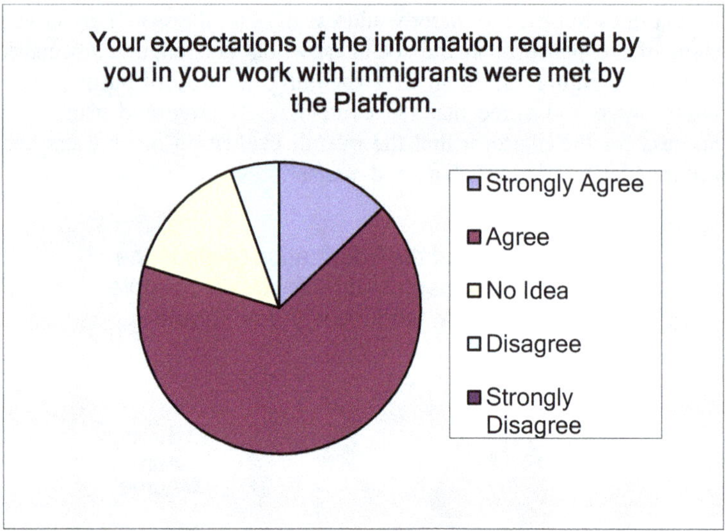

Figure 12.18: The Level of Users' Expectations which is met by the Platform

E-Learning

E-learning (Guided Scenarios) is another component of SONETOR platform which needs to be assessed by the core users. To do so, participants of this study were supposed to see and work with one or more of the four e-learning scenarios which was presented and uploaded in the platform; and then, fill out a questionnaire to assess how they work. Due to the lack of space, a few of these questions are presented here.

The Level of Engagement

It is important to know to what extent the platform could engage its users. Figure 12.19 illustrates that the e-learning section of the platform was not too successful in engaging users. In fact, while just %4 of the users spent between 4-8 hours on the platform, the majority of them (%65) spent less than 1 hour on the e-learning section. It is important since doing an e-learning course in a successful manner requires the participants to spend more time on it. This finding is consistent with the similar findings in the social networks section. In that section, when the users were required to spend more time in the platform and have some contributions, their level of engagement was decreased. Therefore, it could be concluded that users of the platform either in the social networks or in the e-learning section do not tend to spend time on the platform when they are required to do time-consuming tasks. On the other hand, they are interested to do some other works which require them to spend less time on them.

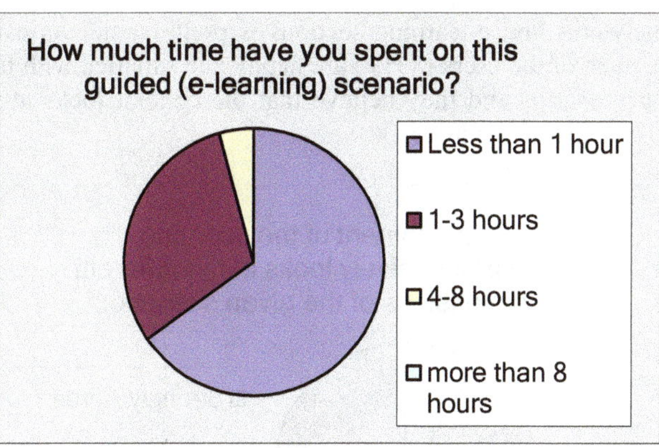

Figure 12.19: The Amount of time which has been spent on E-learning Section by the Participants

Usability Evaluation

User-friendliness of the e-learning section as one of the important aspects of its usability was assessed here. As could be seen in Figure 12.20, majority of the users (%87) do strongly agree and agree that the e-learning design is user-friendly and they can easily track, navigate and pursue their learning in the Platform. This is consistent with the same question which was asked about the user-friendliness of the social networks of the platform. Therefore, in general, we could conclude that the users of SONETOR platform are happy with the usability level of the platform and it could be a good achievement for the project.

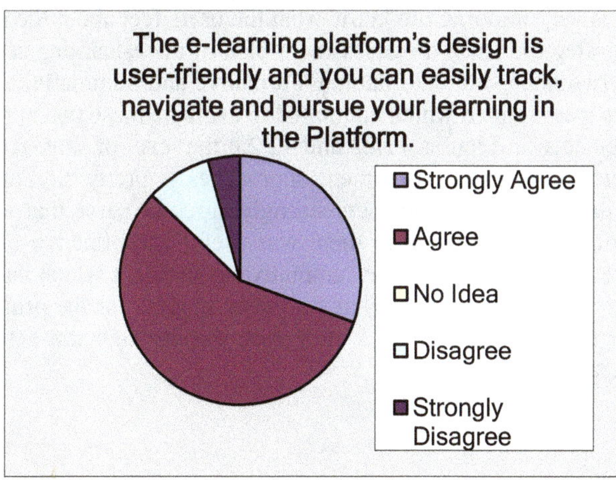

Figure 12.20: The User-friendliness of the E-learning Section

Content Evaluation

In terms of the content, there is a distinction between the e-learning and social networks section. While in the social networks section the content is provided and generated by the users themselves, the e-learning content is initially generated by SONETOR partners. However, the evaluation of the core users of the content of both social networks and e-learning sections is pretty same. As can be seen in Figure 12.21, most of the users (83%) are happy and satisfied with the content of the e-learning scenarios and they believe that the content looks at the different dimensions of the given scenarios.

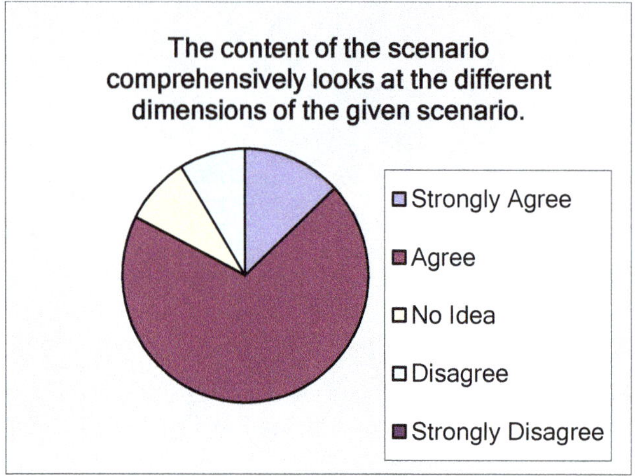

Figure 12.21: Evaluation of the Content of the E-learning Section

Assessment Evaluation

Assessment is one of the most important components of any training program. Therefore, it is very important to know what the users feel about the implemented assessment strategies. Since the assessment plan of the e-learning section is built based on the two main strategies namely Formative and Summative Assessments, two questions were framed which attempted to evaluate these two approaches.

As can be seen in Figures 12.22 and 12.23, the level of satisfaction with the Formative and Summative Assessment approaches is pretty similar. In both of them approximately 70% of the users strongly agree or agree that the formative feedback which has been given to them was useful and effective for improving their initial responses; and also, the summative assessment which has been given by their tutor was good and fair. That's a major success for the project that core users are happy with the feedback they received through these two kinds of assessment approaches.

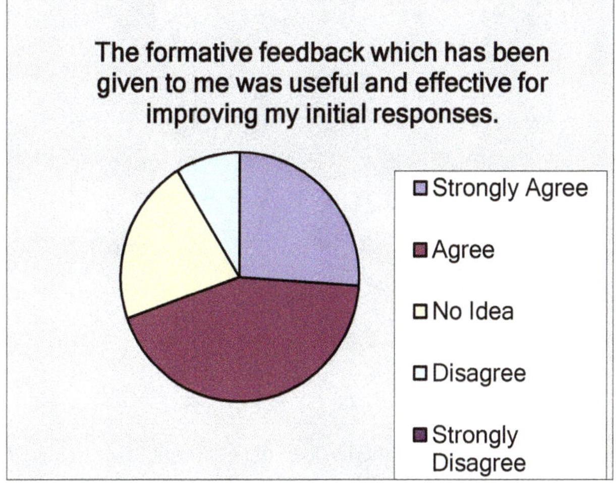

Figure 12.22: Evaluating the Formative Assessment which has been given in the E-learning Section

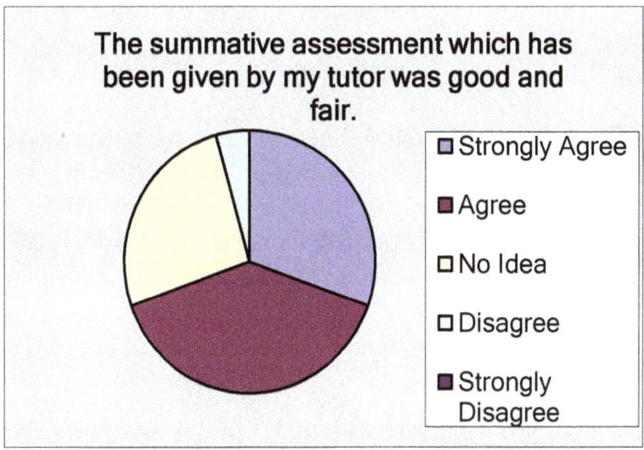

Figure 12.23: Evaluating the Summative Assessment which has been given in the E-learning Section

General

Last but not least, Figure 12.24 outlines the general experience of the core users with the e-learning section. As might be expected based on the results from earlier sections figure 12.20 shows that most of the users (77%) have had a very good or good overall experience with the e-learning scenarios which are provided by SONETOR platform.

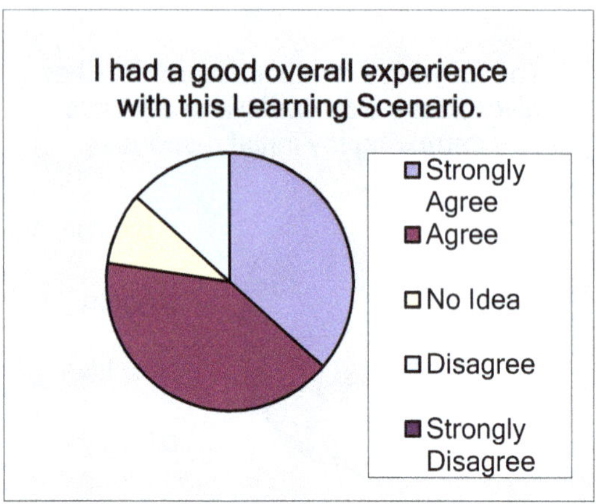

Figure 12.24: The Overall Experience of the Users with E-learning Section

Qualitative Feedback

As mentioned at the outset of the paper the resources which were analyzed in this part of the study were:
The answers to the open-ended questions of the 13 online questionnaires above;

> The reports of SONETOR partners which have been received in the two templates; The discussions of some of the SONETOR core users in the workshops which were conducted by the authors during their work in Ireland; and A high technical review and report which is written by an expert in the area of Information Technologies (IT) and E-Learning Platforms.

Overview

This is a high-level technical and usability assessment of the www.culturalmediators.eu website focusing specifically on the home and the e-learning pages. The culturalmediators.eu website is a web platform with e-learning components designed to assist in the training and professional development of cultural mediators. In summary the current design of the website is quite basic and exhibits significant issues with general site organization and with surfacing relevant content to the user. That said there are some significant "quick win" opportunities for optimization of the design that would rectify these problems and result in a much improved user experience.

General

The following report is based on the feedback we have received from users of the site and from direct interaction with our own group of users in four different cities across Ireland. The following detail is based on the returns so far and we hopefully will have significantly more formal responses when we come to write our final report.

In general the level of engagement with the project site and the training platform has been somewhat less than envisaged at the outset of the project. This however is not due to a lack of interest or seeing the tools as not being useful but that to some extent there is what I will refer to as "project fatigue" in the wider community and in particular with regard to those involved in areas such as migration and the marginalized generally. That said as leader of WP5 I am relatively pleased with the level of engagement with the platform and the site generally.

Project Site

From the feedback we have received we are happy that visitors to the general website are pleased with the content and the ease with which they can navigate the site. Hit counts are not a very reliable source but none the less we have a decent hit rate and interestingly we have several visitors from countries other than those participating in the project. We have had significant interest from Italy and France and some small interest from Canada and the US.

Platform

Generally the reaction to the platform has been positive but like all such developments the reaction will vary from individual to individual. This is also generally associated with the users' engagement with such platforms previously. The content may and will be significantly different but the concept of a learning or training platform was familiar to some. The general breakdown in such instances is that people experiencing such technology for the first time find it interesting and useful. Those familiar with such sites and platforms tend to be a little more insightful in their comments.

People are comfortable with the concept of blocks but in reality are reluctant to use them for some reason which is not readily apparent from the feedback. Similarly with tweets and the primary source of engagement is through the forum section of the platform. Through our own workshops in Ireland we have encouraged people to engage with the other elements but in the final analysis it is the individual who will choose what elements of the platform they will engage with.

As an action we would urge partners to engage with their users and direct them to the different elements apart from forums and request that they test and use these also.

Unguided Scenarios

Users have found these to be useful while noting that their layout in the platform could be more user-friendly. There are also some concerns about developing scenarios and protecting the identity of the players. There was some very favorable comment as to the video scenarios but it should be made clear that they do not relate per se to the written unguided scenarios. The major issue of engaging with this section seems to be the time required. Many individuals have indicated that they would like to contribute but that it does take considerable effort to write one.

E-learning/Guided Scenarios

There has been significant comment regarding this section with the primary issue being one of navigation from the platform to the individual modules. It is very interesting to note some remarks regarding the content. From our analysis it seems that individuals are going straight to the content and are not exploring the instructions pertaining the modules. It is also clear that the comments are based on a cursory engagement with the overall section rather than registering and pursuing one of the modules which would result in tutor support and other additional guidance.

The action from this review is that we will ensure that a number of individuals will actually register for some of the modules and we will get formal feedback from people who will actually pursue the learning rather than review what is available on the platform. We will also advise CTI as to what the users are saying regarding the structure and layout of the e-learning unit of the platform to make it more useable.

Summary

In summary users are generally happy with the learning outcomes they can attain both through casual engagement with the project website and the training platform specifically. There are amendments required to both and we will feed these to the appropriate individuals.

The level of engagement however is still very poor in some partner countries and this will have to be addressed immediately. We have engaged with the national moderators and the lead partner in each partner country and we will be doing so again. It must be borne in mind that while we are developing the work for the end-users – cultural mediators each partner has a responsibility that people in their home countries/cities truly engage with the product.

While we have endeavored to complete the work unfortunately our partners have not responded in a timely fashion despite several reminders. We are still waiting to receive the reports of our colleagues which should have be provided by filling out the two standard templates entitled “National Report Training of the Core Users Group (CUG) Template” and “Training Scenarios Report template”. Obviously, our analysis is not fully completed as we are still awaiting the completed reports from the partners which have been sent again today. We hope for a speedy response to enable us to provide a complete report for our end of project input.

Conclusion

The outputs of the SONETOR project have been thoroughly reviewed both through an extensive study of the views of the users and the assessment of the technical capabilities of its tool by a recognized expert in the field. Based on the quantitative and qualitative assessments we are happy that the outcomes of the project are of a very high standard. This is not just in terms of the technology used but of the manner in which user engagement has been designed and developed.

Europe has long been a multi-cultural society but it is still struggling with the next phase which is to become a truly intercultural society. In its vision for the future the Council of Europe states that a truly intercultural city there will have the following attributes:

- diversity is a source of dynamism, innovation, creativity and growth
- diversity is accepted as the norm and heritage and identity of all people is affirmed
- public spaces, schools, homes, workplaces and cultural forums are designed to enable people from different cultural backgrounds to mix, exchange and interact productively and creatively.
- public consultation, debate and decision making reflect the community's cultural mix - cultural conflict is accepted and dealt with - often at the grassroots level
- politicians and the media encourage citizens' participation in creating a shared identity.

The Council further states that to make this vision a reality, cities must develop an intercultural strategy to transform their policies, public spaces, institutions and the relationships between communities. We would add to this by saying that the key to attaining these goals is through education, training & development. In the outputs of the SONETOR Project there is now a suite of options available to ensure that people can be trained to become cultural mediators who will in turn ensure that through their efforts the city in which they live will take major steps towards achieving the goals which will ensure that the city will move towards the goal of becoming an intercultural city espousing the qualities of a learning and intercultural society.

Part III: Systemic Responses to Mediation: Narratives of Recognition and Validation

Chapter 13: Cultural Mediation in Ireland

Mayte Martín

Cultural Mediation was a concept introduced in Ireland in 2002 by the JOIN Project funded by the European Commission under its Community Action Plan to Combat Discrimination. Led by Finland, the JOIN project lasted two years, from 2002 to 2004. Other partners included Germany and Ireland. With a cross-administrative and horizontal approach, the aim of this initiative was to bring together local authorities and NGOs in order to identify good anti-discriminatory practices. The project sought to develop these practices further and to promote dialogue between discriminated groups and authorities. The JOIN Project targeted different grounds of discrimination including ethnic origin, religion, disability, age and sexual orientation. JOIN specifically drew attention over those cases where people were exposed to multiple discrimination by highlighting the existing similarities in the experiences of different groups. In other words, JOIN, aimed at promoting equality and anti-discrimination through a joint effort regardless of the discrimination ground. In other to do this, the initiative sought to develop new practices and test them. Cultural Mediation was one of these anti-discriminatory practices.

The two-year Cultural Mediation project started with a training program offered to all minorities living in Ireland. The program consisted of a six-month training period complemented by work placements and working sessions. During those two years, one of the difficulties we experienced was to explain to service providers the contribution that cultural mediation (CM) could make in facilitating the access and usage of services among ethnic minorities. Services providers mistook cultural mediation with some sort of interpreting service. Furthermore, many service providers put the difficulties they were experiencing in communicating with minority groups down to language differences rather than to cultural differences. On the other hand, those service providers who understood the challenges culture brought about were at a loss as to how to get help.

While still coordinating the JOIN Project, it was clear that we needed to professionalize and define CM. Unfortunately, projects outside Ireland did not offer much help, in many of them, the roles of the interpreter and the cultural mediators were the same (Martin and Phelan, 2009). This situation was confusing for all parties involved, especially for cultural mediators, whose responsibilities were not clear. Because our participants were working in real cases in the health services, it became imperative for us to define what CM was. We sought to spell out the roles of the cultural mediator and write a code of conduct, which included principles of confidentiality, impartiality and neutrality. A code of practice was and still is important not only to help CM be recognized as a profession but also to protect and guide cultural mediators. In our view, cultural mediators are responsible for the creation of a space of dialogue between service providers and service users so they can establish an effective and respectful relationship (Martin and Phelan, 2009). While they are a valuable resort for service providers, cultural mediators are not supposed to substitute any party or represent any particular interest.

Not all service users from a different linguistic background need or wish to have a cultural mediator although they still might require interpreters if they do not speak the language of the country fluently. CM is needed in order to establish a relationship between services providers and users. Once this is done, cultural mediators are redundant whereas interpreters are always required when service users do not speak the same language as service providers. The roles of cultural mediators and interpreters are different but can complement each other (Martin and Phelan, 2009).

Furthermore, cultural mediation is only an aspect of a global strategy to provide cultural competent healthcare provision. Service providers require training and information to deliver an effective service (Minervino and Martín, 2007). Cultural mediators assist them by providing information about the cultural background of their patients and the way it might affect them when approaching health services. In order words, cultural mediators are a resource for service providers as they help the providers to enhance their intercultural skills. Cultural mediation should not, however, be viewed as the only way to provide cultural competent care or as a substitute for building a relationship with the patients themselves.

Migrants arriving in a new country usually have needs in many areas. It is for this reason that it is important to limit and define the tasks of cultural mediators. Cultural mediators aid health users to navigate the health system and empower them to voice their concerns and decisions but they should not be viewed as the resource to address all their needs. There is no doubt that the job of being in the 'middle' is challenging and cultural mediators sometimes need to work under high emotional pressure. As the JOIN project progressed, we realized that it was also important to develop a structure of support for cultural mediators. By the end of the project we had created several guides and protocols for cultural mediation, including guidelines for those service providers seeking to engage cultural mediators. In addition to the need to professionalize CM, the JOIN project also highlighted the difficulties for service providers and NGOs to access particular vulnerable groups. In Ireland one of those groups were the Roma population.

Ireland, like other European countries has experienced the arrival of Roma people since the nineties. As in many other countries, in Ireland the lack of data collected on the basis of ethnic origin prevents the estimation of the number of Roma residing in the country. According to a 2005 report (Lesovitch, 2005) it was estimated that there were between 2,500 and 3,000 Roma living in Ireland. The enlargement of the EU to Romania and Bulgaria in January 2007 lead to an increase of migration (Martín and Hibernian Consulting, 2007). Approximately

85% to 90% of the Roma in Ireland come from Romania. Before 2007 many Roma arrived to Ireland as asylum seekers hoping to get refugee status. Some succeeded in obtaining it; others were able to stay in the country as parents of Irish born children. Since January 2007, Roma from Bulgaria and Romania acquired the right to free movement across Europe. While Member States at the time of accession could not impede the freedom of movement among the citizens of those countries; they could impose temporary restrictions to enter the labor market, which Ireland chose to do. Roma as well as any other citizen from Romania and Bulgaria after the year 2007 needed a work permit or be self-employed (none of the rest of EU members request work permits). They were not entitled to social welfare assistance or to any other social support.

Although the Irish Government lifted those restrictions in 2012, these measures impacted the Roma particularly because with no accreditation for their skills and high levels of illiteracy, they found it extremely difficult to get work permits. Prejudices and negative stereotypes contribute to further obstruct their integration into the labor market. The first time that the situation of the Roma people in Europe came to the attention of the Irish media was when several families (86 people) camped at a roundabout on the M50 motorway in North Dublin at the beginning of July 2007 (Martín and Hibernian Consulting, 2007). As a result many papers ran articles providing information about the Roma community and their situation in the countries of origin. Unable or unwilling to take any action to assist them, the Irish government opted to repatriate them back to Romania. Even though there is a general lack of information about the socio-economic status of the Roma community living in Ireland, there is some information gathered by different projects. Roma in Ireland, especially those who arrived after 2007, experience great difficulty accessing services (EQUAL Report, 2006). Facing language and cultural barriers, the Roma population often end up in situations of conflict with service providers thus exacerbating prejudices against them (Martín and Hibernian Consulting, 2007; Martín, 2008). The lack of knowledge of the cultural background of the Roma community prevalent among host societies contributes to the misunderstanding and the simplification of their culture and traditions. Their strong patriarchal social structures combined with the pervasiveness of early marriages and the poor attendance of Roma children at school further contributes to the creation of negative stereotypes against them. Even though many might need services, Roma families are reluctant to use them lest they be expelled by the Irish authorities.

Some of the problems that the Roma population faced when accessing services were compounded by low level of education, low socio-economic status, lack of trust in services (due to their persecution in the past), lack of understanding of the services in Ireland, and linguistic and cultural differences. While many difficulties were common to what other minorities arriving in Ireland experienced, in the case of the Roma population, they were more pronounced.

The second cultural mediation project in Ireland was developed with the financial support of the European Social Fund under its EQUAL Community Initiative Program. Managed by the Department of Enterprise, EQUAL was meant to operate as a laboratory to test new practices. The Roma Cultural Mediation Project set out to do just that, to pilot a cultural mediation program for the Roma population. The Roma Cultural Mediation Project (RCMP) aimed at providing

Roma people with greater equality of access to health, social, educational and probation services, and the associated benefits that resulted from their use, while in parallel developing appropriate professional skills and intercultural competences among service providers.

From the beginning of the project, it was very clear that we needed to strive for the professionalization of cultural mediation not only to convince Irish service providers but also to introduce the service among the Roma community. Cultural mediators, in our program all women, needed to be seen as professionals to be accepted by the Roma families with which they were working.

To pursue formal certification in cultural mediation training was one of the objectives of the new project as a way to encourage its professionalization. However, the time requirements that formal certification demands is often difficult to implement. Roma women have a lot of responsibilities in the home and their free time to devote to courses is limited. In our case, our participants could not commit to the minimum length of time necessary to seek a formal certification.

The training was tailored specifically to the Roma population. In a similar way to the JOIN project, the Roma cultural mediators were requested to take work cases as cultural mediators' trainees. Within the EQUAL project we tailored many of the protocols and guidelines created under JOIN. We also developed a pilot project for Temple Street hospitals, one of the best known children's hospitals in Ireland. Some of the cases in which the cultural mediators were involved in the Health service included work in foster care, with teenage mothers, cases of domestic violence, providing support for vaccination awareness, and giving assistance in monitoring medical procedures and treatments. Roma cultural mediators also helped to raise awareness about the needs of the Roma population among police and probation officers as well as teachers.

Overall it was a very successful project and we gathered valuable feedback from service providers and Roma users[1]. In 2008 the Equality Authority selected the Roma Cultural Mediation Project to highlight good practice in Ireland. This project was deemed to meet the Living Together criteria[2].

A comprehensive training program in CM is paramount to attain a professional status. Their job of being in the 'middle' is challenging. It is for this that cultural mediators need to develop several skills; they need to know how to establish dialogue with people from different cultural backgrounds, to be aware of how culture and other factors can hinder access to services; they need to know services well and how to help others navigate them. They need to be aware of different communication patterns and have mediation and negotiating skills.

---

[1] For further details of the EQUAL Roma Cultural Mediation Project, please see the publication,

[2] Criteria that came from the transnational project "Living Together: European Citizenship against Racism and Xenophobia". This initiative was co-financed by the European Commission, Directorate-General Justice, Freedom, Security-Fundamental Rights and Citizenship EU Program (2007-2009). This project aimed at "the promotion of a European discourse of tolerance, based on the generation of a rationale for harmony and respect, on recognition of differences, and on building European citizenship estranged from any kind of racism and xenophobia"
(http://ec.europa.eu/ewsi/en/practice/details.cfm?ID_ITEMS=1870)

Furthermore, they need to be trained in a code of practice and how to behave in a professional manner. It is, after all, this professional and unbiased conduct that helps them to be accepted by their communities and service providers.

While the JOIN and the EQUAL training programs contributed significantly to the recognition of CM among Irish service providers, we realized the need to develop other resources, including a code of practice, a protocol for the service, a description of the role of cultural mediators, as well as guidelines for service providers.

The following guidelines were developed in the context of the EQUAL Roma Cultural Mediation Project:

DEFINITION OF CULTURAL MEDIATION

> Cultural mediation is a dynamic, continuous process through which a third party acts as a cultural broker between two parties and assists both of them in reaching a common understanding and in interacting more satisfactorily. Cultural mediators solve and especially help prevent conflicts caused by cultural misunderstandings and contribute to the creation of a new social reality.

PROTOCOL OF SERVICE

- Selection of a cultural mediator;
- Arrangement of a planning meeting between service provider(s), cultural mediator and project personnel to provide more detailed information about the case and to agree on first contact with client, ensuing actions, timeline and feedback;
- Intervention;
- Evaluation by service providers and clients involved in the intervention.

CODE OF PRACTICE

Cultural mediator shall:

- Maintain confidentiality and boundaries;
- Remain neutral (outcome);
- Behave impartially (process);
- Maintain a high level of performance (mediation techniques, professional attitude, and cultural awareness);
- Facilitate accurate information;
- Not to interfere with the work of service providers;
- Reject cases which cannot be undertaken in a professional manner;
- Respect clients' cultural and religious values;
- Refrain from abusing their power;
- Establish a relationship of trust and confidence with clients and service providers;
- Abstain from accepting any form of payment from clients.

TASKS OF A CULTURAL MEDIATOR

Cultural Mediators will strive to:

- Facilitate communication between service providers and Roma clients
- Assist both parties to reach a common understanding and to interact more satisfactorily
- Help service providers to understand and be aware of culture specific practices
- Establish a relationship of trust and confidence between clients and service providers
- Support and encourage clients to voice their views and concerns
- Help Roma clients to gain a better understanding of the Irish services
- Create a space for mutual understanding and therefore prevent potential conflict between service providers and Roma clients

HOW TO WORK WITH CULTURAL MEDIATORS: GUIDELINES FOR SERVICE PROVIDERS

- Cultural Mediators (CM) are professionals and should be treated as such;
- Strive to create a relationship of mutual respect and trust with the CM;
- Provide adequate briefing about the case;
- Explain the purpose of the intervention and the time commitment expected from CM Make sure you explain what is expected from the CM;
- Review the code of practice of CM in the presence of the CM Clarify any relevant policy or protocol of your agency to the CM;
- Set a strategy for supervision and feedback jointly with the CM for the duration of the case;
- Agree with CM or project staff an evaluation system before the intervention begins;
- Allow more time for appointments assisted by CM;
- Maintain your relationship with your client; ensure you keep regular eye contact with client;
- Ensure that your role and the role of the CM is explained carefully to the client;
- Keep an open communication with the CM and project staff In case of unprofessional behavior from the CM report back to project staff.

References

EQUAL Report (2006). *Training Roma as Cultural Mediators*. (Retrieved from http://ec.europa.eu/employment_social/equal_consolidated/data/document/IE%20-%20training%20roma%20as%20cultural%20mediators.pdf)

Lesovitch, L. (2005). *Roma Educational Needs in Ireland: Context and Challenges*, City of Dublin VEC in association with Pavee Point Travellers Centre and the Roma Support Group. Dublin: City of Dublin VEC.

Martín, M. and Hibernian Consulting (2007). *Fitting In: How Cultural Mediation Supports the Integration of the Roma Community in Ireland*. Funded under EQUAL Community Initiative. (Retrieved from http://www.ideasbank.ie/files/FittingIn.pdf)

Martín, M. (2008). The Roma population in Europe: a brief look at the Situation in Ireland. *Translocations: Migration and Social Change*. *4*(1), 118-127.

Martín, M. and Phelan, M. (2009). Interpreters and Cultural Mediators - different but complementary roles. *Translocations: Migration and Social Change*. *6* (1).

Minervino, S. and Martín, M. (2007). Cultural Competence and Cultural Mediation: Diversity Strategies and Practices in Health Care. *Translocations: Migration and Social Change*. *2*(1).

Chapter 14: Lisbon Community Policing: The Challenge of the Intercultural and Mediation Approach

Mónica Diniz and Cláudia Santa Cruz

"I'm neither I, nor the other one, I am something in between."

- Mário de Sá-Carneiro

A New Paradigm of Intervention for the Lisbon Municipal Police

Security policies and institutions whose role is to maintain and ensure security are facing new challenges, namely the paradigm of prevention, mediation, proximity and partnership. The community policing model embodies these approaches, as a preventive police-citizens response to the new security challenges in our cities. The logic of police-citizens proximity increases the police effectiveness and legitimacy, which according to Oliveira (2006, p. 85) can be analyzed in three dimensions: spatial, temporal and relational. The physical presence of the police officers, through an on foot patrol, in the same territory, taking into account the security priorities and needs felt by citizens in that particular territory (spatial dimension). The police community team working schedules adapted those specific priorities and needs (temporal dimension). The same police officers that are easily recognized by citizens, patrolling and interacting with a more familiar, accessible, transparent and humanized communication style (relational dimension).

The relational proximity of police to citizens, and this humanized dimension addressing security problems, gives a new conception of the police function, with a greater concern for social cohesion when dealing with those problems. Therefore, the police working in partnership with local partners and citizens (in the context of community groups), enables the police to address, in a concerted manner, security problems that have not an exclusively police nature, assuming that security problems can be addressed also through new social practices based on dialogue and leading to the co-production of safety (Oliveira, p.86 cit.

Gleizalm, 1997). In this sense, the police expect partners to contribute in the identification and cooperation in solving community problems that can trigger situations of crime and violence and/or increase the feeling of insecurity (*e.g.* incivilities in public space, truancy or inadequate planning of public space).

Aware of these new challenges, the Lisbon Municipal Police (LMP), a police organization presently with 463 workers (73% police officers, 20% civilian staff and 7% forest rangers), through the implementation of a community policing model, has been trying to find new ways of intervention, to improve security responses in the city, placing emphasis on a crucial aspect, an inside look at its human capital and the need to develop - through a training strategy - the philosophy and practices of the organization.

The Community Policing Strategy

Since 2007, the LMP has been developing a preventive approach through a community policing strategy, seeking the maintenance of public tranquility and the improvement of the quality of life in the city. To this end, the participation of the LMP in community groups has been crucial, since it allows the reflection and definition of concerted intervention strategies with citizens and local partners, engaging the community itself in the process of identifying their main security concerns and proposal of resolutions.

Following this strategy, the LMP has conducted a pilot-experience on community policing in close cooperation with local partners of *Alta de Lisboa*, a northern residential area of Lisbon (with approximately 34,000 inhabitants), composed by social and private housing and with an ethnically and culturally diverse population. In this sense, the community policing "Safer *Alta de Lisboa*", is a policing planned and built together by the LMP and local partners, sensitive to an intercultural approach, promoting awareness for the diversity advantage and for the importance of the active role of all citizens as co-producers of safety on the territory they inhabit.

The project started in 2009, through the integration of the LMP in the Community Group of *Alta de Lisboa* (GCAL), which comprises around thirty community partner organizations (e.g. schools, resident associations – both from social and private housing - health center, child and youth care centers, day care centres for the elderly, NGO's). The community policing in *Alta de Lisboa*, aiming to contribute to the reduction of anti-social behavior and the increase of the sense of security in the community, promotes the involvement of local partners in the process of planning preventive activities in the community. Through these activities, and community meetings, it's encouraged the involvement of citizens in the reflection and discussion about how to create a safer community, incorporating the police those contributions. In this sense, this approach empowers citizens to participate on security at local level, promoting awareness and a participative citizenship on local security issues (Diniz, 2011, p. 57).

The articulation of the police with local partners, also allows a better understanding of the territory vulnerabilities and potentialities, and the design and implementation of responses to the effective needs of the citizens. As a result of this close cooperation, it was created in 2010, a specific working group to deal with the local security problems - the Security Group - in which the local partners and the LMP planned the implementation in the field of a foot patrol by police officers of the LMP – the community policing team. By conducting focus groups with the population, partners and other local actors, the Security Group identified the main problems of the territory, the critical areas and the profile of the police officers needed for the community policing in *Alta de Lisboa*. Based on the results, the police officers were selected and was designed the training program to prepare them to the new community policing approach in Lisbon.

The Intercultural Approach in the Training Strategy

Alongside with the standard technical training in critical areas for the LMP to comply with its mission (*e.g.* law enforcement legislation, road traffic regulation or municipal regulation), the LMP training strategy, in the last years, has been changing, to focus also in the development of personal and social skills to enable the police officers to deal with new urban security problems and social conflict situations. To this end, there has been a strong investment in training strategic police groups, so that they can act on the environment in which they interact as professionals, promoting the awareness of the implicit social responsibility on the quality of their performance, namely in learning skills *"to know"*, *"to do"* and *"to be"*. This latter dimension - learning *"to be"* – as a behavioral dimension of the individual, that influences to a large extent all the other dimensions. So, the LMP officers training has been grounded in the development and improvement of personal, social and relational skills, particularly in terms of assertiveness, communication, conflict management, team work and problem solving, being trained, so far, around 33% (163) of the total police workforce.

In the context of a community policing, where the police officers are more integrated in the social tissue, and therefore acting as social cohesion agents, there is an increasing need of the police to use a preventive approach, in close articulation with other social control agencies (e.g. family, school or social services), since the presence of the police in the community daily conflicts gives it a crucial role in their peaceful settlement (Berlanga et al., 2009).

The training of community policing teams by the LMP takes into account that communities are formed by groups of people who regulate their conduct among each other, based on their social and cultural identity. So, the knowledge of that social and cultural identity of the groups within a given community, by police officers, it's critical to the implementation of the public security policies. To understand the social identity of these groups, it's necessary for the police officers to train social skills and to have the knowledge of their reference values, their goals, their notion of conformity and deviance, their expectations and stereotypes towards others, knowing also the history of their interactions with other groups and also with the group of policemen (Felgueiras, 2009, p. 158). These social skills include social cognitive variables, such as the ability to transform and use information, knowledge of socially competent behaviours, knowledge of social attitudes, knowledge of different types of responses, being able to take the place of the other, or having strategies that enable them to analyze the social behavior of others (Matos, 2000 *et al* cit. Caballo, 1987).

In the case of the planning of the community policing in *Alta de Lisboa*, only after the GCAL security group planning meetings, and the focus groups with the population - for the identification of the expectations, goals, main problems to be tackled and profiling of the police officers for the community policing team - was possible to design the training program. In this case, and taking into account the territory specificities, the training was focused on key areas such as the theoretical model of community policing, interpersonal relationship skills, intercultural competences and conflict resolution and problem solving techniques in community context. In the frame of intercultural competences training, a local partner was invited to speak to police officers on this theme, namely addressing the legal instruments related to immigrant's policies, human rights, statistics on foreign population, communication and cooperation skills. This was the first intercultural approach on the training program of the LMP, seeking the development of competences to the interaction police-citizens with different cultural backgrounds, given emphasis on the peace-keeping function of the police when dealing with community conflicts. For instance, it was made the reflection about culture and identity and on attitudes and behaviors adopted in multicultural contexts, stressing the importance of values such as mutual respect, dignity, solidarity and justice and the value of the cultural diversity.

The community policing training has been targeting not only the community policing teams, but also other police groups of the LMP, so that the model of intervention can be incorporated by all the organization workers. This allows also an opportunity to receive contributions to the model from other police groups - with different professional experiences - diminishing the resistances that often appear towards this model of policing, often seen by other police officers as a social work rather than a police work. Since 2011, were trained, up to now, about 30% (137) of the LMP workers.

The theoretical model of community policing is approached as a policing strategy aiming the quality and efficiency of the police performance, in a citizen-oriented manner, with the objective to provide security and the sense of security, and reduce and prevent crime and public disturbances, maintaining the positive image of the police, and the trust placed in the police at a high level (Virta, 2007, p. 2).

Regarding the interpersonal skills, communication skills play a key role on police officers training. Within a strategy of police intervention in the community, the police communication process is fundamental to the extent that can bring closer the perception that citizens have of the events, with the perceptions of the police. This communication process can be developed also by other actors, for instance, community mediators with recognized prestige by the community (Felgueiras, 2009, p. 159). Besides the training on communication techniques of the police officers with the population and local partners, is also essential training their ability to work together with stakeholders that facilitate also the resolution of community problems.

The importance of the organization develop intercultural competences is stressed in the training as a challenge to the construction of a more inclusive, and therefore, more secure community. In this context, the training sensitizes police officers to the advantages of cultural diversity as a basis for building understanding and awareness for the cultural differences and how to address those differences, by adapting police behaviors to different cultural settings.

In the training session addressing the conflict resolutions and problem solving techniques, it's stressed that the police presence in everyday conflicts, places the community policing teams in a central role, particularly in solving neighborhood problems, which, if not addressed swiftly, can escalate to severer security problems in the community.

The Need for a Police Mediation Culture

Several studies have showed that the role of the police is essential in reducing the occasions for the practice of offenses, namely by the presence of the police officers in the field (Oliveira, 2006, p.82 cit. Wilson and Kelling, 1982; Skogan 1998). Indeed, the proximity and cooperation between the police and citizens, can contribute to the establishment of security priorities and the implementation of preventive interventions (*e.g.* through community meetings in neighborhoods where community spirit is low and crime rates are higher) to strengthen the bonds of trust between the police and citizens, and to increase the informal control mechanisms in the community. As a result, the police action in the field of prevention, allows the extension of the police legitimacy, since the police is no longer required only in case of offenses, but playing also a key role on social mediation.

In this line of thought, since November 2011 - when the community policing team started the daily on foot patrol in *Alta de Lisboa* - the LMP has been planning and promoting, together with the security group local partners, crime prevention activities. These activities, although targeting all community, have been more focused at vulnerable groups (*e.g.* workshops to elderly residents on recommendations about safe behavior; study visits to the facilities of the LMP, to diminish the barriers between youngsters and the police officers or the visit of police officers to schools to debate the importance of the preservation of public spaces or bullying prevention).

The community policing by stimulating the citizen participation in security issues, increases the knowledge of the "other" (both of the police and of the citizens amongst themselves), allowing the police and the citizens to be in a closer contact, becoming the relationships more fluid and bilateral. As a consequence, the police has more support from the population and the population has a better understanding of the police view. Since the police officers have a better knowledge of the community, they are therefore in a better position to address and manage its conflicts. Being the police and justice incapable to solve all conflicts, mediation strategies and a mediation attitude from the police officers can be an important tool to complement the efforts of conflict resolution, namely in cultural diverse communities.

The mediation of conflicts is a way of solving conflicts, legally framed, in which the parties are assisted by a mediator, whose aim will be to find an amicable and negotiated solution to the conflict (Campos, 2008). The benefits of mediation for police officers reflect into a greater understanding of citizens' actions, to the extent that, as mediators, the police officers have the opportunity to hear the versions of the parties in the conflict and then create their own perspective (Kian, 2011). This mediation attitude from the police officers, of communication and active listening, allows the police to be closer to the citizens, contributing to one of the primary goals of the community policing, a trusting relationship between the police and the citizens, aiming the increase of their sense of security and quality of life.

In this sense, alongside with the development of intercultural competences, the training of police officers on mediation skills is of particular importance to the community policing strategy. Since it's a model of policing firmed on the principles of prevention and citizens participation, requires from the police officers a mediation attitude in the community, of active listening and concern in hearing all the people. In the context of cultural diverse communities, this is of a crucial value, where the capacity for police officers to involve all the different social groups in the discussion of local security problems is critical to prevent the feeling of exclusion and to give better and more effective community safety responses.

According to Fachada (2000) active listening means that we pay attention not only to the content of each message parts, but also to the feelings and emotions involved in them, the non-verbal language and the context in which the message is delivered (p. 197). From this idea, it is easy to understand that active listening is of huge importance in a mediation attitude from the police officers, since it is essential that all the parties involved in a given conflict be able to express their opinion and disagreement, being also important to explore the feelings, values and attitudes of all involved, in order to meet the most suitable solution to the situation. The active listening is therefore one of the skills that contribute to the quality and effectiveness of communication process (Ferraz, 2012, cit. Torrego, 2003), since it creates empathy and, in turn, this facilitates and allows a climate conducive to meet satisfactory solutions to a given conflict , revealing itself as a fundamental technique in any mediation process. The lack of training these social skills in police officers, may lead to difficulties in situations of social interaction, namely the level of acceptance of criticism, dealing with citizens provocations, loss of control, or expressing opinions and emotions, essential characteristics for the performance of the police in mediation processes.

The training of these skills it's essential to the extent that police officers are a professional group that is faced daily with citizens and problematic situations that require a proper decision, prior to a suitable action, which is not always possible in high risk and conflict situations. Indeed, the policing teams face on a daily basis, several constraints that affect their performance and are generating stress. So, the police work requires an effective response and a quality performance when addressing the problems identified in the community by requiring, from police teams, commitment and creativity in managing the resources they have at their disposal to help solving the community security problems.

In this context, it's essential to give the police officers tools to allow proper management of their relational and communicational repertoire, for being able to manage conflict situations, using assertive communication styles and conflict management techniques, such as the mediation attitude. This premise becomes even more important when the police officers are integrated in community policing teams, being the daily direct contact with the citizens, their problems and their vulnerabilities, a constant and at the same time, requiring a broad range of skills that they need to use, adapt and adjust according to the settings and situations they have to deal with.

In Portugal, the police officer is by the nature of its profession a natural mediator, someone who is, in general, recognized by the citizens with a fair and legitimate position to mediate conflicts between citizens. In this sense, the mediation skills from the police officers can play an important role, not only to help solving conflicts, but also to promote social cohesion, by improving the relationship of the citizens amongst each other. In conflicts that need to be tackled swiftly, the mediation posture from police officers can allow the creation of dialogue channels between the different parties in conflict so that the communication can be re-established. Therefore, the mediation skills training, addressing conflict resolution techniques, can be an important contribution to the police officers performance, contributing to improve both police-citizen and citizen-citizen interaction.

Since the community policing stresses the importance of the citizens participation and the listening to the other, allowing different looks to the same community problem, a mediation attitude from police officers, can enable the establishing of social bonding, by not just putting all in agreement, but mostly, by putting the different parties in dialogue. In order to do that, the police officers need to develop also competences on how to listen, how to communicate, and how to be able to make themselves heard by different social groups, so that they can, through a mediation posture, create the conditions to address conflicts and allow the citizens in conflict to communicate and be able to listen to each other.

The mediation skills training is therefore crucial to the community policing teams, with a focus on simulation of real situations, in which the essential basis is in putting the police officer in the place of others, accepting their differences and adopting a style of communication marked by assertiveness and active listening.

The community policing pilot-experience in *Alta de Lisboa* allowed a better understanding of the community challenges, helping guiding the LMP training strategy for the near future, namely in how to develop in police officers the skills to sustain and enhance the police-citizen articulation, involving all social groups - particularly in cultural diverse communities - on the identification and building up of local security responses together with the police. In fact, the presence of the LMP, through its on foot policing, closer to the citizens, in the context of the city intercultural events - like *Festival Todos: Caminhada de Culturas* (*All Festival: A Walk of Cultures*) - has proven in practice, a source of learning about different cultures that inhabit the city of Lisbon. This closer contact with different cultural communities in this type of events, raises police officers awareness for the diverse cultural identities, and hence, their self-confidence to cope and manage situations of rising conflict's, being more prepare to take an integrative, facilitator and mediator role, in their management and settlement.

This new model of policing in Lisbon, in closer articulation with the community, shows that Lisbon, as other European cities, is full of diverse cultures, people with different beliefs, values and life experiences, cohabiting all together in the same neighborhood. When conflicts between these different cultures arise, is up to the police organizations in general, and the city police in particular, the ultimate response to maintain security and public tranquility, playing the police frequently a mediation role between the parties in conflict. In this sense, it's of great importance to encourage the citizen's empowerment on security issues, to co-produce security in their own communities, being the cultural competency and mediation skills of the police officers a vital way to promote the social cohesion in the community. The results of this model of policing recommends that, for the police to be able to articulate with the citizens and to establish a trusting relationship in diverse cultural contexts, it's important that the LMP training strategy focus on intercultural learning skills of the police officers, as well as the development of mediation skills in order to address the different conflicts in the community. This training approach assumes that the police officers will be more apt and able to manage conflict and mediate them, knowing that the benefits of the acquisition and/or training of these skills, are not limited only to the promotion of professional skills but also the empowerment and personal growth, that prepare police officers for change, for innovation and to deal with the unexpected and the uncertain.

The steps taken so far, in the community policing strategy, suggest that the success of this intercultural and mediation approach relies on the investment on skills training and lies in key factors such as the level of integration of the police officers in the community, the support of the police hierarchy and the involvement of other police officers - besides the community policing team - in the training activities, which makes this model of policing a core challenge to the LMP, to the citizens and to the city.

References

Berlanga Sanchez, A., Diego Orozco, J.L. (Coord.s) (2009). Buenas Práticas para la Prevención de la Delincuencia: La Mediación Policial. European Commission – Prevention of and Fight against Crime Program. Ajuntament de València, Policía Local de Valencia.

Campos, L. (2008). Mediação de Conflitos: Enquadramentos Institucionais e Posturas Epistemológicas. Mediation in Action – A Mediação em Ação. Coimbra: Minerva Coimbra, 167-195.

Diniz, M. (2011). Práticas Policiais e Cidadania a Nível Local: a Participação dos Cidadãos no contexto do Policiamento Comunitário "Alvalade mais Seguro". ISCTE - Instituto Universitário de Lisboa. (Master Thesis).

Fachada, M. O. (2000). Psicologia das Relações Interpessoais. Lisboa: Edições Rumo.

Felgueiras, S. A. (2009). *Atividade Policial na Gestão da Violência. in Reuniões e Manifestações – Atuação Policial*. Edições Almedina, SA, Valente, M.M.G. (Coord.). Coimbra. 139-162.

Ferraz, F. L. (2012). *A Formação em Mediação de Conflitos no Desenvolvimento Profissional dos Assistentes Operacionais, em Escola Pública do 1º Ciclo do Ensino Básico*. Lisboa: Instituto Politécnico de Lisboa, Escola Superior de Educação de Lisboa.

Kian, M. (2011). *Implementing Conflict Resolution Processes to Enhance Community-Police Relations: Lessons Learned in Convening Mediations and Dialogues*. California: University of San Diego´s Kroc School of Peace Studies.

Matos, M. G. et al. (2000). *Desenvolvimento de Competências de Vida na Prevenção do Desajustamento Social*. Lisboa: Ministério da Justiça.

Oliveira, J.F. (2006). *As Políticas de Segurança e os Modelos de Policiamento: A Emergência do Policiamento de Proximidade*. Edições Almedina, SA. Coimbra.

Virta, S. (2007). *Community Policing Strategy: Strategic Outlines and Objectives of Community Policing and Security Cooperation Development*. Committee's Final Report. Lisbon: Publication of the Police Department of the Ministry of the Interior.

Chapter 15: Co-creation and Inclusion Tools Benefiting Interculturalism of Patras

Maria Andrikopoulou - Rouvali

Introduction

The intercultural character of the city of Patras as a parameter of development plays a key role in the planning of its policies. Patras in recent 20 years, has been inhabited by many people coming from Europe as Albanians, Romanians, Bulgarians, Russians as well as people from Africa & Asia e.g. from Nigeria, Syria, China, India. Since 2008, Patras has been an active member of the "Intercultural Cities" network, coordinated by the Council of Europe very effectively. The successful operation of the network by CoE, has helped Patras to manage multiculturalism as a source of growth. The network is mainly European but has also developed contacts in Canada, USA, Mexico and Japan.

The management of intercultural issues coordinated by the Vice-Municipality of "Support of Citizen, Volunteerism, Gender Equality & Integration of migrants" of the Municipality of Patras and is supported by the "Patras Municipal Enterprise for Planning & Development-ADEP SA". The measures taken for vulnerable groups such as migrants, women and young people, target various fields of actions, including services for citizens, education and culture.

Tools & Structures

With regard to migrants as target group, a key-role "player" in this effort is the "Council for the Integration of Migrants (CIM)" of Patras, a valuable tool for participation, representation and promotion of the views of migrants at the local level.

- It participated in the public consultation on the draft of "National Strategy for Social Integration of third country nationals 2012-2015", with comments and observations

- It collaborates with the new structure of the open multi-clinic of "Medecins du Monde" in the city of Patras
- It is involved in the distribution of printed material courtesy of the Centre for European Constitutional Law Foundation "Themistocles Tsatsos", regarding the multilingual guide on preventive health care, in order to inform and raise awareness among immigrants.
- It supports actively and participates with presentations to all study-visits of experts of the Council of Europe at Patras
- It works actively in all the activities of European projects on interculturalism
- It supports the learning of Greek language to migrants, through initiatives made by both the municipality and by the organizations-members of the local network for interculturalism in Patras
- It organizes sports activities involving all natives and migrants, in cooperation with voluntary organizations and associations
- It collaborates with cultural institutions to develop innovative actions (such as with the Municipal Theatre of Patras for organizing theatrical performance with true stories of migrant women)
- It interfaces with other CIM of Greek cities to exchange information and experiences, such as with the CIM of the Municipality Korydallos (area of Athens). Networking has been created between the two SEMs due to their participation in a PROGRESS project coordinated by National Secretariat of Gender Equality in Greece, focusing on migrant women. Emphasis is put on joint interventions e.g. at the Greek Ministry of Interior Affairs.
- In the same context, a consortium has been established between CIM Patras and NGO "AMKE Support" for the implementation of a PROGRESS project within the measure of "Support to NGOs Women Organization" Operation Plan of "2007-2013".

Regarding specific actions, it is worth mentioning the action of providing food and clothes to migrants who have no economic ability. It concerns 250 migrants three times a week who are given bread donated by bakeries at the city of Patras.
The rate of poverty is increasing day by day in Patras. Therefore, at this stage emphasis is put on charities, utilizing volunteering through the operation of the Department of "Volunteerism & Equality Policy" of the Municipality of Patras.
The role of volunteers for the implementation of actions is determining, considering the extremely difficult economic situation, both in Patras and throughout Greece.

The volunteer members who support the work of the Department, numbering about 650 people, constitute Team "Epsilon" and support various social structures of the Municipality of Patras, such as:

- Organization of the Municipal Wardrobe: It is supported by volunteer organizations of the city, shopkeepers and all citizens. It serves over 1200 families every two months.
- Organization of Social Pharmacy in collaboration with the Pharmaceutical Association, which works with the voluntary offer of

pharmacists. The supply of medicine by pharmacists, companies, voluntary organizations and citizens is exceptional.

- Organization of Social Clinic, working with the voluntary Medical Association, the Medical Faculty of the University of Patras and the Union of Hospital Physicians of Achaia, so that poor and uninsured residents can be examined for free.
- Organization of Social Pediatric Clinic, working with the voluntary assistance of the Association of Private Pediatricians of Patras.

It is noteworthy that the Vice-Municipality of "Education, Transparency & Electronic Consultation" is networked with the "Directorate of Primary & Secondary Education of Achaia prefecture", the "University of Patras" and "Achaia Association of Teachers" in order to support the students, who are children from socially vulnerable families for their lessons. This is called "Social Tutorial" which has been organized into four schools of Patras and involves the voluntary teaching of active and retired teachers and students of the University of Patras, who are members of "Team Epsilon" group of volunteers of the Municipality.

The Municipality of Patras and its organizations are very active in projects. By exploiting national funding, the following social structures have established:

- "Social Grocery " with enriched services based on the pre-existing "Bank of Food" and Municipal Wardrobe", books, toys, school supplies and provision of psycho-social support;
- "Providing food" to 140 beneficiaries on a daily basis;
- "Time Bank " an alternative trading system for the exchange of products and services, with no use of currency;
- "Mediation Office" for providing information and service requests of members of vulnerable groups who wish to exploit the social structures and other actions of the Municipality benefiting them.

Currently, the structure of "Municipal Vegetable Gardens" is being designed which will benefit at least 100 poor families, while giving them the possibility of productive activity.

Providing counseling services to all members of vulnerable groups using the above structures, is regarded as an integral part of the whole process, with particular importance for the beneficiaries. Within this effort, it is important to note the partnership among the Vive-Municipality of "Social Policy, Health and Prevention" and the "Social Organization of the Municipality of Patras" as well as voluntary organizations and social partner organizations of the city.

It is also worth referring to the cooperation with "UNHCR" and the "PRAKSIS" NGO for the implementation of the project entitled "Protection of Children on the Move". The aim of the project was to develop measures for the reception and counseling of unaccompanied children with emphasis on those that do not have access to asylum procedures and other protection mechanisms.

In the same context, recognizing the need to create structures for unaccompanied minors in the city, the Municipality of Patras supported operators of «PRAKSIS» NGO, Red Cross and childcare workers with a proposal to create such a structure. The proposal was adopted by the International Organization for Migration and the respective structure has already started being prepared (it is expected to operate in 2014).

The project on the voluntary return of third country migrants coordinated by International Organization of Migration has launched in Patras, supported by the Municipality. Related space has been allocated for the needs of implementing the program and direct liaison is maintained with the Vice-Municipality in charge. Networking described above regarding all these structures, services and initiatives, is considered as a dynamic process, "open" to all who wish to participate in order to achieve synergy and multiplier effects .

Women as a Target Group

Last but not least, special reference must be made to women as one of the vulnerable groups.

Women's unemployment rate has already reached 30% - unemployment of young women has reached 65%, while unemployment rate of young men has surpassed 50%. The Municipality of Patras has signed the "European Charter for Gender Equality in Local Communities" and retains continuous cooperation with the General Secretariat for Gender Equality. With respect to the basic principles of the Charter, the Municipality of Patras:

- has organized and operates a shelter for abused women (regardless of ethnicity and religion) and their children;
- has successfully implemented a project funded by PROGRESS program in 2012 regarding the incorporation of a gender perspective in the individual strategies of the municipality.

At this stage, Patras Municipal Enterprise for Planning & Development-ADEP SA implements EU projects benefiting vulnerable groups focusing on Roma, migrants, Muslims, women and young people. Local networks of partner organizations are organized for this regard.

Remarks

- Many stakeholders on board is the strongest message (*synergy*);
- If there is no clear political position any communication message would be abstract;
- The genuine intercultural city cannot emerge from disconnected initiatives on policy changes;
- Sustainability and effectiveness of the results also relies on the establishment of partnerships and alliances within each city but also on national and international levels;
- Due to the experience gained as a result of actions at local and European level, the Municipality of Patras is an active partner constantly trying for improvement.

Chapter 16: The Concept of an Intercultural Strategy for Patras: Objectives, Actions, Lessons

Chrissa Geraga

Background: Geopolitical Location

Patras enjoys a remarkable history of engagement with the wider world going back to ancient times, with successive conquests leaving a rich heritage of cultural sediments, like the Byzantine cupola inside the dome of St Andrew's Cathedral. Already a significant port during the Roman empire — its remains still visible in the Odeon — in the last millennium it was embroiled in the Crusades and came under the dominion at different times of Venetians and Ottomans. In the van of the revolution of 1821, it was finally liberated seven years later by a French expeditionary force. The failure of Garibaldi's revolution brought Italians to its shores. This cosmopolitan tradition brought the city to a high level of civilization, joining other major European cultural centers in 1872 in constructing a municipal theatre and opera house, with an Italian stage and co-founded by a Bavarian winemaker.

By the turn of the 20th century Patras had become an important port for the western Peloponnese and in 1922 was to receive an influx of refugees from Asia Minor. The raisin business was to bring an English presence. Cypriot refugees were to flee the troubles which began on the island in the 1960s. Migration in recent decades has brought Albanians, Romanians, Bulgarians and Russians, as well as newcomers from further afield. The University of Patras attracts students not only from across Greece but from other Mediterranean countries. The municipality is twinned with Limassol, the Cypriot Intercultural Cities member, and is a member of the Balcinet network of Balkan cities and the Forum of Adriatic and Ionian Cities.

Patras is thus a Mediterranean gateway, particularly to Italian east-coast cities. This is not, however, supported with adequate infrastructure in its hinterland—most manifest in the railway connection from Athens, truncated by the crisis, which the business community recognizes represents a barrier to development. Even before the crisis, a collapse in the textile industry in Patras in the 1990s led to a surge in unemployment in the city. Around three in ten of the adult population are currently unemployed.

Patras' geopolitical location has of course proved problematic in recent years, as many individuals arriving from north Africa and the middle east, lacking entitlement to remain, have identified Patras as a transit point *en route* to their hoped-for destination of one of the northern European countries, though this may be blocked by their lack of documentation or, if they are seeking asylum, by the requirement that they claim in the EU state of arrival. This humanitarian crisis requires a European solution, characterized by solidarity and burden-sharing.
It does not however prevent Patras embracing the positive nature of its positioning as a cultural bridge in the heart of the Mediterranean and resisting the efforts of those who would scapegoat migrants for the prolonged economic crisis Greece is suffering in the context of European austerity. The municipality recognizes that all the residents of the city are culturally enriched by its contemporary diversity and its distinctive heritage and that its intercultural character is, simply, a fact. Around 8 per cent of the population within the municipality of 215,000 (following the 2011 merger with four small municipalities) are of migrant background, as are 11 per cent of primary schoolchildren. This is reflected in the designation of a deputy mayor with a brief to cover 'volunteerism, gender equality, NGOs, integration of immigrants and services for the citizens', and in the establishment of a Council for the Integration of Immigrants and an Office of Services for the Immigrants. This sends out a strong signal of political commitment at senior level to the intercultural project.

The municipality has developed strong relationships with all the key civil-society actors in the city. Apart from the migrant associations, these importantly include the social partners, cultural actors and the University of Patras. These network connections are invaluable, particularly in the context of a constrained municipal budget, in ensuring intercultural practice is a meaningful reality on the ground. They extend beyond the physical to the virtual, building on the experience in the city of projects on intercultural communication. It will be in activating these connections, with the municipality playing the role of *animateur* that this intercultural strategy will come to life.

Strategic Planning at Municipal Level

Aim

The aim of Patras' intercultural strategy is:

> To develop Patras as an intercultural meeting point, imbued with a spirit of openness, as a co-creation of the municipality, civil society and the residents of the city.

Objectives

It is noteworthy that the key-objectives of the intercultural strategy of Patras are:

1. To foster the social inclusion of all those who wish to make Patras their home and address the humanitarian needs of those only temporarily resident in the city.
2. To model intercultural life in public spaces through festivals, theatre, exhibitions and more generally the performing and visual arts, as well as the internet.
3. To socialize especially young people in Patras into intercultural norms and experiences, via formal and non-formal education and creative use of social media.
4. To address the challenges of on-the-ground diversity through a network of cultural mediators and local partners respecting the diversity advantage.
5. To improve economic security by fostering intercultural innovation and labor-market integration, working with the social partners.
6. To press on the national and European levels for support for Patras in addressing its intercultural commitments.

Activities

- In order to achieve the objectives various activities are proposed, such as:
- Linking Greek language acquisition to the ability of the non-indigenous to speak in their own voice. It will seek to ensure such programs are sustained and broad in coverage, with particular recognition of the needs of women from non-Greek backgrounds.
- Provide primary health care and social support to those outside the national health and social care system, whether they be migrants or refugees, uninsured or homeless or from the Roma community.
- Take into account and try to cover the needs of unaccompanied minors (emphasis on children) arriving in the city.
- Ensure the operation of the planned refuge for victims of domestic violence as a genuinely intercultural initiative, seeking to build on the mutual support which diverse women can give each other.
- Thinking of Roma community and develop an early-intervention program, seeking to ensure Roma children get an equal start in life and recognizing this is much more effective than remedial social interventions later in the life cycle.
- Exploit cultural events of the city (emphasis on Carnival and International Summer Festival) so that to allow citizens and NGOs to consider how that diversity is managed and the contribution they can make.
- Support mother-tongue preservation among minority communities in the city, as well as Greek proficiency, while encouraging basic learning of minority languages among the general population, through specific school projects in which language acquisition becomes a vehicle for intercultural communication and mutual comprehension.

- Organize practical projects as well as formal and non-formal education; school students will be encouraged to develop a spirit of social inclusion for the marginalized.
- Encourage intercultural mediation as key parameter for active inclusion and co-creation
- Involve local media in engaging key public-agency informants with a view to ensuring all reporting is objective and evidence-based and in line with the code of ethics
- Enhance innovation as a key driver of economic progress and newcomers to Patras as a vector of development
- Broker relationships between minority-community associations and science centers, with a view to enhancing further the entrepreneurial contribution newcomers can make to the economic life of the city and region.
- Utilize Patras intercultural character and rich heritage to affirm its distinctive touristic appeal within Greece and the wider region.
- Support the development of projects targeting employment, putting emphasis on social economy initiatives.
- Initiate networking with other municipalities addressing the concerns of migrants (emphasis on youth, women and children).

Governance

In 2010 the Municipality of Patras established the "Council for the Integration of Migrants-CIM", which is chaired by the vice-mayor responsible for integration and which engages the NGOs representing migrant communities. In line with established good practice across Europe,[1] this provides a vehicle for dialogue between the city's political leadership and its migrant members, and for the co-production of events and projects. It also provides a ready-made structure for the co-management of the city's intercultural strategy, its ethos of participation for all ensuring that members of minority communities can be involved on a basis of equal citizenship with members of the 'host' community.

Resources

The Municipality of Patras will for the foreseeable future have to operate within highly straitened budgets in the national context, though EU programs will still be a potential source of support for this strategy. Existing programs and projects can however be examined to see if they can incorporate or develop an intercultural dimension, which will in any event be likely to strengthen them.

The Municipality builds on the extensive experience of ADEP (Patras Municipal Enterprise for Planning & Development) in drawing down EU funding from a range of programs. Patras can draw on a large human resource in support of this strategy through its Dpt. of "Volunteerism & Equality Policy". Established as an office of volunteerism in 2008 and the first in the country, it has now

[1] See Stuttgart Declaration on 'Foreigners' integration and participation in European cities' (2003), at https://wcd.coe.int/ViewDoc.jsp?id=882925&Site=COE

registered 650 volunteers of diverse backgrounds. They already help for the operation of various social solidarity structures operating for the benefit of vulnerable groups of population (migrants included).

Evaluation

Regular monitoring and evaluation of the intercultural strategy by the municipality will indicate the strategic importance of this issue to the political leadership. Specific indicators have been identified for this regard so that to measure outcomes and results, review actions when necessary and address milestones.

Actions at a European Level

Patras is a very extrovert city and it has gained considerable experience both in organizing large scale events as well as implementing transnational European initiatives. Considering the European context and the submission of proposals, it is achieved mainly through "Patras Municipal Enterprise for Planning & Development-ADEP SA". For this regard, ADEP is linked to the respective services of the Municipality of Patras, based on the content of the actions.

The intercultural character of Patras is a fact. It is a reality which has been accepted and it is incorporated in various actions of the Municipality. That is the reason why it had expressed interest by applying for "Intercultural Cities" European program - a pilot joint action of the Council of Europe-CoE in cooperation with the European Commission, in 2008. The activation within this network provided us the opportunity to exchange experience with the other partner-cities, to strengthen cooperation with CoE, to identify weaknesses and fields of action to be improved.

The intercultural character of Patras is revealed in various policy areas such as services for the citizens, media, education, culture, and volunteerism.

More precisely with regard to the frame of the Municipality of Patras, the Vice-Municipality of "Support to Citizen, Volunteerism, Gender Equality & Integration of Migrants" is being operating that contributes to initiatives and encourages common intercultural activities. Throughout this process and as far as "Intercultural Cities" is concerned, it is supported by ADEP SA.

It is noteworthy, that the activation of the city of Patras in "Intercultural Cities" network has enriched cooperation:

▶ "Within" the Municipality of Patras:

- Vice-Municipality of "Support to Citizen, Volunteerism, Gender Equality & Integration of Migrants"
- Vice-Municipality of "Education, Transparency & Electronic Consultation"
- Vice-Municipality of "Health, Prevention, Social Policy"
- Dpt. of "Volunteerism & Equality Policy"
- Council for the Integration of Immigrants
- Patras Cultural Organization
- Municipal & Regional Theatre of Patras / DYPETHE

- Patras Municipal Social Organization / KODYP
- ADEP SA

▶ "Outside" the Municipality of Patras:

- University of Patras / Dpt. of Education
- Hellenic Open University / Schools of Science & Technology
- Communities of Migrants (e.g. Albania, Bulgaria, Romania, Nigeria, Afganistan, Syria, etc.)
- UNHCR
- Medicine du Monde
- Institute of Labor / General Association of Workers in Greece
- Association of journalists / ESIEPIN
- NGOs
- Achaeco Institute of Adult Education
- ASTO
- AMKE Stirixis
- PRAKSIS
- Centre for Care of Family & Child / KEMOP
- CYCLISIS
- Care for Life
- Art in Progress

This networking is a dynamic process, "open" to all those who wish to participate targeting synergy and multiple effects.

The wider Greek crisis makes it impossible to release new revenues for the intercultural strategy at this time. But the municipality will privilege intercultural programs and projects within its budgeting, continue to draw down EU programs (mainly through ADEP) and, in parallel, utilize the developing human resources represented by the Dpt. of "Volunteerism & Equality Policy" and various active local NGOs.

It is noteworthy to refer briefly to such examples of projects:

> -TICTYM: it was implemented for young people highlighting the role of culture linked with active citizenship, as parameters contributing to social cohesion and partnership. Young people from Patras (representatives of theater, music and volunteering) participated in a special international seminar in Limassol (Cyprus), where music was presented as a means to be used for raising awareness on diversity. The project led to the acquaintance of Limassol (Cyprus) on the network "Intercultural Cities", and finally its inclusion as a member-city. Limassol is twinned with Patras and now it has become the core-city of ICC network in Cyprus.

> -SPARDA: it is completed successfully and it helped to eliminate stereotypes regarding diversity. Coordinator was the Council of Europe and Patras was one of the partners. It helped to strengthen relations with associations of migrants and to develop awareness through multiple

products (blogs, video, website, etc.), focusing on interventions in education and society. The awareness campaign exploited not only modern technology but also theater, music, photography and dance, incorporating an artistic character, scoring a direct intervention with great impact in the general population.

-Youth photography for interculturalism: Coordinator was the Lewisham Borough of London and the work was supported by the Council of Europe. Along with Patra partners cities were: Tilburg (Netherlands), Berlin (Germany), Lublin (Poland) and Izefsk (Russia), all being member-cities of the ICC network. The project is based on the idea that successful are those societies that manage to foster innovation and creativity with respect for diversity. In this process, young people play an important role since creativity and innovation characterize their spirit. In this project, photography was the "means" for young people to capture with their camera, how they “interpret” interculturalism in their city. More specifically, Patras organized a seminar on interculturalism, which gave young people the opportunity to address stereotypes, to reflect on basic principles of communication and to apply new forms of outreach. The photos made were exhibited to an Intercultural Centre in Lewisham Borough of London, while the young people within every city and between cities-partners, developed an intensive exchange and cooperation, applying the principles of the project in practice.

-“Support of Roma people of Achaia”: aims at the activation of Roma people in the labour market. It involves the mobilization of local bodies with a view to ensuring the creation of jobs for Roma population after diagnosis of local needs and highlighting of the growth potential in the intervention area. As a result, a social enterprise for recycling materials will be established. The project includes actions on coordination-management, counselling, training, networking and awareness. It is implemented by a Development Partnership (DP) entitled «axaia Roma» coordinated by "Daphne" (Vocational Training Centre). The Municipality of Patras is a partner through ADEP SA. The project falls under Action 3:"Local actions for social inclusion for vulnerable groups" / Intervention Category 1: "Preventing and tackling social exclusion of vulnerable groups" Thematic Priority Axis 4: "Full integration of all human resources in a society of equal opportunities" of the Operational Program "Human Resources Development" 2007-2013.

-“Combating Discrimination in the Field of Entrepreneurship: Women and young Roma and Muslim migrants”: The main aim of the project is to disseminate information on the protection against discrimination, but also to contribute to the creation of anti-discrimination reflexes in society. The aim is also to document the existing situation, the current perceptions and attitudes (e.g. discriminations) regarding the position of female and young Roma and Muslim immigrants in the labour market and to draw some conclusions for the facilitation of their access to it, but also their further development. It is funded by "PROGRESS-Antidiscrimination" EU program and it is coordinated by National Social Research Centre (EKKE) - the Municipality of Patras is a partner through ADEP SA.

-"Communication for Integration: social networking for diversity": The main aim of the project is building and strengthening social mobilization networks to foster public opinion and debate on migration and diversity and combat unfounded (but widespread) myths and misconceptions which undermine the integration strategies at local level. Emphasis is put on local actions to enhance migrants' economic, social, cultural and political participation so that to engage receiving communities in interacting with migrants, based on the mutual respect of their rights, obligations and different cultures. It is funded by grants of DG HOME/European Commission and is coordinated by the Council of Europe (CoE). All partners are members of "Intercultural Cities-ICC" network.

Submission of national and EU proposals is an on-going process.

Challenges and Lessons

The exchange within the network is based on co-creation of actions to tackle identified **challenges** that the city faces:

- To think "out of the box" to find innovative ways to overcome the barriers of financial issues;
- To cultivate an anti-stereotype behavior, putting emphasis on awareness of children and youth;
- To reveal the diversity advantage by identifying real stories of success;
- To involve the business sector in the intercultural approach;
- To establish a permanent and coherent basis for diffusing ongoing information;
- To intervene for the certification of the professional qualifications of the intercultural mediators;
- To apply co-creation and synergy in practice.

However, it is also a fact that because of their geographical location, there exist sub-regions in Europe which by default are gateways for illegal migration. Patras is one such example and the list of related cities is long. This issue affect public opinion, and in parallel complicate the considerable work and effort put into the integration of legal migrants who are inhabitants. To distinguish and clarify the two different situations into the minds of citizens, can also be regarded as a challenge.

The activation is a very live process with strengths and weaknesses and **lessons learnt** so as to become better. More specifically, we may note:

- The role of intercultural mediators in the social inclusion of migrants is of vital importance – invest in them;
- Co-creation is necessary, from the design throughout the implementation and monitoring;
- A municipality cannot substitute the state – there is always a framework that you need to respect which at the same time may present obstacles and delays;
- Concrete numbers and indicators are necessary– in this way, you have the data to monitor your actions, to measure the performance and to persuade others of the importance of continuing them;
- A smile and openness construct an excellent "bridge" to start with.

Putting emphasis on intercultural diversity, the city of Patras is aware that it is not alone. Because of the experience gained, as a result of actions at local and European level, it wants to be a very active partner contributing to effective networking. For this reason, the Municipality of Patras and its organizations remain "open" for collaboration and constructive exchange.

Chapter 17: Doctors of the World: The Role of Cultural Mediator in Combating Social Exclusion

Konstantina Kyriakopoulou

According to the Universal Declaration of Human Rights:

> All human beings are born free and equal in dignity and rights (Article 1).
>
> Everyone is entitled to all the rights and freedoms set forth in this Declaration, without distinction of any kind, such as race, color, sex, language, religion, political or other opinion, national or social origin, property, birth or other status. Furthermore, no distinction shall be made on the basis of the political, jurisdictional or international status of the country or territory to which a person belongs, whether it be independent, trust, non-self-governing or under any other limitation of sovereignty (Article 2).
>
> Everyone has the right to recognition everywhere as a person before the law (Article 6).
>
> All are equal before the law and are entitled without any discrimination to equal protection of the law. All are entitled to equal protection against any discrimination in violation of this Declaration and against any incitement to such discrimination (Article 7).
>
> Everyone has the right to an effective remedy by the competent national tribunals for acts violating the fundamental rights granted him by the constitution or by law (Article 8).
>
> Everyone has the right to freedom of movement and residence within the borders of each state (Article 13§1).

> Everyone has the right to leave any country, including his own, and to return to his country. (Article13§2).
>
> Everyone has the right to seek and to enjoy in other countries asylum from persecution. (Article14§1).
>
> Everyone has the right to freedom of thought, conscience and religion; this right includes freedom to change his religion or belief, and freedom, either alone or in community with others and in public or private, to manifest his religion or belief in teaching, practice, worship and observance (Article18).
>
> Everyone has the right to freedom of opinion and expression; this right includes freedom to hold opinions without interference and to seek, receive and impart information and ideas through any media and regardless of frontiers (Article19).
>
> Everyone, as a member of society, has the right to social security and is entitled to realization, through national effort and international co-operation and in accordance with the organization and resources of each State, of the economic, social and cultural rights indispensable for his dignity and the free development of his personality (Article 22)
>
> Everyone has the right to work, to free choice of employment, to just and favorable conditions of work and to protection against unemployment (Article 23§ 1).
>
> Everyone, without any discrimination, has the right to equal pay for equal work (Article 23 §2)
>
> Everyone has the right to a standard of living adequate for the health and well-being of himself and of his family, including food, clothing, housing and medical care and necessary social services, and the right to security in the event of unemployment, sickness, disability, widowhood, old age or other lack of livelihood in circumstances beyond his control (Article 25§ 1)
>
> Everyone has the right to education. Education shall be free, at least in the elementary and fundamental stages. Elementary education shall be compulsory. Technical and professional education shall be (Article 26§ 1)

The term *Human rights* is a social construction. We refer to the right of "work, health, welfare, education and asylum". However, do we face social justice to all these sectors? The existence of soup kitchens for people with specific ethnic characteristics, the increasing number of homeless people due to economic reasons, the rise of racist violence, the exclusion of people without legal residency papers (immigrants) in Greece from the hospital and generally of public services (see also Law 3386, Article 84 § 1), the bureaucracy and the law as an obstacle for the participation of people in education and employment may appear as isolated incidents nonetheless ever-increasing sum creates a particular context and primitive social gap which requires scientific analysis . In our daily lives even more people need the support from cultural mediator because of communications conflicts that lead to social exclusion.

Social exclusion is a phenomenon and a consequence of specific policies which caused gaps in society and hence disruption of cohesion, equality and therefore freedom. The concept of social exclusion, the content of which is not completely established, comprising as main components of the multidimensional nature of deprivation in many areas of social life, such as access to decent living conditions, education, employment, housing, health and concentration of specific population groups (Kavounidou, 1996). As Levitas (2004) supports «The socially excluded are identified as a group outside the mainstream of society, sometimes even as a group outside the boundaries of the concept itself society (Levitas, 2004: 226). You could say that social exclusion is the process that individuals and groups are excluded from the social, economic and political process that has resulted in the isolation and marginalization of these (Mousourou, 2005). "Social exclusion is precisely that process that occurs as a result of accumulation of many social disadvantages or negative situations (poverty, illness, rupture of the social bond, etc.). This accumulation in turn causes and is caused by the inability to exercise social rights that express and protect human dignity (Papadopoulou, 2004, p. 371).

The provision of cultural mediation in Greece, though a state obligation nevertheless is left in the wider friendly assistance and action NGOs. No policy to eliminate the phenomenon does exist in Greece, apart from the little money given for example in educational centers for the training of cultural mediators. However, the theory must be put into practice in order not to perpetuate a problematic situation. And while the state remains apathetic towards the necessity of cultural mediators in hospitals, training organizations, to legal entities and so on, educational centers such as EAP offer education to cultural mediators expressing in this way the State's obligation to the existence of this institution.

Besides the theoretical context, I wish to highlight some practices which I use as a social worker and cultural mediator in the NGO Medicins Du Monde in Patras.

"Medicins du Monde" is an international, medical, humanitarian, nongovernmental organization. MdM –Greece, maintaining their autonomy, both operational and financial, organize, staff and finance missions through the Greek department. MdM - Greece were established in 1990 and they constitute a unique Greek Organization which follows its own path based to the particularities of Greece, maintaining its economic and administrative independence. At the same time, however, they remain part of the International Net of MdM, which consists of 14 departments; Germany, Belgium, Spain, France, United States, Cyprus ,Greece, Italy, Netherlands, Portugal, United Kingdom, Sweden, Switzerland, Canada, Japan and Argentina.

Completing 23 years of continuous action, MdM have been recognized to the conscience of the citizens as a reliable and effective organization which promotes the feelings of solidarity of the Greek society. With many missions of humanitarian aid in Greece and in developing countries, Greek medicines, sanitary personnel, administrative employees and logisticians offer their services voluntarily. It would not be possible to attempt a complete analysis of the positive points that derive from multiculturalism. However, the most basic conditions of cooperation between the sciences and the state will be given in order to achieve those negotiatory sectors that will bring to the political forefront the necessity for intercultural competence.

In Patras, MdM operated for 6 months in 2011 and for 2 months in 2012 (July and August) within the project called "Care of refugees and asylum seekers in the city of Patras". Since September 2012, a new program of MdM has started. The program "Open Polyclinic" operates with the aim of providing primary medical health care and social support to people who lack access to the National Health Care System (as the immigrants), the refugees without legal license of their stay in the country, the poor people or these without insurance, homeless people and Roma populations.

The program is based on 3 parts including the Primary Health Care, where the medical personnel of the Polyclinic help the patients during its opening hours, the Emergency Cases, which are based on a net of volunteers in all the hospitals of the country, which intervenes in cases of urgent access to the National Health Care System, getting over the bureaucratic obstacles and finally the Drugstore, which provides medicines to the patients A further target of the Open Polyclinic is the protection of target groups as the women, children, minors.

Good Practices of Integrating Refugees/ Asylum Seekers/ Persons in Need of International Protection

- With the translators' aid we provide primary medical care, social support, legal assistance.
- Respecting the country of their origin, their cultural frame of reference, the specific needs, with active listening and empathy, we inform our clients for the obligations and rights arising from the possession of "red card for applying asylum, the opportunity for voluntary repatriation, and the referral to shelters. Furthermore, many of our clients, wanting to achieve social integration, they proceed to actions editing working permits.
- Realizing their living conditions (most of them are homeless) we provide basic hygiene items, clothes and sleeping bags.
- We also make campaigns, and try to aware agencies and residents for the specific target group.
- We Work in collaboration with an organized net of public services and Non-Governmental Organizations. We cooperate with other agencies, civil society organizations in order to make the referral of cases to the appropriate services
- We utilize a network of volunteers composed of doctors from various specialties to cover additional needs of the population
- Considering the demands of our clients, we make proposals for the improvement of their living that will assist them in order to be totally integrated.

- Patras has always been the center of policymaking. Therefore, its role cannot be insignificant but nevertheless it should be described without exaggeration as vital. In fact Patras is the receiver and the channel input and output both for immigrants and from Europe, but also ideas. Moreover, Patras is a city with high unemployment rate, and a high rate of poor and homeless. However, practices that promote multiculturalism and its beneficial outlook is a sign that can bring our town as the capital for hospitality, a center for welfare of all those who benefit by their presence in this place.

"Doctors of the World", operating in this context and understanding that multiculturalism is not only related to the immigrant or refugee, but also to the person that comes from a different socioeconomic status, implement programs with a twofold objective: to prevent multi-problematic situations, and on the other, they offer medical care to all those who are excluded from the public health system.

References

Kavounidi, T. (1996). Social exclusion: Definition, community initiatives, Greek experience and political dilemmas. In D. Karantinos, L. Maratou-Alibranti and E. Fronimou (Eds.), *Dimensions of Social Exclusion in Greece* (pp. 47–96). Athens: EKKE.

Levitas, R. (2004). *Η έννοια του κοινωνικού αποκλεισμού και η νέα ντυρκεμιανή ηγεμονία».* Στο Μ. Πετμεζίδου & Χ. Παπαθεοδώρου (Επιμ.), Φτώχεια και Κοινωνικός Αποκλεισμός, Αθήνα: Εξάντας.

Mousourou, L. (1998). Social exclusion and social protection. In K. Kasimati (Ed.). *Social exclusion: The Greek experience.* Athens: Gutenberg.

Papadopoulou, D. (2004). The nature of social exclusion in Greek society. In M. Permezidou & H. Papatheodorou (eds). *Poverty and social exclusion* (pp. 367-398). Athens: Exantas

Part IV: Mediation in Schools

Chapter 18: Educational Studies and Cultural Mediation: Notes to a Case Study from Rhodes, Greece

Eleni Skourtou

Introduction

At any educational department in Greece students get engaged in compulsory practical exercise for a certain period of time. The school environment gives undergraduate students the opportunity to become familiar with educational activities *in the field.* It offers them the opportunity to work with diverse age groups or/and with students of diverse cultural and social origin. This kind of practical exercise follows a schedule that aims to prepare students for their future educational duties; pedagogical concepts, methods, strategies, materials are employed as integral parts of small scale projects in order to make prospect teaching cognitively and socially effective. In this context, 'effective' is equal with a teacher teaching the content of a subject matter and with students dealing with it. As for the social effect, this refers mostly to inclusion. Inclusion may have clear limits as culturally diverse students will be included as long as they passively or dynamically adjust to the mainstream model of educational participation.

There are a series of challenging issues that go hand in hand with diversity in school. In the last few decades, the educational studies in Greece have been enriched with undergraduate and graduate programs of intercultural or inclusive education to meet the challenge. Since the 1990's there are large scale EU funded inclusive educational programs in the country. These programs deal with specific target groups, i.e. Roma (http://www.keda.gr/roma/ and http://roma.eled.auth.gr/en/node/4), Immigrants & Repatriate (Εκπαίδευση Παλιννοστούντων & Αλλοδαπών Μαθητών) and Muslim minority students in Northern Greece (http://museduc.gr/el/). A lot of research findings that refer to issues of diversity in school and society were and still are generated in the context of these programs. As for the Roma population in Greece there is an increasing research interest and an emerging bulk of research reports and papers that deal with many aspects of life, work and education of Roma in Greece. Teacher training in respect to inclusive education for Roma students represents an expanding field of educational and research work (see Georgiadis & Zisimos, 2012).

In some cases these programs were/are interwoven with graduate or undergraduate educational studies. In this way, university students have the opportunity to get involved in research and educational activities with a specific target group of school students. This is the case, which we are presenting here; undergraduate students' involvement in literacy supporting activities for Roma school students in Rhodes/Greece.

More specifically, during the academic years 2012-2013 and 2013-2014 undergraduate students attending a Literacy Seminar[1] were given the opportunity to choose how they would be evaluated, i.e. they could (a) either take a written test or (b) write an essay or (c) participate in literacy supporting activities for Roma children. In the first academic year, 70 students participated, and in the second academic year 120 students participated (out of +/- 500 students) in literacy supporting activities for Roma students. Their assignment was to support Roma students in matters of school literacy in Greek and to reflect on their involvement. The supporting activities took place either in the school or at home.

The Objectives of the Project

The main objective of the project was to investigate literacy practices and modes of learning and teaching in a pedagogical relationship between mainstream teachers and Roma students. The focus was on undergraduate students during their involvement in literacy supporting activities, in order to see how far stereotypes rather than pedagogical concepts guide them and to examine whether they move towards a transformation of their attitudes and actions as result of their involvement in the project. A transformative point would be if the undergraduate students would be able to build bridges, i.e. to help to construct a continuum between home and school (Hornberger, 2004), community knowledge and school literacy (Wells, 1999 & 2008). The hypothesis is that in doing so the tutors would become aware of their students' prior knowledge and would learn to appreciate and to employ it as a basis for teaching new content (Cummins 2000 and Cummins et al 2006). Mediation skills would be the outcome of this process.

Who Are the Mediators and What is Their Duty

The notion of mediation reflects the efforts of building human bridges between cultural groups in order to work in an inclusive and collaborative way. Looking closer at mediation process, we should note a paradox. The mediation process is designed by mainstream researchers and educators, but it is directed to community people with an expectation that they perform the duty of mediation themselves. These people are usually of low socioeconomic status although they have experienced inclusion and social engagement at least to some extent. Their duty is to help their community peers to communicate with mainstream

---

[1] A joint seminar between the Department of Primary Education and the Department of Preschool Education and Educational Design

individuals and institutions in order to gain access to resources and experience social inclusion as well. The mainstream school is a major institution where the mediators are expected to work towards integration. What we are arguing here is that mainstream teachers themselves should be trained to act as mediators through regular involvement in joint activities with members of a specific group. This involvement would lead to a pedagogical relationship that allows for respect, tolerance and interpersonal negotiation in constructing knowledge and in developing literacy skills.

Methodology

The research methodology used was participatory research with participants who kept record of their involvement and evaluated themselves in the end. Participants were introduced to tools of 'new learning' (Kalantzis & Cope, 2012) in order to be able to focus on certain aspects. Prior to this, a sample of 50 undergraduate students had to answer an open question as part of a written questionnaire. They were asked whether (and why) they would consider it easy or difficult to teach literacy to Roma students.

Assignments and Tools

The students that took part in the activities were asked to support an individual child or a small group of Roma children in their literacy assignments for school or in their literacy activities for kindergarten. In this way the students became tutors for Roma children. As soon as they became tutors, undergraduate students were asked to keep a diary of their educational involvement in a twofold way:

> (a) they were given a table to fill in on a day to day basis, with all necessary data for each child; (b) they were asked to keep a more personal diary recording observations, thoughts or fears the tutors might have had or might have made during their involvement.

As for (a), i.e. the diary in table form, it provided the tutors with an easily readable account of their daily activities: date/time, place, kind & content of the activity, name/age of the child, short remarks that give a clue whether something worked or not. As for (b), i.e. the diary in a form of detailed entries, tutors had the opportunity to elaborate on their everyday activities and observations.

Finally, tutors were asked to deliver (c) their own evaluation of the whole activity. They had to focus on their educational relationship with the Roma children they worked with. Specifically they were asked to focus on themselves (what attitudes, knowledge, skills they had brought into the pedagogical relationship) and on what they have learned from the Roma children (i.e. any prior knowledge the Roma children had brought into the relationship and helped them to step on it in order to teach new content).

In keeping diary and evaluating the way they deal with literacy issues tutors were supposed to report on how: (i) they were 'experiencing the known and the new'; (ii) they were 'applying appropriately and creatively'; (iii) they were able to 'conceptualize using theory and by naming'; (iv) they were able to analyze 'functionally and critically' the context, their specific doing and its outcome (Kalantzis & Cope 2012).

Initial Findings

Questionnaire

The questionnaire prior to the main project gave a contradictory but interesting insight into students' attitudes about teaching literacy to Roma children. Out of a sample of 49 students (n=49), 18 answered that it would be difficult even impossible to teach Roma children literacy because they lack a cultural background of literacy. 12 students answered that their 'well organized orality' would serve as a basis for teaching them literacy. 7 students answered that it would be easy to teach Roma children literacy because they were 'an unwritten piece of paper'. Finally 12 students could not decide, and they suggested segregated classes, where Roma students would be 'helped' in literacy matters.

We see that in the questionnaire the students expressed rather extreme viewpoints. We thought that it would be interesting to follow up in the main project the attitudes that referred to 'organized orality', as a basis for learning literacy (n=12) and the attitudes that referred to Roma children as being 'an unwritten piece of paper', (n=7) that made them easy to teach to, because they offered a 'zero knowledge basis' for starting.

The responses that refer to literacy as an impossible mission (n=18) and the responses that referred to segregated classes (n=12) were not included to our priorities in the main project for the following reasons: (a) since the students signed up to participate in the literacy activities, we assumed that they would not think of teaching literacy to Roma students as a hopeless task; (b) since the students had to adjust to a given context, they had no option of defining the form of schooling.

Main Project

The whole activity offered an opportunity to the tutors to come closer to Roma students and to their everyday life in the community and in the school. Through supporting their Roma students at home the tutors came in contact with the family and their community daily life. By talking with parents and children, they were given the opportunity to participate in intercultural communication, to ask questions, to formulate suggestions, to try out ways of teaching, to record emerging skills. Above all, the close social and educational contact offered the material for reporting on experiencing 'the known and the new'. Diaries, (assignments a & b) served as tools in helping tutors monitor their own involvement day after day. Self-evaluation (assignment c) turned out to be a more complicated task that on the one hand reflected an overall positive educational and social experience and on the other hand lacked information about the kind of knowledge Roma children brought into the pedagogical relationship.

Focus on Stereotypes

In both the diaries and the self-evaluation we could observe a shift towards challenging social stereotypes. None of the tutors had any experience with working with Roma children, while they had expressed initial reservations about the project and, as we could see in the initial questionnaire, some extreme attitudes. There was a distance between the initial findings through the questionnaire and the final outcomes of the project. Former attitudes were based on the lack of personal experience. This led students to express attitudes towards an abstract collective subject (i.e. Roma in general). Later, attitudes were expressed after involvement in the project that offered the opportunity to become acquainted with real people. The abstraction Roma was transformed to concrete persons with name/surname that have parents and siblings with names/surnames as well. The abstract Roma camp with negative connotations became the real home of a concrete family.

Preliminary Evaluation

Referring to their Roma students by name and not as members of their cultural/social group, the tutors demonstrated a shift from stereotyping towards recognition, tolerance and acceptance of their culturally and socially diverse students.

Referring to their own experiences in a positive way, the tutors demonstrated a genuine emotional involvement in the educational relationship.

Observing and assessing the actual school knowledge and literacy level of their students, tutors were able to spot the diverse knowledge gaps, but they did not recognize or value Roma students' prior knowledge which was culturally oriented. It seemed that what the Roma students did not know in comparison to their mainstream peers was visible to their tutors as a missing module in a clearly defined school curriculum. What the students knew seemed to be comprehensible to their tutors only as far as it was similar or identical with school knowledge. In any other case, it seemed that tutors were not able to identify any prior knowledge. In comparison to the initial questionnaire tutors did not refer to the orality experiences of their Roma students. What they had reported in the initial questionnaire as 'organized orality' that would serve as a basis for learning literacy did not appear to be operational in the main project. Thus, orality as an experience was not conceptualized as prior knowledge. An explanation might be that tutors lacked sufficient tools that could enable then to recognize prior knowledge.

An Opposite Example

The example we are presenting here refers to supporting an older child in the Roma community. The tutor reports of her work with S., who is a 15 years old boy and who had some years of school experience but not regular school attendance in the past. Currently, S. is too old to go to Primary School and has too limited knowledge to attend High School. The initial idea was to support S. to catch up with age / grade appropriate school literacy level in order to give him a motive for coming back to school. The supporting activities took part at S.'s home and lasted 12 weeks, once or twice per week.

The tutor was introduced into following tools:

i. Cummins's framework for academic expertise with the triple focus on meaning, language and language use. Prior knowledge would be the basis for it, especially for focus on meaning and on language (Cummins 2000, 2001).
ii. Kalantzis & Cope's framework for 'new learning' with emphasis on the modes of learning and more specific focusing at least on 'experiencing the known and the new' (Kalantzis & Cope, 2012).
iii. Wells's (1999) concept for making meaning
iv. Hornberger's (2004) concept for the 'continuum of biliteracy'
v. Garcia's (Garcia & Wei, 2014) concept of translanguaging.

With regards (i), (ii) and (iii) the tutor was asked to focus on the pedagogical relationship with S.; she was asked to follow not only S.'s academic progress in it, but also her own transformation, if any. As regards to points (iv) and (v) the tutor was asked to focus on her student's actual use of his languages during the sessions.

According to tutor's diary, S. came to the project having a strong willing to learn. He knew exactly what he wanted to learn and why. Though the project was aiming to support school literacy in Greek, S. asked for support in learning English in order to develop skills for working in tourism business during the summer time. The tutor responded to S.'s wishes and started teaching him essential English. As she puts it, she started from point 'zero'. At this point we see no clear connection to any of the proposed frameworks/concepts above, apart from tutor's respect of her student's wishes.

Soon enough, the tutor starts asking S. for any prior knowledge in English and any connections between English, Greek and Romani. She puts herself in a position of learning from her student what connects his English with his Greek and his Romani knowledge. She gives a few lightening examples: she writes that S. "wrote down a series of similarities between English and Romani, like the Romani word 'kat' that means 'scissors', something that helped him to remember the English verb 'to cut'. She also reports that S.'s orality was helpful when she applied a translation game between oral /written as well as between Greek/English/Romani. Tutor's description of S.'s language use and learning reflects S.'s translanguaging performance and his dynamic way to make meaning beyond one or two languages (Garcia & Weil, 2014). The tutor also reports of the multilingual home environment where she and her student were interacting during the sessions, but she does to conceptualize it neither in terms of the concept of *continua of biliteracy* nor in terms of the translaguaging concept.

Nevertheless tutor's work and self-evaluation respond to more than one concept: they respond to Cummins's concept of focusing on meaning using prior knowledge and on Kalantzis & Cope's concept of 'new learning' and experiencing the known and the new. The tutor managed to go a step further towards applying appropriately and creatively. Furthermore, the tutor's initiative responds to Wells's concept of 'making meaning'.

The most interesting issue was the way the tutor reports of her own learning process. The tutor starts with speaking about her student and swifts gradually to speaking about their pedagogical relationship. She ends up speaking of herself. It seems that a transformation process took place for both, tutor and student. The Roma student found somebody who respected his wishes and needs. The tutor, following the needs of her student, moved away from initial intentions to 'teach the essentials' to a gradually more and more sophisticated syllabus where three languages and community knowledge were multimodality involved. Tutor and student established a mutually enriching pedagogical relationship. The aspects 'analyzing functionally and critically' of the new learning concept were rather potentially than actively addressed. Nevertheless, the distance that was covered between the starting point and the end point is worth noting.

It is obvious that we cannot generalize on the basis of a single example. On the other hand, this example worked, and it may be further examined as a good practice and as a potential scenario.

Follow Up of the Opposite Example

After the tutor has completed her work, she took the initiative to support S. further, but in a different context. She talked to the English teacher at her university department, asking for permission in order to have S. as a guest in the English seminar. A small group of students, along with the original tutor, would support S., both in matters of learning and in matters of social integration. They would act as a coaching team around him. At this point, we cannot say what we should expect, as this attempt is in progress.

Back to Mediation

Speaking of education, we often refer to it as mainstream. Speaking of teachers in the context of education we often assume that they represent this mainstream. We think that this is not entirely accurate. Being a teacher, i.e. practicing teaching as such, requires a constant negotiation of identities. This represents an act of cultural mediation. To our opinion, teachers stand and function between contexts. As stated earlier, we suggest that mediation becomes part for education and training of teachers, not necessarily as a discrete skill that has to be applied separately, but rather as an integral part of the definition of the teachers' profession.

References

Cummins, J. (2001). *Negotiating Identities: Education for Empowerment in a Diverse Society*. Los Angeles: California Association for Bilingual Education (2nd Edition).

Cummins, J. (2000). *Language, Power, and Pedagogy: Bilingual Children in the Crossfire*. Clevedon: Multilingual Matters.

Cummins, J., Chow, P. and Schecter, S. (2006). Community as Curriculum. *Language Arts*. /83(4), 297-307.

Garcia, O. and Wei, L. (2014). *Translanguaging – Language, Bilingualism & Education.* Hampshire & New York: Palgrave & Macmillan.

Georgiadis, F. and Zisimos, A. (2012). Teacher Training in Roma Education in Greece: Intercultural and Critical Educational Necessities. *Issues in Educational Research, 22(1),* 47-59.

Hornberger, N. (2006). The Continua of Biliteracy & the Bilingual Educator – Educational Linguistics in Practice. *International Journal of Bilingual Education*, 7(2 & 3), 155-171.

Kalantzis, M. and Cope, B. (2012). *New Learning – Elements of a Science of Education* (2nd Edition). Cambridge: Cambridge University Press.

Wells, G. (1999). *Dialogic inquiry: Towards a sociocultural practice and theory of education.* Cambridge: Cambridge University Press.

Chapter 19: The School Mediation to Confront Violence and Bullying due to Cultural Diversity

Georgios Nikolaou, Theodoros Thanos, and Eleni Samsari

Introduction

Violence and aggression have been examined systematically over the years, taking into account their powerful connection with human nature. School violence is considered to be a phenomenon which concerns teachers, parents and students as well. However, incidents of violence, which were observed within the school environment, were initially approached by jurists, as they were related to juvenile violence and delinquency (Αρτινοπούλου, 2001; Πανούσης, 2006).

During the last decades school bullying appears as a special form of school violence and attracts international attention of scientists in the field of education, who examine the complicated aspects of the phenomenon and realize the seriousness of the problem. Although the findings of recent studies allow us to become aware of the issue and to understand some of its basic features, the relation between school bullying and cultural diversity is still an object of investigation.

The confrontation of the phenomenon is difficult especially when non-native students are involved. Regardless of the various anti-bullying programs or policies that are applied nationally or within the school unit, school mediation could be the starting point in order to deal with each incident of school bullying, focusing on its unique and on its different aspects.

Defining School Violence and School Bullying

The term of "violence" varies according to the scientific approach, but also according to the social and the cultural context in which it appears (Αρτινοπούλου, 2001;·Θάνος, 2012;·Πανούσης, 2013). The concept of "violence" is defined as an intentional behavior which is exerted by someone, in order to threaten or to cause physical or psychological damage towards another person or even towards himself (Καρύδης, 2003).

Specifically, “school violence” refers to a series of infractions which take place within the school context (Πανούσης, 2013). Some of its primary features are the imposition of will, the cause of damage or injury and the threat of bullying, of maltreatment and of abuse (Αρτινοπούλου, 2001). Students tend to describe school violence as the cause of physical damage, annoyance, insult or as a form of threatening, blackmailing and coercion. However, the majority of students report that the appearance of violence is not related to specific causes (Θάνος, Νταλάκας, & Γιαννούλη, 2013). Although incidents of school violence are often observed and the presence of the phenomenon within schools is verified, the amount of evidence for the expansion of the problem is not sufficient (Γεωργούλη-Κούκκου, 1995). Various methodological issues which appear throughout the research, lead to unambiguous conclusions as for the dimensions of the problem (Αρτινοπούλου, 2001;·Κουράκης, 2009).

The most common forms of school violence are physical, verbal, non-verbal violence, psychological violence, teasing, exclusion, rumor spreading, sexual violence and cyber-bullying (Κουράκης, 2009). Vandalism is also included as a form of school violence. According to teachers of primary education, students tend to use mostly verbal violence, teasing and physical violence (Θάνος, 2012). “School bullying” is considered to be a special and a harmful form of school violence (Νικολάου, 2013). Comparing school violence and school bullying, it is clear that school violence has a wider content and such incidents do not usually have a great duration. Although there are plenty of definitions for the phenomenon of school bullying (see Rigby, 2008; Σπυρόπουλος, 2011), there are some basic features which characterize “school bullying”. Specifically, school bullying includes repetition, duration, desire/intention to cause harm and tendency to demonstrate power (physical, affective and cognitive power) and prevalence towards weaker students (i.e., imbalance of power) (Κουράκης, 2009).

However, there is not a consensus among scientists as for the definitional characteristics of school bullying. For example, according to Rigby (2008) the attitude that incidents of school bullying are not serious, when they take place only once, is completely wrong and the phenomenon should not be ignored even in this case. Other studies (Αρτινοπούλου, 2001; Θάνος, Νταλάκας, & Γιαννούλη, 2013; Κουράκης, 2009; Πανούσης, 2013) prove that an important problem is the reaction of children-victims. The majority of them remain silent and they do not report the incident to anyone. Therefore, the perception, which prevails as for the expansion of the phenomenon, does not respond to the real situation and it becomes even more difficult to deal with the problem.

Another parameter of school bullying which is not deeply investigated according to Rigby (2008, p. 45) is the justified or the unjustified aggression towards the victim. This factor concerns substantially students-victims, as they cannot understand the motives of bullies for their aggressive behaviour and the reasons of bullies’ actions towards specific students.

Some severe forms of bullying are racial and ethnic victimization. These take place, when the negative behavior of the bully is addressed to a person belonging to a racial or to an ethnic minority group (Rigby, 2008). Incidents of school bullying might appear due to the different ethnic, racial or cultural characteristics of some students, who do not belong to the majority group, specifically due to the bias towards the different race or nationality (Σαμσάρη & Νικολάου, 2013).

These forms of violence are present, when there are ethno-cultural differences between the bully and the victim. Specifically, in racial victimization the victim experiences repeatedly and intentionally discrimination and exclusion, due to his racial identity (Rigby, 2008). As the causes of the phenomenon could not be easily detected, it is usually questionable to prove each time that the negative behaviors hide racial or ethnic victimization.

School bullying is a difficult problem which requires a careful and a well-planned handling. For example, some schools, which aim to achieve the integration of students from different cultural backgrounds, adopt solutions that might lead to opposite results, increasing the discrimination among native and non-native students and failing to establish the necessary conditions of equity and respect for diversity (Νικολάου, 2005). Thus, Olweus (as cited in Rigby, 2008) supported that the problem of school bullying could be reduced through the application of a program which aims for the prevention and the confrontation of the phenomenon through the participation of all those who are directly or indirectly involved (e.g., students, teachers, parents, headmaster, school's staff etc.). The objectives would be the awareness of the problem, the improvement of interpersonal relationships, the mediation as a means to deal with the phenomenon, the application of concrete rules, the support and the protection of the victims (Σπυρόπουλος, 2011).

School Bullying and Cultural Diversity

The appearance of school bullying in relation to ethno-cultural diversity is a complex social phenomenon, because it includes the different culture and the nationality of students from minority groups and possible bias or stereotypes towards them. Cultural diversity is described as the diversity of the cultural background and the presence of different ethno-cultural identities among people. Ethno-cultural identity is a part of a broad cultural identity of the person, which is created through the experiences and through the interaction with the direct social and cultural environment, where the person lives (Οικονομίδης & Κοντογιάννη, 2011).

Investigating the relation between school bullying and cultural diversity, there are various studies which lead to contradictory results. Generally, there is not sufficient evidence for the involvement of students in incidents of school bullying, taking into account their ethnic, racial or cultural background and their socio-economic status. Several studies show that there is a significant relation between the two factors, proving that non-native students are systematically victimized (Graham & Juvonen, 2002; Pagani, Robustelli, & Martinelli, 2011). Racist and stereotypical beliefs, which prevail in the society, cause the expression of prejudiced forms of behaviour and biased attitudes towards minority groups and such behaviors are also replicated within the school environment towards students from different cultural backgrounds (Cobia & Carney, 2002; Pagani, Robustelli, & Martinelli, 2011).

The results of other studies show that native students are those who are more likely to become victims in an incident of school bullying (Strohmeier & Spiel, 2003; Strohmeier, Spiel, & Gradinger, 2008). Finally, some other studies prove that a significant relation between school bullying and cultural diversity does not exist or it cannot be detected (Eslea & Mukhtar, 2000; Fandrem, Strohmeier, & Roland, 2009). According to the findings of a more recent study (Nikolaou & Samsari, 2013) non-native students are involved in incidents of school bullying (either as victims or as bullies) more systematically compared to native students. Thus, incidents of school bullying tend to appear more often in a school context, where there are students from different ethnic or cultural backgrounds (Nikolaou & Samsari, 2013).

Comparing the contradictory findings of the previous studies, it is clear that the relation between school bullying and cultural diversity is still an area, which is not completely examined. However, it would be wrong to ignore the different social, psychological and cultural conditions which influence the context of each study and the different research methodology which has been possibly adopted (Nikolaou & Samsari, 2013). Consequently, the research has yet to reveal a lot of aspects of the issue, in order to form a clear scientific point of view as for the nature of the relation between the two factors.

School Mediation as an Alternative Means against School Bullying

During the last decades countries all over the world have begun to realize the seriousness of school violence and bullying which are prevalent in schools of primary and secondary education and they have focused on the design and the application of measures and practices in order to deal with the phenomenon.

Specifically, in Europe several countries adopt various policies which are divided in three levels: a) national policies which are controlled by the political authority and include specialized services, national actions aiming to confront school failure and abandonment, and national programs aiming to reduce xenophobia and racism within the school context and to improve the quality of education, b) local policies which are designed by local authorities in order to establish a positive relationship between school and local community and c) policies and initiatives which are applied by the school units and include programs of peaceful confrontation of conflicts and the application of mediation to deal with disputes or with incidents of school bullying (Αρτινοπούλου, 2001).

Although school bullying also concerns Greek society specifically during the last decades, anti-bullying intervention programs have not been applied yet. The phenomenon is present in Greek schools and it is more intense in a multicultural school context, because there is a higher risk for students from different cultural backgrounds to be involved either as bullies or as victims in incidents of school violence and school bullying (Nikolaou & Samsari, 2013).

However, the confrontation of school violence and school bullying is attempted indirectly through the implementation of various programs, such as the function of "Second Chance's" schools, programs of remedial teaching, programs of creative occupation, the function of National Centre for Vocational Orientation (Αρτινοπούλου, 2010a) and the recent creation of "Observatory of School Violence and Bullying" under the supervision of Greek Ministry of Education and Religious Affairs. Generally, policies towards school bullying and programs related to school mediation are not applied systematically, but they appear sporadically in some schools of the country (Αρτινοπούλου, 2010a).

School mediation is considered to be an alternative means to face school violence and school bullying as compared to traditional disciplinary forms, which are used in order to confront the phenomenon. It is included in the context of restorative justice, aiming to restore the relationships among those who are involved in incidents of school violence and school bullying (Αρτινοπούλου, 2010a; Αρτινοπούλου, 2011). School mediation is a structured process which has specific limits and aims for the efficient solution of the conflict or of the dispute among two or more students who participate actively and communicate directly with the help of one third neutral person called as "mediator" (Αρτινοπούλου, 2010b).

The process of mediation begins with the request of a student who usually experiences the incident as a victim and addresses to the mediator. Then, the mediator gets in contact separately with both sides (two or more students) who are involved and after their agreement is assured, he sets the date for their mediation. When the mediation takes place, both sides (bully/bullies and victim/victims) are initially introduced, they agree with the principles of mediation and they report the problem according to their point of view and their sentiments that they felt about it. The mediator summarizes and asks from both sides to propose various solutions, so that one would be eventually chosen as the final solution and another would be chosen as the alternative solution. Afterwards, they set the date of meeting in order to discuss about the progress of their agreement. The mediator reads the contract and both sides sign it (Αρτινοπούλου, Καλαβρή, & Μιχαήλ, 2010; Θάνος, Κολοφωτιά, & Χατζάκη, 2011).

In Greece, school mediation is applied in several schools of primary and secondary education, having positive results. The assessment of the application of these programs shows that students who participated in the process of mediation, are satisfied, as they managed to find a solution to the problem, they did not have conflicts anymore and they became friends with each other. According to their reports, the mediators were friendly, neutral and they were interested to hear everything that students said and revealed in confidence. Several students usually seek an alternative solution, as they find it futile to deal with the phenomenon all alone or they hesitate to disclose the problem, having the fear that the bullies would punish them or they would take revenge for that.

Specifically in primary education, school mediation is applied in some schools of the country. One of these schools is the 5th Primary School of Ioannina, where school mediation was applied during the school year 2012-2013 and continues to be applied during the school year 2013-2014. The final assessment of the program's application proved positive and encouraging results. Students, who participated, supported that after the process, a solution was given to the problem, they did not fight again with each other, their interpersonal relationships were improved and the mediation was preferred as a way to solve their disputes (Θάνος, Νταλάκας, & Γιαννούλη, 2013).

Mediation is one of the most appropriate methods in order to deal with school bullying (Αρτινοπούλου, 2010a), taking into account its basic principles (volunteerism, confidentiality, trust, equality etc.) (Αρτινοπούλου, Καλαβρή, & Μιχαήλ, 2010). Besides, these principles also serve the need of intercultural communication and especially the need of equality.

One of the basic features of school bullying is the imbalance of power between the bully and the victim (Κουράκης, 2009) and the most important obstacle to the confrontation of the phenomenon is the fact that victims do not ask for help and protection from their school (teacher, headmaster) and they do not report such incidents to their parents (Πανούσης, 2013). It is not surprising that such features are even more intense in the context of ethno-cultural diversity. Victimization of "different" students is observed at school, when the minority group feels weak and hesitates to ask for help, thinking that the school community would probably support the students who belong to the majority group.

When students who are involved in an incident of school bullying, accept the suggestion for mediation and agree to participate in the process, they have to accept its principles, so that the process would be continued. If the students are not consistent with the principles and with their application, the mediation stops. Besides, one of the principles of mediation, which requires the agreement of the bully and of the victim, is that all those who are involved in the process, are equal and any child is not stronger or better than someone else. If the student-bully agrees with this principle, then the imbalance of power between the two sides (between the bully/bullies and the victim/victims) does not prevail anymore. Consequently, one of the substantial features of school bullying –the power differential– is eliminated, as both sides participate and attempt to find a solution to the problem in a context of equality.

The confidentiality is also one of the primary conditions of school mediation, required for its successful application. Both sides should accept this principle in order to participate in the process. The mediator reassures that the discussion would be applied in an atmosphere of confidentiality and he tries to highlight that mediation is just a normal and an ordinary process. This fact creates gradually a sense of security, so that all students who are involved would feel comfortable to talk about the problem. This is very important for students-victims, as they would feel safe to reveal their victimization. Generally, according to the findings of the study conducted by Nikolaou and Samsari (2013), victims avoid talking to their parents or to their teachers about their victimization and prefer to remain silent. Silence is one of the main obstacles to the confrontation of school bullying, which usually accompanies the appearance of the phenomenon and tends to be one of its component features. Confidentiality as a basic principle of school mediation allows the victim to break his silence. Even if the process cannot lead to a sufficient solution, it seems to be the threshold, so that students would discuss about the process.

The voluntary participation in school mediation is another important principle. When the bully wants to participate in the process voluntarily, he activates his desire to face and to resolve the problem. The mediation gives bully the opportunity to propose alternative solutions beyond the aggressive forms of behaviors, which he was used to exert, as he has "learned" to solve his disputes in this way. On the other hand, the process of mediation allows students of both sides (bullies and victims) to express their feelings. This is very important for two reasons. Firstly, the findings of various studies prove that bullies derive from families, where the violence dominates within the family environment (aggressive parents) (Κουράκης, 2009; Rigby, 2008). Furthermore, investigating the climate in the school environment, it is clear that the feelings which are prevalent in students-bullies are sorrow and distress (Θάνος, Νταλάκας, & Γιαννούλη, 2013). Thus, these children have experienced negative feelings within their family and they do not feel pleasure, when they are involved in such incidents. Secondly, during the process the bully has to repeat the side of the problem, in the same way as it is reported by the victim, either he agrees with the student-victim or not. Therefore, the bully sees the problem from the point of view of the victim and comes into his position, so that he would learn to develop his empathy. Empathy is considered to be a basic principle of intercultural education, which is usually absent at these children (Κουράκης, 2009).

Although prevention against the appearance of school bullying is probably the best solution against the phenomenon (see Σαμσάρη & Νικολάου, 2013), school mediation seems to be an effective process to deal with a specific incident of school bullying, especially when native and non-native students are involved. Even if an adequate solution to the problem cannot be found, students, who participate in the process, will learn to accept the important principles of school mediation, which are the same or they are additional to the principles of intercultural education.

Conclusion

Incidents of school violence and bullying take place within the school context, having various forms of appearance. The presence of such incidents is more intense when students from different cultural backgrounds are involved, affecting their emotional and their psychological health and having negative consequences at the school climate and at the relationships among students. Today, teachers and parents have begun to be aware of the problem and to detect such incidents in schools. Although the realization and the understanding of the problem is an encouraging starting point to focus on the phenomenon, it is necessary to find and to apply concrete solutions in order to deal with the problem effectively.

Consequently, it is obvious that school mediation could be an effective means to compensate for some important reasons, which create obstacles during the efforts to reduce incidents of school bullying where native and non-native students are involved. The program of school mediation in combination with some other school's practices and actions, such as the awareness of school violence and bullying, could help efficiently to the prevention and to the confrontation of the phenomenon.

References

Cobia, D. C., & Carney, J. S. (2002). Creating a culture of tolerance in schools: Everyday actions to prevent hate-motivated violent incidents. *Journal of School Violence, 1*, 87-104.

Eslea, M., & Mukhtar, K. (2000). Bullying and racism among Asian schoolchildren in Britain. *Educational Research, 42*(2), 207-217.

Fandrem, H., Strohmeier, D., & Roland, E. (2009). Bullying and victimization among Norwegian and immigrant adolescents in Norway: The role of proactive and reactive aggressiveness. *Journal of Early Adolescence, 29*(6), 898-923.

Graham, S., & Juvonen, J. (2002). Ethnicity, peer harassment, and adjustment in middle school: An exploratory study. *Journal of Early Adolescence, 22*(2), 173-199.

Nikolaou, G., & Samsari, E. (2013). School bullying and ethno-cultural diversity in Greek Schools. *Proceedings of International Conference Breaking Classroom Silences: Addressing sensitive issues in education,* European University Cyprus Department of Education Sciences, Nicosia, 11-12 October 2013 (publication in preparation).

Pagani, C., Robustelli, F., & Martinelli, C. (2011). School, cultural diversity, multiculturalism, and contact. *Intercultural Education, 22*(4), 337-349.

Strohmeier, D., & Spiel, C. (2003). Immigrant children in Austria: Aggressive behavior and friendship patterns in multicultural school classes. *Journal of Applied School Psychology, 19*(2), 99-116.

Strohmeier, D., Spiel, C., & Gradinger, P. (2008). Social relationships in multicultural schools: Bullying and victimization. *European Journal of Developmental Psychology, 5*(2), 262-285.

In Greek:

Αρτινοπούλου, Β. (2001). *Βία στο σχολείο. Έρευνες και πολιτικές στην Ευρώπη.* Αθήνα: Μεταίχμιο.

Αρτινοπούλου, Β. (2010a). *Η σχολική διαμεσολάβηση. Εκπαιδεύοντας τους μαθητές στη διαχείριση της βίας και του εκφοβισμού.* Αθήνα: Νομική Βιβλιοθήκη.

Αρτινοπούλου, Β. (2010b, 11 Μαΐου). «Σχολική διαμεσολάβηση με κατανόηση και διευθέτηση των προβλημάτων». Συνέντευξη στον Θ. Θάνο. *Κρητική Επιθεώρηση*, σ. 12.

Αρτινοπούλου, Β. (2011). Η διαμεσολάβηση στο πλαίσιο της επανορθωτικής δικαιοσύνης. Στο: Θ. Θάνος (Επιμ.), *Η διαμεσολάβηση στο σχολείο και την κοινωνία* (σελ. 15-25). Αθήνα: Πεδίο.

Αρτινοπούλου, Β., Καλαβρή, Χ., & Μιχαήλ, Η. (2010). *Η κοινωνική διαμεσολάβηση. Προσαρμογή για το ελληνικό σχολείο (Πρωτοβάθμια Εκπαίδευση)*. Αθήνα: Ελληνικό Κέντρο Κοινωνικής Διαμεσολάβησης.

Γεωργούλη-Κούκκου, Α. (1995). Παιδιά πρωταγωνιστές νέων μορφών βίας. Θύτες ή θύματα. *Σύγχρονη Εκπαίδευση, 82-83*, 119-122.

Θάνος, Θ. (2012). *Αποκλίνουσα και παραβατική συμπεριφορά των μαθητών στο σχολείο*. Θεσσαλονίκη: Αφοί Κυριακίδη

Θάνος, Θ., Κολοφωτιά, Σ., & Χατζάκη, Μ. (2011). Πιλοτική εφαρμογή της διαμεσολάβησης σε δημοτικό σχολείο. Στο: Θ. Θάνος (Επιμ.), *Η διαμεσολάβηση στο σχολείο και την κοινωνία* (σελ. 47-76). Αθήνα: Πεδίο.

Θάνος, Θ., Νταλάκας, Χ., & Γιαννούλη, Ε. (2013). Σχολική διαμεσολάβηση. Εφαρμογή και αξιολόγηση. *Εισήγηση στην Επιστημονική Ημερίδα με θέμα Σχολική διαμεσολάβηση. Θεωρία, Εφαρμογή, Αξιολόγηση* που οργάνωσαν το 5ο Δημοτικό Σχολείο, το Π.Τ.Ν. και το Εργαστήριο

Μελετών Απόδημου Ελληνισμού και Διαπολιτισμικής Εκπαίδευσης Πανεπιστημίου Ιωαννίνων, Ιωάννινα, 18 Οκτωβρίου 2013.

Καρύδης, Β. (2003). Προλεγόμενα. Στο: Σ. Δημητρίου (Επιμ.), *Μορφές βίας*. Αθήνα: Σαββάλας.

Κουράκης, Ν. (2009). Μορφές νεανικής βίας και δυνατότητες αντιμετώπισής της. Στο: Θ. Θάνος (Επιμ.), *Πρακτικά Επιστημονικής Ημερίδας με θέμα Παιδική παραβατικότητα και σχολείο* (σελ. 85-104), Ρέθυμνο 1 Απριλίου 2009. Αθήνα: Τόπος.

Νικολάου, Γ. (2005). *Διαπολιτισμική Διδακτική. Το νέο περιβάλλον. Βασικές αρχές*. Αθήνα: Ελληνικά Γράμματα.

Νικολάου, Γ. (2013). Σχολικός εκφοβισμός και εθνοπολιτισμική ετερότητα. Στο: Η. Κουρκούτας & Θ. Θάνος (Επιμ.). *Σχολική βία και παραβατικότητα. Ψυχολογικές, κοινωνιολογικές, παιδαγωγικές διαστάσεις. Ενταξιακές προσεγγίσεις και παρεμβάσεις* (σελ. 51-77). Αθήνα: Τόπος.

Οικονομίδης, Β., & Κοντογιάννη, Δ. (2011). Υποβοηθώντας τη μετάβαση από την οικογένεια στο νηπιαγωγείο: Η διαχείριση της εθνοπολιτισμικής ετερότητας μέσα στην τάξη. *Επιστήμες Αγωγής, Θεματικό τεύχος 2011*, 105-124.

Πανούσης, Γ. (2006). «Ταξικοί» αγώνες με ή χωρίς διαιτητή; - Βία στα σχολεία. *Ποινική Δικαιοσύνη, Τεύχος 1*, 75-85.

Πανούσης, Γ. (2013). (Ενδο)σχολική βία: Χωρίς όρια και χωρίς ορίζοντα. Στο: Η. Κουρκούτας & Θ. Θάνος (Επιμ.). *Σχολική βία και παραβατικότητα. Ψυχολογικές, κοινωνιολογικές, παιδαγωγικές διαστάσεις. Ενταξιακές προσεγγίσεις και παρεμβάσεις* (σελ. 21-34). Αθήνα: Τόπος.

Rigby, K. (2008). *Σχολικός εκφοβισμός. Σύγχρονες απόψεις* (Επιμ. Α. Γιοβαζολιάς, Μτφ. Β. Δόμπολα). Αθήνα: Τόπος.

Σαμσάρη, Ε., & Νικολάου, Γ. (2013). Σχολικός εκφοβισμός και εθνοπολιτισμική ετερότητα: Πρακτικές και δράσεις για την πρόληψη της εκδήλωσης του φαινομένου. Στο: Π. Γεωργογιάννης (Επιμ.), *Πρακτικά 16ου Διεθνούς Συνεδρίου του ΚΕ.Δ.ΕΚ. του Πανεπιστημίου Πατρών Οργάνωση της Διοίκησης της Εκπαίδευσης, Διαπολιτισμικότητα και τα Ελληνικά ως Ξένη Γλώσσα,* Πάτρα 28-30 Ιουνίου 2013, Τόμος ΙΙ, σελ. 502-515.

Σπυρόπουλος, Φ. (2011). *Σχολικός τραμπουκισμός*. Αθήνα: Αντ. Σάκκουλας.

Chapter 20: Peer Mediation: Application to a Primary School

Theodoros Thanos and Charalampos Dalakas

Introduction

In Europe the last 15th years and more precisely after the European Conference of Utrecht (1997) the theme of school violence was put on the agenda of the European Commission (Artinopoulou, 2001). During this period an intense interest in this theme was noted which is reflected in the "bibliographic explosion" on school violence and bullying as well as the policies for presentation and combating them. A similar tendency appeared in Greek bibliography after 2005. The references, however, for the prevention and the handling of the phenomenon are very few (Artinopoulou, 2010).

The prevention and the handling of school violence and school bullying is associated with feelings of security in the school and indicates the prevailing culture, democracy and solidarity (ib). The various practices –mainly traditional- that are used for dealing with them, are usually ineffective (Thanos, 2010). Punitive practices have been unsuccessful. They have been abandoned by teachers since they contradict the new educational theories and principles, create bad relationships between teachers and pupils and aggravate problems instead of solving them (Thanos, 2012).

Inclusion practices are used today (Kourkoutas & Thanos, 2013) at the antipodes of the punitive paradigm which are known as "good practices". These offer an alternative, peaceful management, of conflicts between pupils. The restorative justice is used in this context. It aims at restoring the damage caused by the offender redressing the relationships among the offender and the victim as well the school community and the inclusion of the offender in it (Mc Evoy, Mika & Hudson, 2002).

Restorative Justice and Social Mediation

The restorative justice presupposes the acceptance of the act by the involved and mainly from the side of the offender and aims at restoring the relationship between the offender and the victim (Mirsky, 2003). Violation, in the context of restorative practice, is seen as damage of the interpersonal relationships which must be restored (Braithwaite, 2001). The concerned parts use the consequences of the damage (Marshall, 1996) for the restoration of their relationships as well as their reconciliation (Cameron, 2005). The programs of restorative justice require the involvement of the whole community for the solution of the conflict through an equal participation in the process (Artinopoulou, 2010). The participation of all the parties of the community aims at showing that the violation of the offender is a damage insult addressed not only to the victim but to all the members of the community (Carp & Breslin, 2001).

Many attempts have been made to define restorative justice but there is no a community accepted definition so far. However all the definitions have a common ideological stance according to which justice is the restoration of the damage done to the victim, of the relationship between the offender and the victim and the re-inclusion of the offender in the commonly through the restoration of the damage constitute the main characteristic of the restorative practices. The community functions according to be "family model" and cares for the good of all the members without any exclusion as it happens to the family (Carp & Breslin, 2001).

One could say that the restorative justice constitutes an "umbrella concept" that includes a wide spectrum of practices among which is the mediation between the offender and the victim in different social contexts like school, family etc. These practices cover a variety of situations among which is school violence (Artinopoulou, 2010). The evaluation and the meta-analysis of the programs of restorative justice in different countries that used them, have shown that there is a higher sense of justice among offenders and the victims. The offenders tend to accept the suggested solution to a great degree in comparison to the others forms of justice (Latimer, Dowden & Muise, 2001; Artinopoulou, 2010).

The Mediation in the School

Mediation as a means of peaceful conflict solution is an old practice (Roumpea, 2011). It is a strictly structural process, which, as we said, aims at the restoration of the damage and the relationship of the involved parties and it is discussed in the context of restorative justice (Artinopoulou, 2011). The structural character of mediation secures the context of a genuine expression of the two parties and the satisfaction of their needs. The role of the mediator is, among other things, to secure the structural context which is abided by specific norms and principles (Artinopoulou, 2010).

The school is regarded as an ideal community for induction of mediation and restorative justice more generally in the themes of children's involvement in delinquent activities. Peer mediation or school based mediation constitutes a kind of mediation that is applied to the school as an alternative, peaceful way of facing conflicts which substitute the traditional punitive practices (ib). Usually, punishment inflicted on pupils is not followed by some educational activity and doesn't offer the possibility of restoration to the offenders. As a result of this the transgressive pupils are need such action and, in many cases, they pursue them (Johnson & Johnson, 1995).

School mediation is a structural process of peaceful solution of conflicts between two or more pupils by the help of a third impartial pupil (Artinopoulou, 2010). During the process of mediation with the help of a mediator two or more parties which disagree express their own view and their emotions for the case and then they suggest solutions. Among these solutions, they will select and adopt one of them in order to restore the damage that the victim suffered and their relationships (Wall, Stark & Standifer, 2001). Mediation is characterized by a voluntary participation of the involved parties, equality, confidentiality and trust among all the parties including the mediator (Fredrickson & Maruyama, 2006). The participation of the disagreed and the mediator on equal grounds expresses the respect and the support to the offender (Artinopoulou, 2010).

Mediation offers a context of experimental and active learning and of internalization of norms (Karp & Breslin, 2001). Especially, the mediation enhances critical ability, active learning and the self-directed behavior of pupils. In addition to this, it enhances the dialogue and change the way of solving conflicts. Moreover, a preference for the model of negotiation is developed and the ability of students to listen to others is enhanced as well as the sense of self-concept. Finally, the spirit of collectivity is encouraged and co-operation is improved (Artinopoulou, 2010). The programs of school mediation that are implied in various European countries are aimed at encouraging the participation of pupils in confronting and solving conflicts, in decreasing prejudices and in accepting the difference and the formulation of rules for the function of the school community (ib).

The first attempts of application of school mediation appeared in the context of developing and extension of restorative justice to the schools during the decade of 1990 (Morrison, 2007). These were supported by national and regional policies of European countries and the Council of Europe (Artinopoulou, 2010). The application of the program presupposes the involvement of all members of the school community: pupils, teachers, parents and the administration of the school (holistic approach). The teaching staff is informed about the program, the principles and its structure, attends in-service seminars and actively support its implementation. Pupils are also informed about the program and those who are chosen are trained in the role of mediator. Parents are informed about the program and encourage the participation of their children in it. The support of the program from the administration of the school is important: since two committees –the steering and the monitoring one- monitor its development (Artinopoulou, 2010).

The application of the program of school mediation depends on its organization, on the program of training of the mediators, on the group of mediators. This group must be representative of the school population, on the support of the program by the school community and its continuous application (Fredrickson & Maruyama, 2006; Skiba & Paterson, 2000). Two are the main approaches to the program of school mediation: The holistic one (the total school approach) which requires the training of a group of pupils. Usually this group is representative of the school population (Artinopoulou, 2010).

The mediation starts by the submission of a request by a pupil who is involved in a problem. Then, the mediator informs both sides, guarantees confidentiality and, if they are agreed, the date of mediation is arranged. During the process of mediation the two parties are mutually introduced and then the mediator which the involved must agree in order to proceed the process. Then, each side gives his or her own view and expresses his or her feelings about the problem. The mediator asks the involved parties to select the best of the suggested points and to form a third solution that contains the most viable of the suggested points. This procedure does not end up with winners and losers but with all winners. After that they agree on the date of feedback, right down their agreement which is signed by the participants in the process of mediation (Artinopoulou, 2010; Artinopoulou, Kalavri & Michail, 2010; Thanos, Kalofotia & Xatzaki, 2011).

The results of the application of school mediation are generally satisfactory. However, teachers do not seem to use this practice as frequently as other practices. Two may be the reasons for this: the lack a) of relative information and training of teachers who are interested in school mediation and b) of time required by its application (Artinopoulou, 2010). However, peer mediation constitutes the most frequently studied program of conflict solution in schools (Gerrald & Lipsey, 2007).

Application of School Mediation Programs in Greece

The first programs of school mediation appeared in U.S.A. during the 1980's. Later they appeared in many countries of Europe, Canada, Australia, New Zealand etc. Their results were very positive regarding the decrease of school violence, the increase of pupils' self-control, of cooperation and group work (Artinopoulou, 2010). In Greece the first programs of school mediation appeared rather late, after 2005 and especially in the context of health education programs of secondary schools. I mention the following secondary schools: 2nd Gymnasium of Aspropyrgos (2005-2006 school year), Ionidio school (2008-2009), 14th Gymnasium of Larisa (2008-2009), 5th Gymnasium of Stavroupoli (2009-2010), Varvakio Experimental Gymnasium (2010-2011), German school and 2nd Gymnasium of Zefyri (2011-2012), Gymnasium of Fyli and 2nd Gymnasium of Ano Liosia (2011-2012).It is obvious that the program of school mediation in secondary schools have been implemented mainly in private and public schools of mainly West Attica. The results of these programs were very satisfactory regarding the lessening of school violence, the improvement of the relationships among students, the improvement of cooperation, of dialogue, the group spirit etc. (Thanos, Tsatsakis, Stagaki & Katsioulas, 2013).

Similar programs have been implemented in primary schools such as: Primary School Armenon Rethymnon of Crete (2009-2010 and 2010-2011) the 5th "Valanio" Primary School of Ioannina for two years (2012-2013 and 2013-2014). The evaluation of the program "School Mediation" of the first school was very satisfactory. The pupil mediators expressed the view that their training in mediation was interesting and adequate since they did not find serious difficulties in the process of mediation. Furthermore, they said that they were friendly and impartial towards their peers who participated in the process of mediation. They found interesting what their peers were saying and had a sense of satisfaction of their own mediation. The pupils who participated in the mediation said that they found a solution to their problem, that the relationships between them were improved and their differences were minimized. Regarding the mediators they said that they were friendly and neutral and they entrusted them.

The participation of pupils in the process of mediation either as mediators or as involved in it, recognized elements of change in their character: better control of their anger, more sensitive to the view of others and understood better their position. Moreover, they tried to a greater extend, to avoid conflicts and to seek solutions to their problem through dialogue. Finally, they said that they started to use some aspects of mediation in out of school situations, especially in their family (ib).

Application and Evaluation of Mediation in the 5th "Valanio" Primary School of Ioannina

The application of the school mediation program in the 5th "Valanio" Primary School started in the school year 2012-2013. Its phases were the following: a) informing the school community about the program, b) Investigating the school climate, c) Selecting and training pupils in the process of mediation, d) realization of mediation and e) the evaluation of the program. As a good mediation program depends on its continuity (Skiba & Paterson, 2000), we decided to continue its application for a second year (2013-2014) with pupils as mediators and the selection and training of new pupils in the process of mediation.

Informing the School Community

A special meeting was held before the start of the program in order to inform the teachers of the school about the rationale of the program. Then parents were informed by a letter and pupils by the teachers of the school. At the same time, an attempt was made to involve the local community in the context of the holistic approach. This was done by the organization of one day conference entitled "School Mediation for Confronting School Violence". The participants of this conference were: the teaching staff and the association of parents of the school, the association of primary school teachers of the prefecture of Ioannina and representatives of the University of Ioannina. The conference consisted of two parts: the first concerned school violence and ways of dealing with it and the second the strategy of mediation. The phenomenon of violence was approached by an interdisciplinary way where educational sciences such as psychology, sociology, philosophy, criminology, etc. contributed to its illumination. The conference was welcomed by people as this has been shown by people who attended it, its publicity in mass media (newspapers and TV). The conference was addressed by representatives of local community and education. At the beginning of the next school year (2013-2014), a second conference was held as we had committed. Its title was "School Mediation. Theory, application, evaluation". We presented the results of the implementation of the program in the school. Teachers, parents, students of higher education, specialists and pupils of other schools expressed their interest about the results of program.

Investigating School Climate

Mediation and the programs of restorative justice in general are adjusted to the special characteristics of the school because it contains actions directed from the bottom to the top. In this context the investigation of school climate and the cartography of violence in the school are necessary for training pupils in mediation as well as the information required by the school community (Artinopoulou, 2010).

The majority of the pupils who acted as observers referred to the frequencies of various forms of violence as follows: verbal threats 47,3%, mocking 42,7%, exclusion 36%, physical violence 34%. The pupils who experienced violence (victims) gave the following frequencies: mocking 25,3%, verbal threats 19,3%, physical violence 18,1%, exclusion 14%. The pupils who were offenders gave the following frequencies to the various forms of violence: physical violence 5,3% and the verbal threats 2,7% (Figure 20.1).

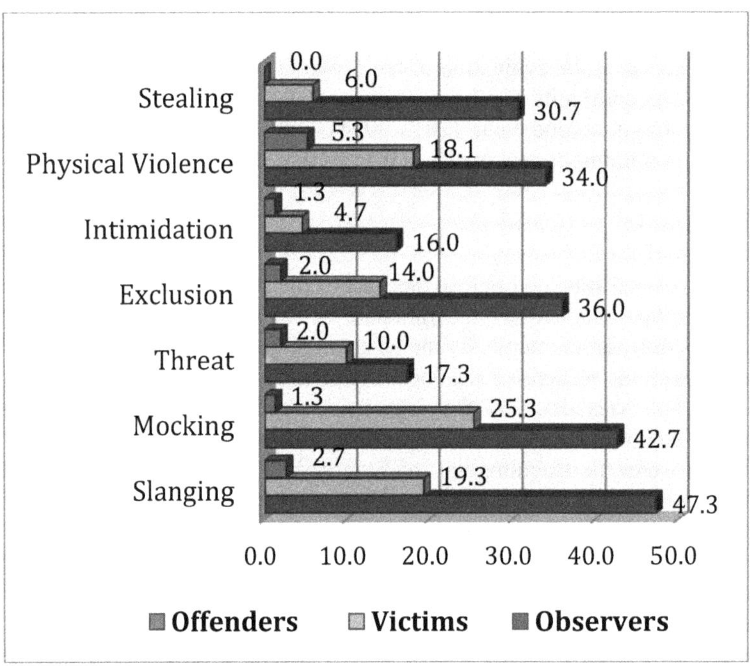

Figure 20.1: Frequency (%) of Reference to various Forms of Violence by Pupils

As it can been seen in the figure the frequency of reference to the various forms of violence differ according to the pupils as observers, victims and offenders. The observers referred to a greater frequency of all the forms. A small percentage of pupils accept that they are offenders. The same happens with the offender pupils. This may mean that these two categories of pupils are not willing to speak about acts of violence. It may also be attributed to the fact that the offenders-pupils practice violence to many victim-pupils and many more observer-pupils are sensitive to their pressure (Thanos, Dalakas & Giannouli, 2013).

Violence is usually taking place in school yard as this is found in already all the relative research (Spyropoulos, 2011). Other places where a high reference of incidents of violence takes place are the classroom and the excursions. A few incidents of violence take place on the way to school whereas a greater number of such incidents take place when pupils leave school. This may represent an attempt to solve disagreements and conflicts between pupils which have not been solved during school time. Another possibility may be that pupils tend to avoid showing transgressive behavior on their way to school because the victims may refer them to their teachers and suffer the relative consequences. There is not such a possibility of having such consequences on leaving the school. The frequency of school violence is lower in toilets and staircases (Figure 20.2).

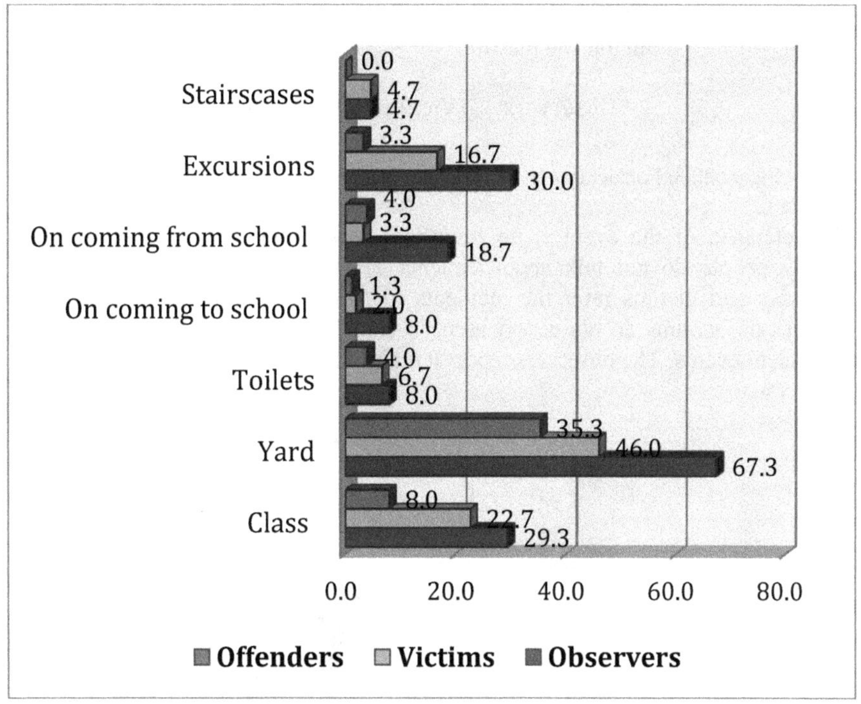

Figure 20.2: Frequency (%) of School Violence in various Places

The incidents of violence happen mainly during intervals according to the answers of pupils of the school (observers, victims, offenders). This may be attributed by the fact that pupils find it difficult to handle situations of disagreement without the direct supervision of teachers. This leads them to the adoption of transgressive behavior. There is a small percentage of school violence during the lessons (Figure 20.3).

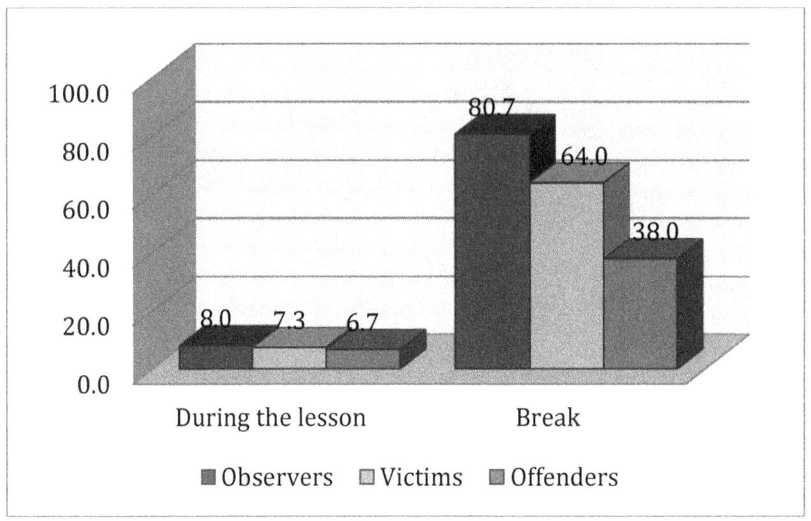

Figure 20.3: Frequency (%) of School Violence by Place of its Appearance

The reference of the event is an important requirement for its solution since usually people do not talk about violence (Panousis, 2009). The majority of observers and victims refer the incidents to their teachers and to their parents whereas the victims do not report them to somebody. Peers follow in reporting the violent events. The observers report it mainly to the director (Figure 20.4).

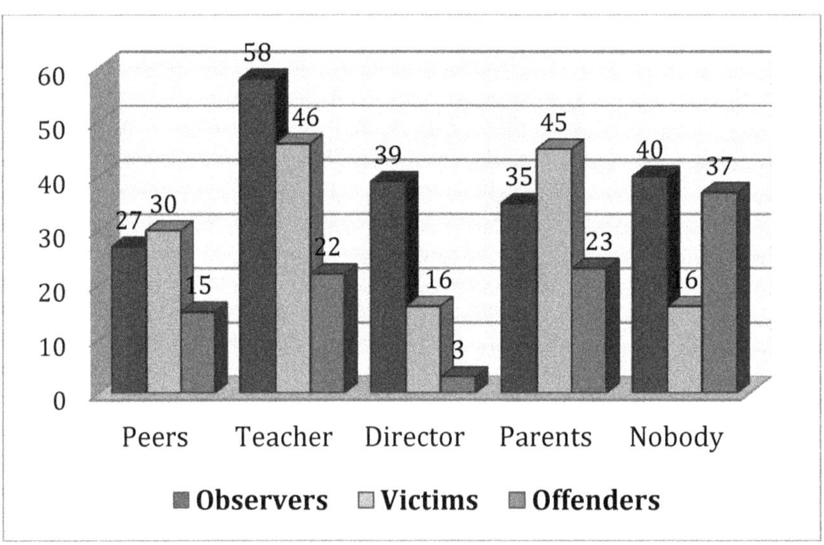

Figure 20.4: Frequency of Reporting Violent Incidents

The fact that pupils do not report the violent events to their peers may be due to the relations of trust between them. The majority of pupils believe that their teachers trust them and declare that they trust their teachers. However, this belief in reciprocity of trust does not exist among the pupils (Figure 20.5).

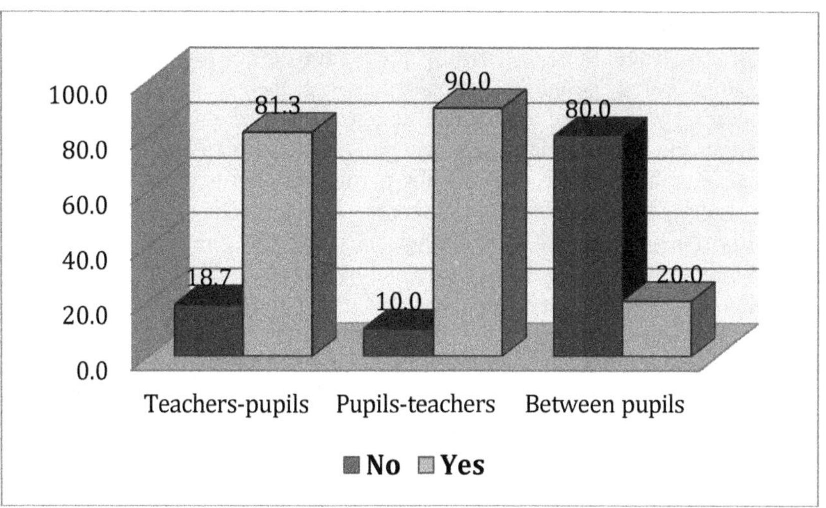

Figure 20.5: Frequency of Trustful Relationships among Teachers-Pupils, Pupils-Teachers and Pupils-Pupils

Selection and Training of Pupils and Presentation of the Program

The selection and the training of pupils in mediation is one of the most important elements for the application of the program (Fredrickson & Maruyana, 2006). These matters were arranged in collaboration with the Department of Preschool Education of the University of Ioannina (Artinopoulou, 2010). The selection of pupils for training in mediation was based on the approach of cadre which is related to the program and combined the classroom model and elective courses. The reason for selecting the cadre approach is the luck of time and trainers who could apply the total school approach that is the training of the pupils of the school. However, the further aim is the total school approach. This will be achieved when the program continuous for several successive years and when at least a whole class of children is trained every year. In our school we chose the pupils of 5th grade (26 pupils, classroom model) divided in two groups. The criteria for dividing the class were: the age of pupils and the continuation of the program the next school year. An important criterion for selecting the grade of pupils was, among others, the willingness of the teachers to participate in the program. The mediation was realized in the context of the health education (elective course and model), as this is applied in all the cases of application of the program in schools of Greece (Thanos, Tsatsakis, Stagakis & Katsioulas, 2013).

The training of pupils took place in a period of more than four months (from October 2012 to the beginning of February 2013). The teaching was amounted to about 25 hours although the relative bibliography suggests 10 to 20 hours in a period of 30 days (Artinopoulou, 2010). The greater length of our period of training is due to the fact that we adopted the classroom model where the training took place in the context of a certain subject that is taught only one hour per week according to the official curriculum. Another reason for the duration of 25 hours is due to the relatively greater number of pupils.

The training in mediation was based on an experiential way by means of video, role plying, drama, various exercises etc. It also included teaching of theoretical knowledge. More specifically, the main points of training in mediation were the following: a) definition, forms of violence, their characteristics and the ways of dealing with school violence, b) the acquisition of vocabulary related to the mediation and its principles, c) the recognition and the expression of emotions and the development of the capacity for participating in another's feelings or ideas (empathy), issues of identity, difference and acceptance, e) communicate skills-skills of active listening and f) principles, rules, structure etc. of the process of mediation (Artinopoulou, 2010; Artinopoulou, Kalavri & Michail, 2010).

On the completion of their training, the pupil mediators in collaboration with the principal of the teachers of the school presented the program to the other pupils of the school. They entered the other classes of the school and informed the pupils for the mediation (aim, principles and the process) and the documents related to it. Moreover, they played relative games and represented a virtual mediation (Thanos, Dalakas & Giannouli, 2013).

Incidents Referred to Mediation

A total of 37 incidents of pupils were referred to the process of mediation during the school years 2012-2013 and 2013-2014. 28 of them were requested by boys and only 9 by girls (Figure 20.6). This may imply that boys are more frequently involved in violent incidents than girls, as it suggested by research data (Paraskevopoulos, 1985; Zafeiropoulou & Mati, 1997; Andreou, 2005) The mediators concerned mainly incidents of pupils of the same sex (Figure 20.7).

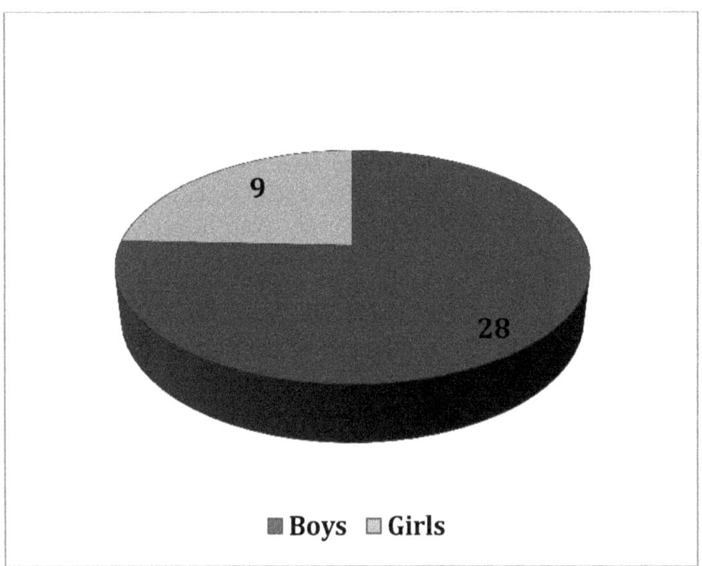

Figure 20.6: Requests of Mediation by Sex

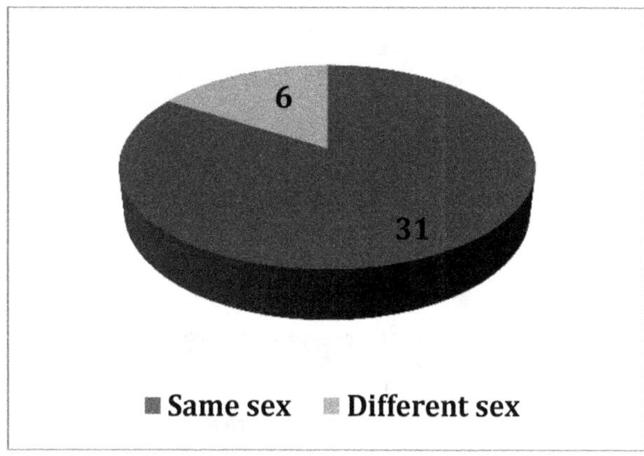

Figure 20.7: Requests of Mediation by Sex

The pupils who submitted requests for mediation were mainly for younger children. On the contrary, the number of children from the upper grades of the school were small (Figure 20.8). The majority of requests concerned incidents among pupils of the same classes (19 incidents). Requests where the involved pupils of different grades (8 requests) are usually submitted by younger children and ask older children for mediation (7 requests).

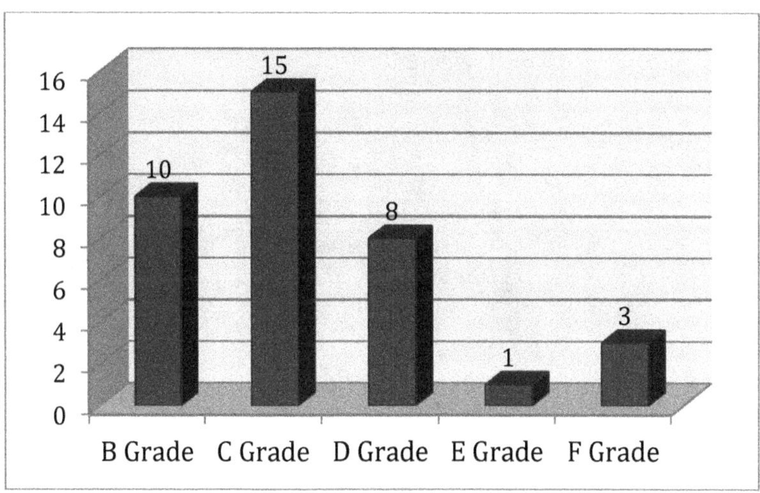

Figure 20.8: Frequency (n) of Requests by Grade

The requests for mediation that were submitted by pupils, concerned incidents of physical or verbal violence (Figure 20.9). This corresponds to the findings of the investigation of school climate and of other research as well. The main forms of violence that take place in the Greek school is the physical and verbal violence (Artinopoulou, 2001; Drosinou, 1995; Fakiolas & Armenakis, 1995).

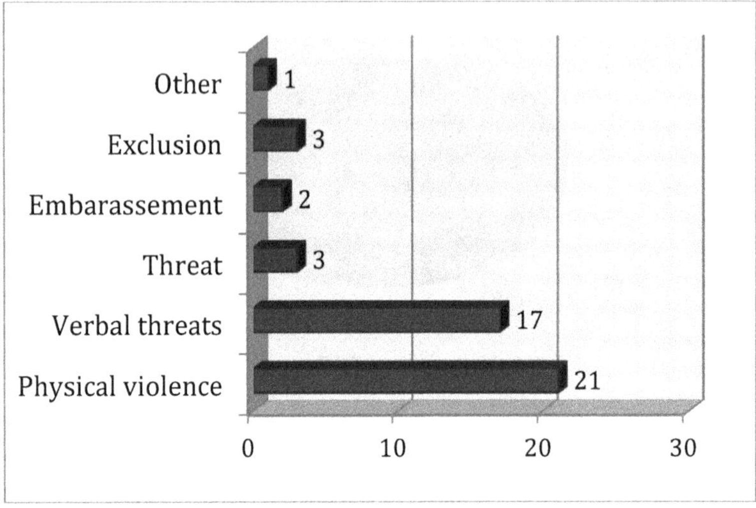

Figure 20.9: Frequency (n) of Requests and form of Violence

The emotions that the two parties - the pupil who submitted the request and the pupil who is called for mediation - were generally common. Bothe felt sorrow, anger from the event and sadness. Other emotions do not appear frequently and are differentiated between the two parties. Furthermore pupils who submitted the request felt pain and misfortune whereas the called - to mediations – usually the offenders' pleasure and hatred (Figure 20.10).

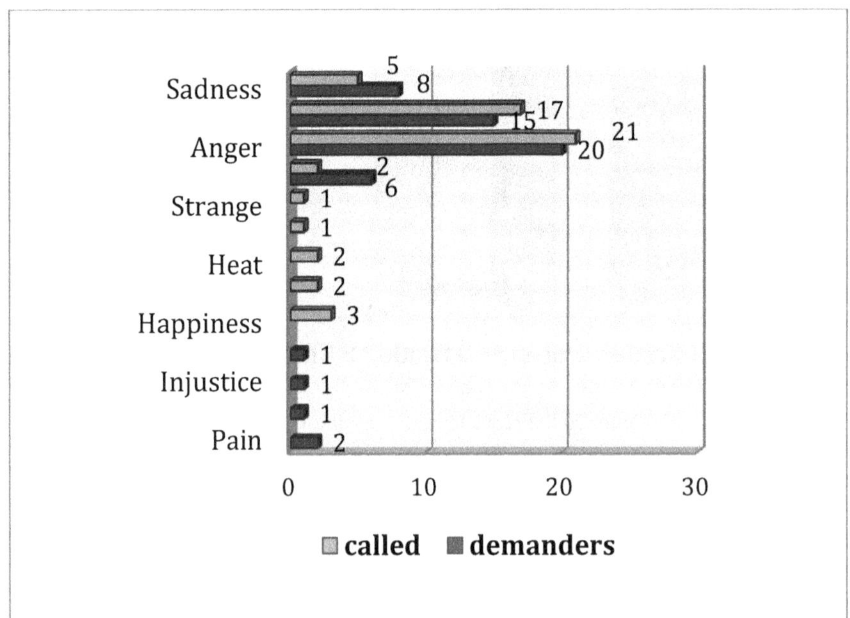

Figure 20.10: Frequency of Emotions of the Pupils

The pupils who were fighting suggest and propose as solution to become friends, to stop conflicting and to shake hands or to forget the incident that caused negative emotions (Figure 20.11).

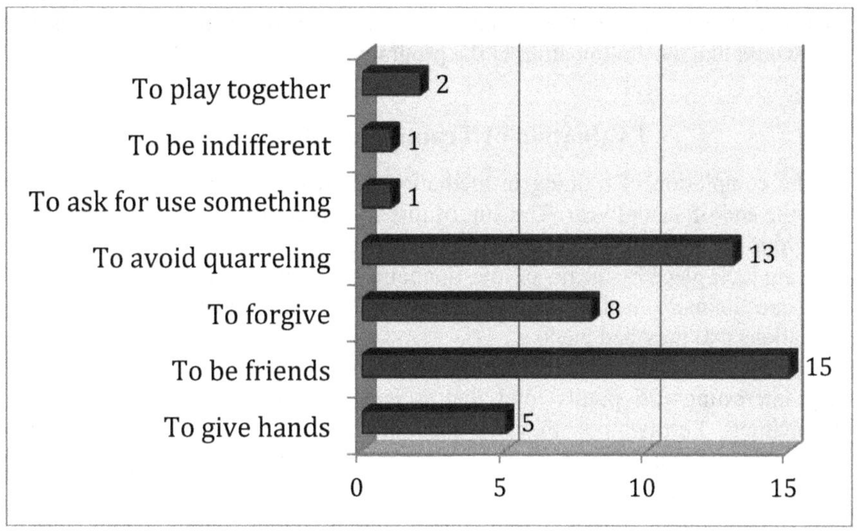

Figure 20.11: Frequency of Solutions Suggested by the involved during the Mediation

Evaluation of the Mediation Program

In the end of the first school year the program was evaluated by pupils who participated in mediation in order to solve their differences. 21 pupils completed a questionnaire. The questions concerned the solutions to the problem, the mediators and the changes in their behavior. 18 of the pupils who chose mediation said that they found a solution in their disagreement or that found a solution in many cases. Three of them said that they did not find a solution to the problem or they did not find solutions in the most of the cases. It is important that after mediation all the pupils stopped fought (18 pupils) or fighting fewer times (3 pupils). This fully corresponds with the solutions suggested by pupils during mediation.

During mediation the pupils-mediators followed the principles of mediation. Most of the pupils who participated aid that the mediators were sufficiently or very friendly (17 pupils), they trusted them and felt secure (15 pupils). The number, however, of pupils who felt a little or no trust is higher in relation to the rest of the cases. This may be attributed to the low percentage of trust among pupils, as it came out from the investigation of the school climate. In addition to that, they said that the mediators were impartial and did not support of one or the other and they said everything they wanted to say.

The aim of all the programs of school violence is the prevention of transgressive behavior. Although the period of application of mediation was relatively small-about 3 months- many of the pupils who participated in the program showed a modification of their behavior: better control of their nerves, consideration of the possibility of the other being right, attempt to avoid conflicts, listen to his or her opinion and try to find solutions. A substantial number of pupils said that they try to understand the position of the other. Finally, a great number of pupils (19 out of 21) said that they did not change their mind in relation to the mediation, they liked it as a means to solve their differences and they would like the continuation of the program next year.

Evaluation of Training in Mediation

On the completion of training in mediation, pupil mediators continued to meet until the end of school year. The aim of this was to get feedback and to reinforce the group of mediators. At the end of the school year, an evaluation of the program took place by means of questionnaire which was completed by 26 pupils. The questionnaire had a dual purpose: to evaluate their training and the mediations that they had made.

Pupils declared that their training program in mediation was sufficiently or very interesting (26 pupils) and that it met sufficiently or very much their expectations. Furthermore, they felt that their training was sufficiently or very satisfactory (Figure 20.12) and they found no or little difficulties during mediations (Figure 20.13).

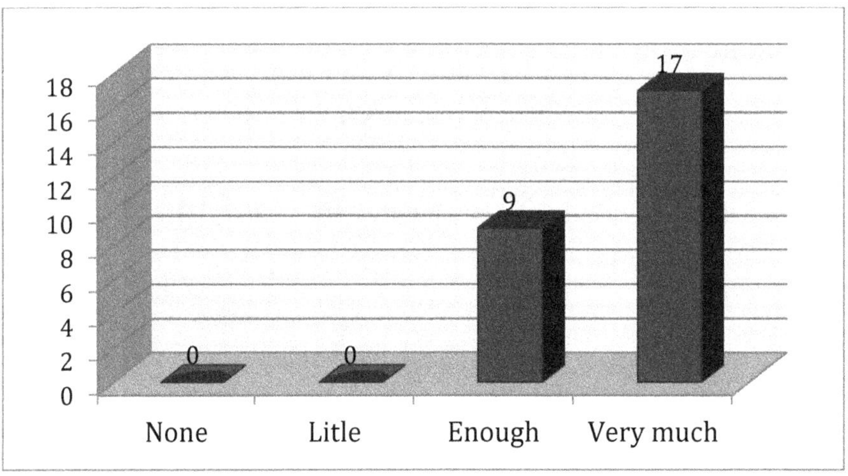

Figure 20.12: Pupils Answers regarding the Adequacy of the Program of Training

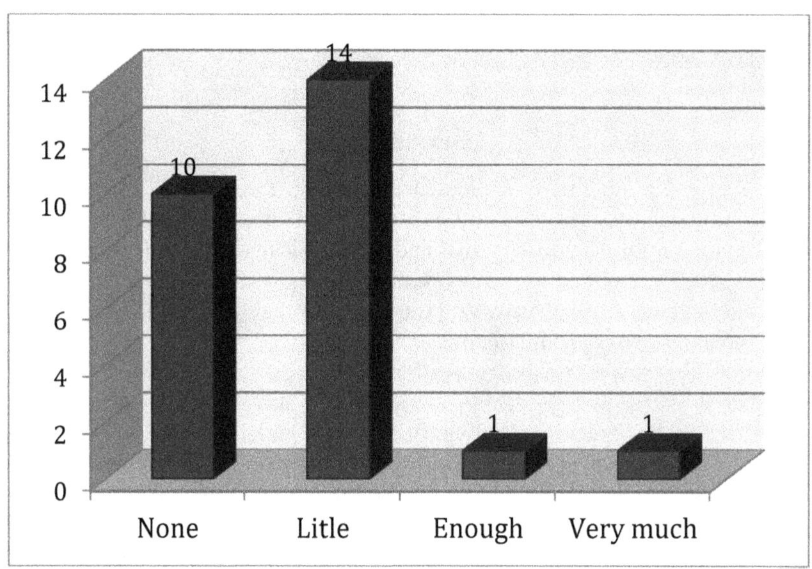

Figure 20.13: Pupils Answers related to the Difficulties of the Role of Mediator

The application of the program showed that whatsoever reservations existed at the beginning of its application concerning the ability of pupils to undertake the demands required by the role of the mediator were not justified, although the program is just applied for a second year in a primary school in Greece. Furthermore, 24 out of 26 pupils said that their mediations was successful (Figure 20.14).

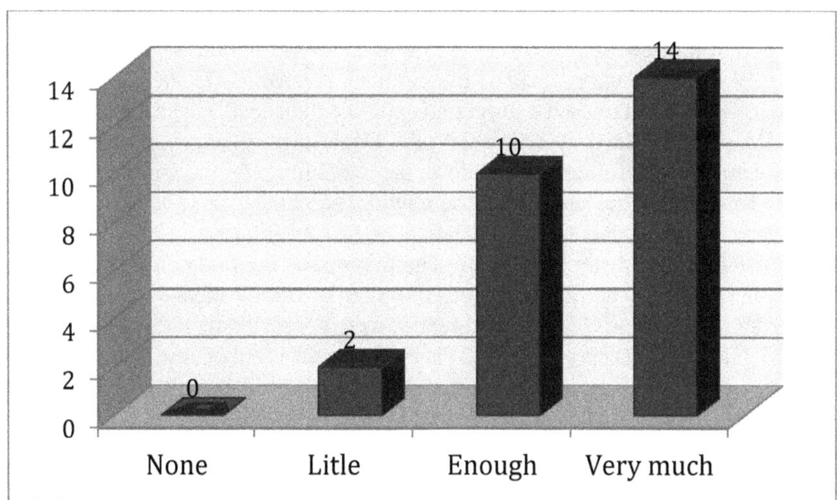

Figure20.14: Views of pupils mediators concerning the success of their mediation

The mediators said that during mediations they were sufficiently or very much impartial (24 out of 26 pupils) and friendly and thought that they were entrusted (26 pupils). Furthermore, pupils thought that their mediation was successful.

These results are in line with the results of other evaluations of training programs of pupils (Thanos, Tsatsakis, Stagakis & Katsioulas, 2013).

Discussion

Today a growing anguish is expressed concerning the increase of violence in schools, although research data in Greece show. This phenomenon to be rather limited. Its main forms are the verbal and the physical violence (Panousis, 2009; Kourakis, 2009). Despite this, however, parents, teachers and polity express their invasiveness about it. Their ways and the practices that are used for dealing with school violence seem to be ineffective (Thanos, 2012).

From 2005 onwards o program of school mediation have been applied in some schools of secondary education. Although in has been applied in very few schools, the results are very positive: decrease of violence, improvement of the relationships between pupils, change of school climate etc. (Thanos, Tsatsakis, Stagakis & Katsioulas, 2013). The application of the program revealed that pupils' main interest is not the punishment of other children but to overcome what separates them and become friends (Giannatou, 2011). The application, therefore, of restorative programs aimed at restoring the relationships between disagreed parties (Artinopoulou, 2010) are the most suitable for managing school violence. These programs are included in the context of restorative justice and seek to solve problems that exist between pupils and to develop skills like cooperation, dialogue, respect for and acceptance of difference (ib). It is for this reason that such programs must be applied quite early in life, from primary school and even from pre-primary school.

In Greece, the program of mediation was applied for two school years (2009-2010 and 2010-2011) in the Primary School of Armenon Rethymnon where pupils were trained in mediation (Thanos, Kalophotia, Stagakis & Katsioulas, 2013). From the school year 2012-2013 a mediation program is implemented in the 5th "Valanio" Primary School of Ioannina and which is the only primary school in Greece where such a program is applied (Thanos, Dalakas & Giannouli, 2013). It is applied in cooperation with the Department of Pre-school Education of the University of Ioannina. Before the beginning of the program all the involved parties-school and local community, parents, pupils and the teaching staff-were informed about the application of the program by suitable means as lectures, letters, and two conferences. The purpose of the first conference was to inform the involved parties about the program of school mediation and of the second about the results. These conferences were organized by the Association of Primary School Teachers and the Parent's Association of the 5th "Valanio" Primary School. Various representatives addressed the conferences such as the Principal and the vise Principal of the University of Ioannina, the Director of Primary Education, School Supervisors, the representative of the Town Hall etc. The involvement of school and local community was thought necessary for the better application of the program in the context of the holistic approach (Artinopoulou, 2010).

The mediations that took place during the school years 2012-2013 and 2013-2014 (until this moment) concerned incidents of physical and verbal violence or a combination of them in many cases. Both, offenders and victims expressed negative emotions during their involvement in instances of violence. The prevailing emotions were sorrow and anger. Their suggested solutions concerning their differences were: to become friends and to stop quarreling. It is obvious that pupils restore their relationships and this is line with the aims of restorative justice (Mc Evoy, Mika & Hudson, 2002). The evaluation that took place at the end of the year showed that pupils who participated in mediation said that mediation helped them to find solutions to their problems, to improve their relationship with their fellow pupils, to stop quarreling or to quarrel fewer times. Finally, they said that the mediator were friendly, impartial and were actively listening what they are saying.

Conclusion

- The support of the program by all the members of school and wider local community is necessary for the application of the program. The school community as well the wider one showed a great interest for the program and supported it in all its phases.
- The selection and the training of pupils must be based on the unique characteristics of the school. This is necessary for changing the traditional direction from the top to bottom to a direction from bottom to the top. The investigation of school climate is very important for this change.
- The principles and the structure of school mediation encourage the development of feelings of respect, equality, trustfulness and security of pupils, as this comes out from what pupils who participated in mediation have said that these qualities helped them to find creative solutions to the human conflicts.
- Pupils involved in conflicts found solutions to their problems, improved their relationships and stopped repeating them. This is a valid reason for applying this method to the school. It has implications for improving the social climate as well the kind of society we desire to appear in the future.

References

Andreou, E. (2005). Combination of factors of family with aggressiveness which is manifested by the first school age. *Researching the world of children* (OMEP), 5, 9-22.

Artinopoulou, V. (2001). *School Violence. Research and Policies in Europe.* Athens: Metaixmio.

Artinopoulou, V. (2010) *The School Mediation* (In cooperation with Kalavri, Ch. & Michail, H.). Athens: Legal Library.

Artinopoulou, V. (2011α). The Mediation in the Context of Restorative Justice (15-25). In Th. Thanos, (Ed.), *Mediation in the school and society.* Athens: Pedio (in Greek).

Artinopoulou, V. (2011β). School based mediation and restorative justice (39-46). In Thanos, Th. (Edr), *Mediation in the school and society*. Athens: Pedio (in Greek).

Artinopoulou, V. Kalavri, Ch. & Michail, H. (2010). *The social Mediation Adaption to Greek School* (Primary Education) [Educative Material]. Athens: Greek Centre of Social Mediation.

Braithwaite, J. (2001). Reconciling Models: Balancing standards and principles of restorative justice practice. In H. Mika & McEvoy (Eds), *International perspectives on restorative justice conference report.* Belfast: Queen University.

Drosinou, M. (1995). The Violence in School. *Modern Education,* 85, 76-79.

Fakiolas, N. & Armenakis, A. (1195). Participation of users of toxic substance to violence. *Modern Education,* 81, 42-50.

Fredrickson, J. & Mauyana, G. (1996). Peer mediation programs: benefits and key elements. *Center For Applied Research and Educational Improvement Research/Practice Newsletter,* 4 (3), University of Minesota [http://www. cehd.umn.edu/carei/publications/documents/PeerMediation.pdf]

Gerrard, W. M. & Lipsey, M. W. (2007). Conflict resolution education and antisocial behavior in U.S. Schools: A meta-analysis. *Conflict Resolution Quarterly,* 25 (1), 9-38.

Giannatou, A. (2011). The function «peer mediators» in 2o Gymnasium Aspropirgou (103-112). In Th. Thanos (Ed.), *Mediation in the school and society*. Athens: Pedio (in Greek).

Johnson, D. W., Johnson, R. T. (1995). Teaching students to be peacemakers: results of five years of research. *Peace and Conflict: Journal of Peace Psychology*, 1 (4), 417-438.

Karp, D. & Breslin, B. (2001). Restorative justice in school communities. *Youth and Society,* 33 (2), 249-272.

Kourakis, N. (2009). Forms of school violence and possibility of its confronting (85-104). In Th. Thanos (Ed.), *Juvenile Delinquency and School.* Athens: Topos (in Greek).

Kourkoutas, I. & Thanos, T. (2013). Integration of adolescents with antisocial and delinquent behavior in school: Macro social and psychosocial dimensions (189-237). In E. Kourkoutas, & Th. Thanos (Ed.) *School violence and delinquency*. Athens: Topos (in Greek).

Latimer, J., Dowden, C. & Muise, D. (2005). The effectiveness of restorative justice practices: a meta-analysis. *The Prison Journal*, *85* (2), 127-144.

Marshall, T. (1996). The evolution of restorative justice in Britain. *European Journal of Criminal Policy and Research*, 4, 21-43.

McEvoy, K., Mika, H. & Hudson, B. (2002). Introduction, practice, performance and prospects for restorative justice. *British Journal Criminology*, 42, 469-475.

Mirsky, L. (2003). Albert Eglash and Creative Restitution: A Precursor to Restorative Practices. *Restorative Practices E-Forum, (on Web, 13.01.2013)* http://www.realjustice.org/library/eglash.html.2003,

Morrison, B. (2007). Schools and restorative justice (325-337). In G. Johnstone & D.W. Van Ness (Eds), *Handbook of restorative justice.* UK: Willan Publishing.

Panoussis I. (2009). School violence: without limits, without perspective? [Lecture Reference]. In Th. Thanos (Ed.), *Juvenile Delinquency and School.* Athens: Topos (in Greek).

Paraskevopoulos, I. (1985). Progressive Psychology. Athens

Roumpea G. (2011). Training Pupils Mediators (91-102). In Th. Thanos (Ed.), *Mediation in the school and society.* Athens: Pedio (in Greek).

Spyropoulos, F. (2011). *Bullying at school. Theoretical approach and preventive policies.* Athens: Sakkoulas (in Greek).

Thanos, T. (2012). *Deviant and delinquent behavior of students at school* (G. Panousis, Preface - Addendum).Thessaloniki: Kuriakidi (in Greek).

Thanos, T., Dalakas, Ch. & Giannouli, E. (2013). School mediation. Application and Evaluation. In the scientific conference titled: "*School Mediation. Theory, Application, Evaluation*" which was organized by the Department of Pre-school Education of University of Ioannina and the 5th Primary School of Ioannina at 18-10-2013 in Ioannina (in Greek).

Thanos, T., Kolofotia, S. & Xatzaki, M. (2011). Pilot application on mediation in Primary School (47-76). In Th. Thanos (Edr), *The mediation in the school and society.* Athens: Pedio (in Greek).

Thanos, T., Tsatsakis, A., Stagakis, B. & Katsioulas, K. (2013). The mediation in the Primary School. Evaluation of training program an its application (317-335). In E. Kourkoutas, & Th. Thanos (Eds) *School violence and delinquency.* Athens: Topos (in Greek).

Thanos, Th., (2010, 5th of May). School Mediation. Peaceful Solution of Conflicts in School. *Crete Review.*

Wall, J., Stark, J. & Standifer, R. (2001). Mediation: a current review and theory development. *The Journal of Conflict Resolution*, 45 (3), 370-391.

Zafeiropoulou, M. & Mati, E. (1997). Definition and parameters of transgressive behavior of pupils in the school (65-81). In Society of Educational Sciences of Komotini (Ed), *Psychological and Social problems: Disorderly, aggressiveness, violence, criminality in School and Society.* Komotini (in Greek).

About the Contributors

Maria Andrikopoulou-Rouvali. Since, 2011 she is vice-mayor in municipality of Patras-Greece, managing areas of volunteerism, gender equality, NGOs, inclusion of migrants and services for the citizens. At the same time, she is the president of "Patras Council for Inclusion of Migrants" and participates in the managing boards of municipal organizations of social and cultural character. She has represented the municipality of Patras in conferences and high-scale events organized by local, regional and national authorities in Greece as well as by international bodies abroad.

Georgia Antonelou graduated from the Department of Mathematics of the University of Patras. She received her first M.Sc. degree in "Mathematics of Computation and Decision Making" in 2010 and her second M.Sc. degree in Technologies of Informatics and Communications in Education" in 2013. She also holds a certificate from the annual distance education course "Adult Education", of the Open Education Foundation of Athens, she has the Michigan Proficiency in English and she was currently certified as a user/creator of digital courses in LMS / LCMS systems. She is an attested excellent handler of computers, with programming knowledge and ability to handle different educational software packages. During 2007-2012, she worked as a part-time teacher of Mathematics in High schools and in Second Chance Schools, as a trainer in training educational programs for adults and as a course assistant in the Department of Mathematics of the University of Patras. She participates in the Research Group of the European project SONETOR and coordinates actions organized by e-CoMet Lab and the directorate of Secondary Education of Achaia Patras. Her research interests include applications of data mining - EDM, intelligent systems, ICT in education, creation - design - support-management of online courses, study development methodology of the algorithmic thinking and evaluation learning processes, designing learning activities. She also has publications in International and Nationwide Conferences. Since 2011 she has been collaborating with e-CoMet Lab (2011-2012: at the Systems and Technology Division, 2012-2013: at the Educational Material and Content Division).

Eugenia Arvanitis is lecturer at the Department of Educational Science and Early Childhood Education, University of Patras. She teaches at the Post Graduate Program "Adult Education" of the Hellenic Open University. She has been involved in policy development for intercultural, adult and immigrant education at the Greek Ministry of Education (2006-2012). Dr. Arvanitis lived for a decade in Australia gaining valuable experience in multicultural educational and ethnic language maintenance policies. During 2001-2004, she was co-ordinator of the Greek Language and Cultural Studies Program (BA International Studies) at the School of International and Community Studies, RMIT University and the Manager of the Australian-Greek Resource and Learning Centre at RMIT University, Melbourne (www.rmit.edu.au/greekcentre). She is an Associate &

Research Partner in several scientific organisations such as PASCAL International Observatory, RMIT Globalism Institute and the University of Illinois (Common Ground & Learning by Design project teams). Most recently, she has helped to establish the web based platform, 'Nea Mathisi' (http://neamathisi.com), supporting professional and intercultural learning in school-based teachers' training. Finally, she is the author of several research papers and the editor/author of three books (*Bonegilla: Memories and Recollections of an Insider* by Zac Vogiazopoulos (2006), *Greek Ethnic Schools in Australia in the late 1990s: Selected Case Studies* by Eugenia Arvanitis (2010) and she edited the Greek version of the book *New Learning: Elements of a Science of Education* by Kalantzis & Cope (2013).

Mara Aspioti has a Bachelor in European Culture Studies by the Hellenic Open University and is soon finishing her postgraduate studies and getting the Master in Cultural Organizations Management at the HOU. She has had vocational training in Educational Psychology and in Education on Translation at the National and Kapodistrian University of Athens. She is a certified Researcher on European Governance trained at the Jean Monnet Centre of Excellence and has contributed as a Rapporteur in the Research Paper published by the Jean Monnet Centre of Excellence entitled: *"Exit from Crisis: Applicable Alternative Proposals"*. She has worked as an independent freelance translator from 1998 till 2012 in Greece and worldwide. She has been an approved freelance translator by the European Union for 7 years. She is a trained Cultural Mediator having attended TIPS ("Practising and Enhancing Cultural Mediation in a Pluralistic Europe" / Training as a Cultural Mediator) and she is a registered member at the Registry of Trained Cultural Mediators. She has worked out and published a number of research papers, articles and reports in Humanities and Culture and she has translated many books and students' handbooks in Informatics and Medicine. She is a researcher at the Hellenic Open University/e-CoMeT Lab and since February 2013 is assigned with the role of SONETOR National Moderator for Greece. She speaks English, Italian, German, French, Spanish, Romanian and Japanese.

Jeries Besarat is a PhD student at the Department of Computer Engineering and Informatics, University of Patras, Greece. He has also worked as an external researcher at the Computer Technology Institute and Press "Diophantus" (CTI) since 2012. His research interests include Augmented Reality, Pervasive and Mobile Computing, Web Technologies and Social Networks. In 2011 he received his Master's degree in Computer Science and Technology from University of Patras, Greece.

Catherine Christodoulopoulou is project manager at the Directorate of Telematics and Applications for Regional Development, inComputer Technology Institute & Press "Diophantus" – CTI. Catherine Christodoulopoulou holds BSs in Business Administration (major Management and Organizational Behavior) and a MA in Strategic Decision Making (University of Leeds). She is working in National and European Programs Department of CTI's Directorate of Telematics & Applications for Regional Development. She is Technical manager of the implementation of projects related with regional development and interregional collaboration. She has adequate experience in day to day administrative and financial management of European projects related to Information Society (INTERREG IIIB MEDOC, INTERREG IIIC SOUTH and WEST INTERREG IIIB CADSES, LEONARDO etc). She also has able experience in preparing and coordinating proposals for collaborative European and National programs. Her previous experience includes the provision of services as Business Consultant (SWOT Analysis, Marketing strategies, Management strategies). Some indicative papers and publication of Catherine Christodoulopoulou are: "Creation of telecenters to support learning, entrepreneurship and access to Information Society, in isolated areas. The TELEACCESS project", Accepted to Ruralearn 2007, Chios, Greece 24 – 27/6/2007; "Horizontal ICT interregional collaboration activities in the region of Western Greece. Impact on Regional Development", Accepted to: "Shaping EU Regional Policy: Economic Social and Political Pressures" international conference (organized by the Regional studies association www.regional-studies-assoc.ac.uk), June 2006; "Virtual 3D Tools in Online Language Learning" International conference "Learning a Language in Virtual Worlds A Review of Innovation and ICT in Language Teaching Methodology "Accepted to: "Learning a Language in Virtual Worlds A Review of Innovation and ICT in Language Teaching Methodology " Warsaw, Poland, November 2011

Dermot Coughlan is professor emeritus at the University of Limerick in Ireland where he previously served as Director of Lifelong Learning & Outreach. Prior to assuming this position he worked in human resources management for almost 30 years. He was a Member of the Ireland's National Adult Learning Council. He holds a Master Degree in Law & Employment Relations from the University of Leicester and is a Chartered Fellow of the Chartered Institute of Personnel and Development. He is a recognised expert in the field of Lifelong Learning and within this area he has published widely and delivered several papers at international conferences. He has led and participated in several EU Funded Projects dealing with issues such as, Work-based Learning, the Recognition of Prior Learning, Quality Management, next generation employability and issues pertaining to the Learning Region concept especially issues associated with social regeneration. He is actively involved in reviewing educational systems across Europe and the implementation of qualification frameworks

Claudia Santa Cruz obtained a Master's Degree in Clinical Psychology and Psychopathology at the Institute of Applied Psychology, worked in Social Inclusion Projects of the Lisbon Municipality and is Trainer in the Behavioral Field, particularly in Stress Management, Conflict and Motivation and responsible for Profiling Community Policing Teams.

Charalampos Dalakas (Med, PhD) is the director of the 5th "Valanio" primary school of Ioannina. This school is involved in piloting a new national curriculum and also in applying a peer mediation program. His main interests cover the relationship of educational theory-especially psychology. Sociology, educational management, multicultural education, citizenship- and teaching practice. He is a member of the Greek Educational Society and of editorial board of the professional journal of primary and Pre-primary school teachers of the area of Ioannina, entitled "Indicators of Education". He has presented papers in various Greek and international conferences. He is authorized to teach in in-service courses for teachers and in the National Centre for Public Administration. Finally, he has published articles of educational interest in journals and newspapers.

Mónica Diniz, is the head of strategic development of the Lisbon Municipal Police at Lisbon Municipality. She is a Sociologist with a master degree on Sociology and Planning with a thesis in the field of police practices and citizenship at local level. Her current post involves:

- Conduct of studies on police-citizen relationships and community policing.
- Development of the organization training strategic plan.
- Trainer on community policing models.
- Participation in community groups in the framework of community policing, promoting police and civil society partnerships to identify, prioritize and solve security problems.
- Developing national and international partnerships to share knowledge and best practices on police-citizen relationships (e.g. in the field of Interculturality, CPTED-Crime Prevention Through Environmental Design, Community Policing, Gender Violence and Domestic Violence and Mediation).
- Design and implementation of Monitoring & Evaluation systems (internal performance indicators and evaluation of police interventions in the community).

John Garofalakis is professor at the Department of Computer Engineering and Informatics of the University of Patras, as well as Director of Computer Technology Institute's Directorate for Telematics and Applications for Regional Development. He was also General Director and Information Technology-Telecommunications Manager of the Patras Science Park. He has worked for Evaluation and Review of European Commission proposals "Telematics Applications Program - Libraries" and the IST, for the Commission of the EU. He is responsible and scientific coordinator of several recent IT and Telematics Projects.

Chrissa Geraga is the head of programming-networking & international affairs at the Patras Municipal Enterprise for Planning & Development-ADEP SA. She shares valuable experience in the submission and implementation of projects in topics related to equal opportunities, social cohesion, interculturalism, youth, employment, tourism and culture. She organises and operates networks of organisations benefiting multiple effects. Member of "TEAM EUROPE" experts on EU matters coordinated by DG COMM / European Commission (Representation office in Greece).

Krzysztof Gurba, PhD is associate professor and deputy director of the Institute of Journalism and Social Communication, at the Pontifical University of John Paul II in Krakow, as well as chief of the Department of Journalism. He teaches journalism and multimedia both on BA and MA studies. He is responsible for international projects management and he specializes also in distance learning and e-learning methodology. Since 2006 he was elected the European Area Representative of the GUIDE Association (Association of Global Universities in Distance Education). He was co-organiser of Thematic Workshop on "Excellence Models for a Global University Network" and is an author of many studies and papers concerning the question of quality of lifelong education systems. He is also a director of the Institute for Research on Civilizations. He was organizer and co-organizer of many international projects, including LLP projects in the domain of e-learning, and Polish Aid projects financed by Polish Ministry of Foreign Affairs. Member of editorial staff of Studia Socialia Cracoviensia. Magazine. Member of Polish Journalists Association (Secretary of Krakow Branch). Member of Executory Council of Polish Radio in Krakow, member of Advisory Council of Polish Television in Krakow.

Achilles Kameas, is associate professor of Educational Content Methodology & Technology Laboratory (e-CoMeT Lab) Hellenic Open University and the SONETOR Project coordinator. Achilles D. Kameas received his Engineering Diploma (in 1989) and his Ph.D. (in 1995) from the Department of Computer Engineering and Informatics, Univ. of Patras, Greece. Since 2003, he is an Assistant Professor with the Hellenic Open University (HOU), where he teaches Software Engineering. Since 2007 he is Director of the Educational Content, Methodology and Technology (e-CoMeT) Lab with HOU (http://eeyem.eap.gr), which currently employs more than 40 researchers with an average annual budget of more than 1MEuro. Since 2010, he is directing the Career and Employment Centre of HOU (http://dasta.eap.gr). He is also the Director of Research Unit 3 / DAISy (Dynamic Ambient Intelligent Systems) (http://daisy.cti.gr) at the Computer Technology & Publications Institute "Diophantus" (CTI), attracting funding of more than 1,5MEuro during the past 10 years. He has participated as researcher / group leader in several EU and national R&D projects. Examples are the IST (FP5, FP6 and FP7) projects e-Gadgets, Astra, Plants, Social and Atraco (he was the scientific coordinator of the first two), the LLP projects TIPS, VAB, PIN, CompAAL, EngAGEnt, CRITON and SONETOR (he is the coordinator of the latter) and the national project ADVENT (as coordinator). He is responsible for the project that led to the development of the National Registry of Certified Cultural Mediators. He has published over 100 journal articles, conference papers and book chapters, and authored and co-edited more than 10 five books and conference proceedings. He is a member of the program committee of several international conferences and of the editorial boards of acclaimed international scientific journals. His current research interests include applications of ICT in education, ubiquitous computing, semantic modeling and ontology matching.

Andreas Koskeris is holding a BSc on Computer Engineering and Informatics (University of Patras) and an MBA from the Hellenic Management Association. He is currently vice director of Computer Technology Institute's Directorate for Telematics and Applications for Regional Development, with the main task to act as coordinator of all Department's R&D projects. He is also certified adult education evaluator.

Konstantina Kyriakopoulou, is social worker and coordinator of the Open Polyclinic in Patras, Doctors of the World- Medicins du Monde. Her post as co-ordinator involves registration of social elements and requests of the beneficiaries, creation and information about the records of social service, provision of social services - social intervention. Intervention to situations of crisis, social advisory and Support, Material aid at cases, information about educational and training issues as well as professional orientation, work with public service and Non-Governmental Organisation, collaboration with a net of social service. She is also a researcher in Pollster Company.

Charikleia Manavi, is social anthropologist, career counsellor and adult educator. Charikleia Manavi holds a bachelor's degree in Education, Philosophy and Psychology and a master's degree in Education, Social Pedagogy and Social Anthropology from Aristotle University of Thessaloniki. She is currently working towards her Ph.D in Training and Continuing Education for Guidance Counsellors and Teachers in Inter-cultural Approach to Career Counselling, under the guidance of Zarifis G. (Assistant Professor of Continuing Education in the Department of Education/School of Philosophy & Education, Faculty of Philosophy/ Aristotle University of Thessaloniki). She is Certified Adult Educator (National Certification Qualifications and Vocational Guidance (E.O.P.P.E.P.), Assessor in Educational Committees for Instructor and Administrative staff of Vocational Guidance & Counselling Services (SYY) and Assessor in Certification Committees for Adult Training. In the last two decades she has been involved in various nationwide and European projects in the areas of developing local strategies for the promotion of migrants employment, teaching and counselling migrants, social workers and researchers who interact with migrants. She collaborates (on a freelance basis) with educational institutions, training centers, NGOs, public administrations and local authorities. Several times her job has direct bearing on European integration.

Mayte Martín has extensive experience managing European funded projects aimed at combating discrimination including the Roma Cultural Mediation Project funded under the EQUAL Community Initiative. She has been instrumental in the development of a cultural mediation model for the Irish health sector since 2002. Previously, Mayte lectured for several years in the School of Applied Languages and Intercultural Studies, Dublin City University.

Georgios Nikolaou, is associate professor at the Pedagogical Department of Primary Education, University of Ioannina, Greece. Dr Georgios Nikolaou is born in 1964 at Ptolemaida. He studied at the Marasleion Education School of Athens and at the Department of Sciences of Education at the University of Lyon-Lumière II, where he finished his undergraduate degree (Maîtrise, 1986) and his Master's degree (DEA, 1988). He is nominated Doctor of the Department of Primary Education in the University of Athens at 1999. Dr Nikolaou has taught at the Primary and the Higher Education in Greece and in France. In January of 2000, Dr. Nikolaou is elected as an Assistant Counsellor of Intercultural Education at the Pedagogical Institute of Greece. Since September 2001, he is member of the academic staff at the Department of Primary Education of the University of Ioannina. Today he is an Associate Professor in Intercultural Education in the same Department. He is the writer of three books and many papers, published to Greeks and international reviews. He is also a member of the Greek Pedagogical Association, of the Greek Association of Special Education and President of the Greek Observatory for Intercultural Education.

Akrivi-Irene Panagiotopoulou, is R&D Executive in Training and Consulting Research and Development, Department Olympic Training and Consulting Ltd. Akrivi-Irene Panagiotopoulou has a bachelor degree in Educational & Social Policy – Special Educational Needs and is mainly active in projects promoting migrant integration, as well as in the design of European programs. Interculturalism and languages are her special foci of interest.

Zampeta Papadodima is currently engaged (2012-2014), as PI Researcher in the audiovisual research project "Mapping the now here" of the politics in the European South metropolis (European Cultural Foundation/ University HfBK Hamburg/ UCM- Madrid). MSc in International Migration Politics from the University of Buenos Aires (2009). Research and Teaching activities at University of Buenos Aires (2007-2012), University of Jujuy (2010-2012), University of Patras (2012), University of Zaragoza, Humboldt University of Berlin (2011-2012), HfBK Hamburg (2012-2014). Co-Founder of Research Centre for Migration "Espacio de Estudios Migratorios" in Buenos Aires. Main areas of research and teaching geopolitics of migration, regional integration, critical theory and urban policies in Southern Europe and South America. Articles and informs on migration policies and regional analysis. Editor of the scientific Journal on Migration "Miradas en Movimiento" (2008-2013).

Vasiliki Papageorgiou has studied Ethnology at the Democritus University of Thrace and has completed postgraduate studies and her PhD at the department of Social Anthropology and History of the University of the Aegean in 2009. She has specialized in migration, cultural identities and interculturalism. Her research work has been published as a book under the title "From Albania to Greece, Place and Identity, Interculturalism and Incorporation, an Anthropological Perspective on Migratory Experience" (Athens: Nissos, 2011). She currently teaches Cultural Theory and Cultural Management in the Department of Digital Media and Communication at the TEI of Ionian Islands.

Konstantina Polymeropoulou has a degree in Business Administration from University of Patras in 2007. She is currently a postgraduate student in Cultural Organizations Management of the HOU School of Social Sciences. Since 2007, she has working experience as assistant project manager in ICT European projects. Since 2008, she has been working with e-CoMeT Lab, submitting proposals in a national and European level and managing several Lifelong Learning projects -Leonardo Da Vinci such as TIPS, VAB, PIN, SONETOR, CompAAL, Learn Play Manage, engAGEnt, CRITON, eCult Skills, TAKE CARE and e-Virtue. She has also participated in the national project "Human Network of training and education in the administration of the informatics projects" as a project manager (financial management, organization of the seminars) and in the Project 1.1.b/11 "Creating a Register of trained Intercultural Mediators and networking Intercultural Mediators through an electronic Platform" of the European Integration Fund. She has presented her publications entitled as "Using the TIPS platform to train Greek cultural mediators" at the Conference "Social Applications for Lifelong Learning" that was held in Patras, Greece on 4-5 November 2010 and the «PROINTERNET: SKILLS FOR INTERNET-RELATED JOBS» that was held in Athens , Greece on 27 April – 1 May 2011 at the Conference "CAREER-EU 2011". Finally, she has organized several events that took place within the projects' context.

Morteza Rezaei-Zadeh, is a PhD researcher in University of Limerick, Ireland in the area of e-Learning and Entrepreneurship. He was awarded a full scholarship (€120,000) to do his PhD study which aims to design and develop an e-learning platform with the support of 27 new pedagogical processes which could positively affect students' entrepreneurial competences through a hidden curriculum. Morteza published 3 books and also presented and published around 30 papers in the peer-reviewed academic conferences and journals over the last 5 years. One of his papers was selected as the best paper of 2013 International Conference on Information and Education Technology" (ICIET 2013) which was held in Brussels on 12-13 January 2013. He is also a member of International E-Learning Association (IELA) which is based in New York – USA. His interest is also in the cultural aspects of education and he published a book in this area as well. In terms of the research methodology, his main interest is in the area of qualitative research methodologies. His research is one of the first efforts of using Interactive management (IM) as a qualitative methodology in the area of entrepreneurship. He published a book about this methodology as well and guided a group of postgraduate students to use IM in their academic research.

Andrica Rozi, is R&D Executive, at the Training and Consulting Research and Development Department, Olympic Training and Consulting Ltd. Andrica Rozi has a bachelor degree in European and International Studies from Panteion University of Social & Political Sciences in Athens, Greece, and speaks five languages. She has been working for Olympic Training & Consulting Ltd since 2012 and has since participated in the implementation of EU-funded and national projects in the fields of Interculturalization, Entrepreneurship & Adult Training.

Eleni Samsari, is teacher of Primary Education & Postgraduate Student at the Pedagogical Department of Primary Education, University of Ioannina, Greece in the field of "Special Education & Intercultural Education". Proficient user of English, French and German language. She has presented her work in numerous international and national conferences related to Sciences of Education in Greek and in English. Her articles have been published in national and international refereed conference proceedings.

Eleni Skourtou, is professor for linguistic and cultural diversity at the Department of Primary Education / University of the Aegean, Rhodes/Greece. Her research and teaching focus on language diversity in education and on orality/literacy and learning. She is involved in projects dealing with the education of Rom children.

Theodoros Thanos, is assistant professor of Sociology of Education in the Department of the Pre-school Education of the University of Ioannina. His academic interests cover subjects of child socialization in the family and the school, of the relationships between education and social reproduction, the transition of young graduate to work, school violence and school mediation. He has organized educational conferences, and published various articles. He also has taken care of two collective volumes concerning social inequalities in education, school violence and mediation. Finally, he is the author of the books: Sociology of social inequalities in education (publ. by Nisos), Deviant and delinquent behavior of students in school (publ. by Kyriakidis), and Education and social reproduction in post-war Greece (publ. by Kyriakidis).

Index

T

U

www.ingramcontent.com/pod-product-compliance
Lightning Source LLC
Chambersburg PA
CBHW060032030426
42334CB00019B/2288
* 9 7 8 1 6 1 2 2 9 4 7 5 9 *